Straight Outta Scotland

A True Story of Fakery, Money and Betrayal
in the Music Industry

Gavin Bain

WITHDRAWN

SIMON &
SCHUSTER

London · New York · Sydney · Toronto

A CBS COMPANY

First published in Great Britain as *California Schemin'* by
Simon & Schuster UK Ltd, 2010
This edition published by Simon & Schuster UK Ltd, 2011
A CBS COMPANY

1 3 5 7 9 10 8 6 4 2

Simon & Schuster UK Ltd
1st Floor
222 Gray's Inn Road
London
WC1X 8HB

www.simonandschuster.co.uk

Simon & Schuster Australia
Sydney

A CIP catalogue record for this book is available
from the British Library.

ISBN: 978-1-84739-652-5

Typeset by M Rules
Printed in the UK by CPI Cox & Wyman, Reading, Berkshire RG1 8EX

In loving memory of
Robert Gardiner Bain, Robert Dean Bain,
Brian Robertson, Elizabeth Dean Bain, Skye Russo,
Duncan Thomson and Ivan Friedman

Acknowledgements

There is no accurate way to measure the appreciation, respect and unconditional love I have for my family. My career and life's work will always be, in some way or another, for my mother and father Norah and Hugh Bain who have bankrupted themselves in the past at the drop of a hat to keep my music career alive. For my sister Laurette, the most rebellious spirit I've ever known. For my sister and best friend Michelle who has been like a guardian angel to me, saving my life on a number of occasions. I sincerely apologise for all the worry and anxiety I have caused you all. I'd also like to thank my Uncle Bill, my Uncle Gordon and of course I can't forget my dear granny Hannah May Thomson. To my gorgeous fiancée Natalie Ould for making me feel human again and helping me realize that Gavin Bain didn't need Brains McLoud to fall in love again. She is the greatest.

I'd like to thank Decca Aitkenhead for her excellent Guardian article 'California Schemin'' back in May 2008 which got the ball rolling on all of this and allowed me to drive up enough interest in my story. Decca's title was just too good and impossible not to use. I'd also like to thank my producer and close friend Tom

Aitkenhead for alerting his sister to my story and for his continued faith in my music.

A debt of gratitude to my agent Patrick Walsh for his support and guidance. To Nick Duerden for helping me make sense of all this mess. To Paul Duane and Avril Macrory for knowing a good story when they see one and to the legendary Irvine Welsh and Dean Cavanagh for being inspired enough by my story to want to take it all the way to the big screen.

To Mike Jones for *believing* me and handling my crazy emails, Katherine Stanton for her time and energy on the project, Rob Cox, Anna Robinson, everyone else at Simon & Schuster and Gina Rozner for being a hot-shot publicist.

To Jonathan Shalit for his confidence in Silibil N' Brains and for being an instrumental link between my twisted mind and the short-sighted. To Jay D and Del Conboy for 'getting' us and for putting their necks on the line for my insane schemes.

To my best friends and brothers in Hopeless Heroic whose unfaltering support has pulled me through two incredibly stressful years. I can't thank them enough for writing the soundtrack of this story with me. To Rob Bailey for everything we've shared over the last few years, for holding my head together until the ambulance arrived and for being the best drinking partner an alcoholic could have. To my guitarist Grant Magnus, the funniest man alive, whose life has been inspirational to me. Tony Sabberton and David Knight, the future is ours. I'd also like to thank Grant Dickson for all of his help, Owen Packard at Hero PR, Richard Poet, Kyle Howe and everyone who has helped me turn my vision of Hopeless Heroic into reality.

A special thanks to Gordon Donald for sticking with me for the whole ride from Silibil N' Brains to Hopeless Heroic and Andy Patrick for shining a light on some of my darkest moments and helping me find my way back into the studio. I will repay you both for your loyalty and respect.

To all my former band members from Silibil N' Brains, Gordon, Colin Petrie and Greg Keegan for lying for me to protect my lies – we'll always have Brixton. To Danny O'Malley, John 'Chic' Harcus and Matt Netherington for supporting Silibil N' Brains and not hating us for disrupting PMX's progress by what could only be described as common band member thievery.

To Big Mark and Ian Martin for keeping Silibil N' Brains alive on the road.

To Murray Buchanan for looking out for my best interests.

To my cousins Warren and Byron Bain for not only documenting all of the mayhem but also attempting to keep me sane in my most demented of times. I know watching two of your best friends fall apart must have been heartbreaking.

To Grace Stanley for drawing me out of the shadows when everything went black.

Thanks also to Caroline and Darren Saunders for your continued support, Steve Warby, Dan Miller, Nickie Banks, Stuart Reid, Andy Carrington, Biscuits, Emily and everyone at The Dairy, The Svengali Team, Jane Graham and Victoria McArthur, Mark 'Skinny' Adjacan, Paul Greenwood, Calvin Talbot, Fingers, Skills, Wayne Beckford, Brendan and Garth Barnes and everyone from Crash Car Burn, Fabian Sing and Bret. Alex and Chris of Delica Black and Mike and the boys from Hypo Psycho. Mary Boyd, Zenga Boyd and the boys Gary and Shaun and their grandfather Bill. Lisa Webb, Blair McAfferty, Chris Boyd, Craig 'Spit' Arnott and the rest of the boys from the Albany terrace days.

For their musical inspiration I'd like to thank Eminem & D12 (RIP Proof), Pharcyde, DJ Shadow, Billy Talent, Muse, My Chemical Romance and Rage Against The Machine.

Gavin Bain

And now to thank my greatest friend, Oskar 'Bravo' Kirkwood, my sparring partner who has had more confidence in me over the years than anyone in my life, including myself. He is without a doubt the darkest, funniest poet there is, a true genius and his words continue to spark creativity in me. Our deal is still on.

And finally
To Bill
Porcupine

Some names and dates have been changed to protect the privacy of individuals.

Prologue

Afterwards, they would call it a suicide attempt – and that's if they would call it anything at all. Mostly they chose never to speak about it, at least not in my company. Friends protected me, or wanted to, by drawing a polite veil of silence over a night most of us would like to forget – a night I still dream about vividly, whether I like it or not.

It was a Saturday, the end of August 2006, and a hot summer's night. Eagle's Nest was empty. No girls tonight, no parties, no marathon sessions on the PlayStation, just spent beer cans and bottles of Jack on the stained wood floors, ashtrays overflowing with roaches, and everywhere balled-up tissues and the lingering smell of stale breath. I was on my own, as I so often was these days, watching television. Reading Festival was showing live. Muse were headlining – making an awful lot of noise, for three small men. A crowd of 65,000 were moving as one to the music, a great rolling wave that filled the television screen like an electric, pulsing thing. This was Muse's defining moment: no longer just another band with potential, but now one of the major players on the world stage. I'd met Muse a couple of years ago at a party with Bill. One of our songs, most likely 'Losers', had come over the speakers. The bassist was all smiles, and told us that the song was amazing, brilliant, a sure-fire future Number 1. He said that Bill and I, Silibil N' Brains, would be huge. We couldn't help but agree with him.

But Silibil N' Brains never did become huge. We'd died, unofficially and acrimoniously, more than a year ago now, and I hadn't seen Bill since. The record company weren't returning my calls any more, all the money was gone, and I was alone, by myself, on a Saturday night. On television, Muse launched into 'Newborn' and the crowd approached frenzy. *This* was huge.

I hurled the remote control at the screen, and as I drew my arm back in I felt a sudden tightness. My chest began to constrict; I couldn't breathe. The room span. Out of nowhere came a crushing migraine, and my eyes filled with tears. I ran downstairs to the kitchen and the drawer in which I'd stashed all my medicine, my co-codymol, my co-dydramol, my precious, precious painkillers. I found three bottles: white ones, yellow ones, red and yellow ones. I tipped the contents of each into my palm and then rammed them into my mouth like skittles, washing them down with warm milk – the closest thing to hand. They filled my throat like the jackpot payout from a fruit machine, and then they were gone.

Back in my room, and Muse had just finished playing 'Plug in Baby' and were now three silhouettes leaving the stage to endless cheers. There was blinding light on the screen. The credits rolled. Did I really hurl the television on to the floor then, and attack it with a cricket bat, screaming with rage as I did so, or did I just fantasize about doing that? I lay down shakily on my bed, sank into the mattress and kept on sinking, through the floor, down through the front room and into the earth below. The migraine was receding. I was attaining bliss.

I have no idea how much time passed, but I became slowly aware that I was now awake but unable to move. My limbs were heavy as lead. I began to thrash my body left and right, but this was agonizingly hard to do, like swimming in sludge. With enormous effort, I managed to roll over, off the bed and on to the carpeted floor. I dragged myself slowly out of the room and towards the stairs, using only my arms – my legs useless behind me – breathing hard through my open mouth. I couldn't stand up, couldn't even sit, so I rolled my body down the stairs, on my front, my face and my shoulders, and ended up flat on my back on the landing, looking up at the hall light, a naked bulb that hung from a long stretch of cord whose base had come loose from the ceiling.

I didn't want to die. Not like this, not now.

I crawled into the bathroom in darkness, then up the side of the bath, hitting the cold shower tap on the way, and collapsed into it. Freezing water fell on my face. I was sinking again, my muscles mulch and my bones putty. My teeth began to chatter, my body to convulse. And it was like this that I fell again into sublime semi-consciousness. The water continued to fall, a waterfall – Victoria Falls, perhaps, thousands of miles away, my African youth, a summer holiday I never managed to take but always wanted to . . .

From somewhere, a sound. My name.

'Gavin? What the hell are you doing?'

My sister, Michelle. She turned on the light. It blazed.

'*Gav*? Oh shit, Gavin! What have you done?'

She stopped the water, and pulled me by my sodden T shirt up and out of the bath, screaming my name and slapping my face. But I was miles away, and she couldn't reach me. I felt myself being dragged, out of the bath and down the stairs, the floor hard beneath my head. She left me in the hall then, and I could hear a car start outside. She came back, still calling my name, and pulled me into the back seat, where I lay sopping wet, still in search of my final private bliss, only that. Beneath me I felt the speed of the wheels. Blurred light filled the window, the sound of honking horns puddled in my ears.

I slept.

Memory is a funny thing. You can call upon it or ignore it at will, and you can change what you remember to suit any particular situation. Over the past few years I've made up all kinds of memories, for all sorts of reasons, and a great many of them were, as I saw it, entirely necessary, as if nothing less than my life depended on their existence. I have *chosen*, then, not to remember now much of what happened later that night. I have no recollection of arriving at the hospital, nor of the rigmarole of admission, a gurney, a bed, concerned nurses, frowning doctors. But then I don't need to. By this time I'd had enough experience of hospitals to know that they were all the same. I would be fixed up and, somewhere along the line, admonished, spoken down to, offered counselling. The mental scars would heal, the physical ones would fade in time. I don't recall what these latest doctors and nurses said to me, nor even whether my stomach was pumped. I do know, because she later told me, that Michelle when she spoke with the doctors felt it crucial to play down the seriousness of the occasion, suggesting that I'd simply been drunk and confused about my medication. This was true. I was on a lot of medication. There was no mention, to my knowledge, of depression, no official whisper that I had tried to take my own life. I was not to be detained any further. I could go.

I was discharged the following lunchtime, Michelle waiting for

4

me with a change of clothes and an exhausted, disappointed expression on her face. The sun was shining and hot, and I was happy to be alive, but I'd felt better. I slumped in the back seat, the fabric beneath me still damp from the night before, and Michelle drove me home wordlessly. I saw nothing of the journey back, registering only the bumps in the tarmac along the way and a low growl in my stomach that had nothing to do with hunger.

At home, Michelle opened the curtains in my room. I drew them again. The television that had so taunted me the night before was still there on top of the chest of drawers, unharmed by cricket bat. I lay down on my bed, and stared up into nothing. I thought nothing, and felt nothing. Michelle went downstairs and came back up with a cup of tea, turning the light on as she entered. I asked her to turn it off again. I didn't want the tea, and I didn't want to see anyone. I never wanted to think about music again. I wanted only darkness, somewhere to hide.

I'll be honest. I'd never thought things would turn out like this for me. I was twenty-five years old, the age by which I had always envisioned I would be famous, a superstar, my name in lights, my cheeky genius analysed on television, in magazine and newspaper profiles and on a thousand fansites. But that one little lie – that one little necessary lie – had over the course of two years grown and mutated out of all proportion, and had turned me into something I wasn't, someone I no longer recognized. Because of it I had lost everything. I hated myself.

I was in a living hell.

One

My first real memory is of blood.

She was my nanny, one of many in Montclair, and I regret that I no longer recall her name, but I do remember the night she came staggering up to the house in pieces. She'd had an argument with her boyfriend, and he had taken a machete to her arms, her chest and back. I was seven years old, and this was fascinating. Blood was pouring out of her in great frothing arcs. She wasn't screaming out loud, but rather wailing pitifully, as if more in distress than pain, which confused me. Didn't it hurt? Before my mother bundled me out of the way and ordered my sisters to take me back to my room, I caught sight of the wounds up close, the dark brown of her skin contrasting somehow obscenely with the shocking white of bone. By the time she was inside the house, my mother taking towels to her wounds, the bedroom door had slammed shut in my face and my nanny's wailing had become horrified screams. She would be gone by morning, and I would never see her again.

A few months later, and it was my father's turn. It was late at night, in the middle of the week, and he and my uncle Duncan had still not returned home from work. My mother grew increasingly concerned; she had already put in the usual round of phone calls, but nobody had heard from him. We sat pointedly not watching television while she paced the room until at last we heard noises from outside. We rushed to the window as one and saw him and my uncle striding purposefully towards the porch. My father is a lean man, but broad with it. You wouldn't mess with him, though many foolishly did. He walked up the steps and, as light fell on him, we recoiled. His face and shirt were full of blood. He was smiling. My mother screamed.

'Hughie! What the hell happened?'

'Don't worry, Norah,' he said in an oddly calm voice. 'It's not *my* blood.'

Surprisingly, it wasn't Uncle Duncan's, either. Instead it was the blood of a business associate – by now, presumably, a *former* business associate. They'd had a dispute over money and it had turned ugly. Like many Scottish people, even those relocated to the other end of the earth, my father liked to settle his disputes (and he had many) not with dialogue or even his fists, but with his forehead. Tonight, he had stuck his head into a disagreeable great oaf of a man for daring to mess him about. A bar brawl had ensued. My father used to take pride in his inability to back down when challenged – in his industry, this kind of thing happened all the time. He was always getting into scrapes, most often with Uncle Duncan, with whom he ran a construction company. Anything could set them at one another's throats. Drunk and argumentative one night, my uncle threw him over a balcony. He fell two floors and landed on top of a big shed, which collapsed under his weight. He got up, dusted himself down, and laughed mercilessly. And then he went for my uncle. The following morning, they both groggily regained consciousness to find

8

themselves side-by-side in an unheated hospital ward. Policemen were waiting to ask them questions.

He's from Paisley, my father. What can I tell you?

I was born in Durban, South Africa, in 1981. Nine years before the release of Nelson Mandela. I was raised in an almost genteel existence of postcolonial comfort, far from my parents' native Scotland and blissfully oblivious to any local tensions. After years of working for others, my father and Uncle Duncan were by this time co-running their own construction business, and were doing well. Our families lived across the street from one another, and ours was a life of sunshine, swimming pools and beaches. Our houses were big and spacious; we drove nice cars. I had a succession of nannies, each of whom I loved dearly. We were as tight as only families can be, and, though my father and uncle were always at war, Duncan's sons, Grant, Warren and Byron, were my closest friends, more like brothers than cousins. We spent every evening together, and most weekends. I enjoyed school, and I thrived at sport – football, cricket, surfing. I loved the beach, and had a year-round tan. I had many friends, many of whom were, like us, originally from somewhere else. My only connection to what my parents still liked to call *home* was notional at best. My bedroom walls were covered with Rangers posters. I idolized Ally McCoist. The only way I could ever imagine relocating to Scotland was in order to follow McCoist's footsteps as an Ibrox legend.

I was twelve years old when things began to change. Unbeknown to the rest of us, the family business had been struggling for some time; and now, suddenly, went bankrupt. We were stunned, and then we panicked. There were all sorts of reasons, my father insisted – ask-no-questions reasons, mostly – but I knew it had something to do with a disagreement between my dad and Duncan. There was no way back, my father claimed. The business was damaged beyond repair. His brother would be a stranger to him from now on.

All of a sudden, we had to tighten our belts. We started to go out less. I no longer surfed at the weekend.

For the next two years, my father tried to claw his way back into business on his own, but with little success. We were running on empty and it was only a matter of time before there was nothing left. But then, in 1993, an opportunity came my father's way. A close friend of his offered him a share in a biltong bar, which, if it thrived as anticipated, could well go on to become a chain of biltong bars. How was my father, in 1993, to know that this proposed chain would go on to become one of South Africa's biggest, and that biltong (dried meats) would go on to become a thriving export? Had he invested the last of his savings in this venture, he would have been a millionaire many times over by now. But my father was ignorant to all this back then, and so he said no, insisting that we go back *home* instead. South Africa was no longer the country he had settled in seventeen years previously. He craved a return to his roots, and, no, he wouldn't be talked out of it. We were going.

My mother has never forgiven him.

I was thirteen years old in 1994. Durban, specifically suburban Montclair, was the only life I'd known – a good life, and so very uncomplicated. It felt full of opportunity, too. With our school no longer segregated on grounds of race, we now had more children, and a formidable football team, and I had myself a whole new circle of friends. I told my father that I didn't want to leave. I begged him. I told him that he could go on without me. I was staying here. His response was to laugh. 'Think of Ibrox,' he said.

Straight Outta Scotland

In April of 1994 Kurt Cobain, a man who was to mean more to me in the years after his death than he ever did alive, had just blown his brains out, and I was wrenched from my place of birth, this golden country, to somewhere bleak and alien and far, far away. Worse, it was going to be *cold*. My father related this fact to me as if it were a boast. 'So cold it will put hairs on your tits.' For this reason and so many more, it felt fundamentally wrong to leave South Africa. To get on that plane was a grave error that would surely alter everything. I couldn't find the courage to tell my friends that I was leaving, because that would be admitting the truth of it, and so I never did. My South African childhood ended one lazy, hot afternoon. I left the school gates with a wave to my friends, saying, 'Bye, see you tomorrow', as if that really would be the case. Then I went back to pack sullenly alongside my sisters, and would never see many of them again.

The Durban sky was cloudless when we left it for the last time, an endless cobalt blue, and then it was black, pinpricked by a million bright stars. But the sky we arrived in many hours later was grey and malevolent, with clouds that threatened rain. Stepping off that plane was like coming out of a sauna and diving into an icy lake; the wind was uncompromising and froze a disgruntled frown on my face. When we finally reached the dark estates of North Motherwell, our new home, it was close to midnight. There were no stars here, just the endless concrete silhouette of the estate only partially lit by the sodium glow of the few working streetlamps. We walked up the stairs to my grandmother's flat, and we could hear screaming arguments, glasses smashing in the street, the occasional scream, dogs barking and, from a distance, a wailing police siren. It was freezing, our breath clouding before our faces. The only warmth was an ember: the smile of greeting on my grandmother's wizened face. Everything else was bitter and bleak.

North Motherwell is not Scotland at its most radiant, and shall never be a European destination of culture. It is not bustling and metropolitan like Glasgow, nor beautiful and cobblestoned like Edinburgh, but rather a featureless crater smack-bang in the middle of the country that I could not believe I would warm to. The council estate on which my grandmother lived had been nicknamed Little Bosnia by the locals – and with good reason. It was a place that the local drunks and drug addicts treated simultaneously as their playground, their place of business and a toilet that they forever failed to flush. The lifts rarely worked, and whenever you climbed the stairs to our floor you'd inevitably encounter some native wildlife along the way. On a good day you'd be asked for change. On a bad day you'd be mugged for it.

We had arrived in April, early spring. April in Durban was already hot, hotter than your average British summer, and glorious. But in North Motherwell that year it was unseasonally cold. There was a petulance, somehow, to the eternally driving rain, and the sneering wind that blew it sideways taunted you with its December chill. Lying still on my tiny bed that first night, looking up at a much paler, smaller moon than I was used to, I had a sense of foreboding that you don't normally expect to experience at thirteen years of age. I realized that I had left paradise, to paraphrase Joni Mitchell, for a parking lot. Excuse me for saying this, Dad, but fuck Ally McCoist and fuck Ibrox.

The tenement block we were now calling home looked straight out of the nineteenth century. Great sections of it were barely habitable, but somehow there was a waiting list for eager new tenants to move in whenever the bailiffs moved somebody out – the incomers presumably arriving from even bleaker places than this. We were a family of five, squeezed alongside my grandmother, in a place built for two at best. It was cramped and poorly heated. The hot-water tap offered mostly cold, tinted the colour of rust. The fact that my grandmother had tried her best to be house-proud in a place that didn't deserve her efforts pierced me to my core. My parents slept on the couches, my sisters shared a bedroom and I was lucky enough to be holed up in my uncle Billy's old room, where I found solace in the pages of his old comic books. Weeks later I found his record collection and this was the first time I had heard real heavy metal, the likes of Motörhead, Maiden and Sabbath. I had no idea what I was listening to but I loved it: it was as if I had just discovered a new world. In troubled times to come, I would find myself withdrawing from everyone and everything, locking myself in my uncle's room and disappearing into this new world, a world of heroes and heavy metal, a world far from North Motherwell.

My parents perennially sniped at each other, we saw little of my older sister Laurette, whose ability to make instant new friends took none of us by surprise. Michelle was brooding and depressed, as homesick for Durban as I was. She spent most of the first few weeks curled up in her bed, facing the wall. Depression infected us all, though my father refused to acknowledge it. Everything, so I was convinced, had conspired to make us comprehensively unwelcome here. A simple trip to the corner shop was fraught with danger, awkwardness and embarrassment. I dreaded the inevitability of school. Even at home we were exposed to a frosty reception. My grandmother's senile cat was a mean fat fucker who failed to disguise its displeasure at our arrival. This was a cat that liked to maul, and my mother's legs were the perfect battleground, her varicose veins target practice for claws that refused to be blunted by age.

The night before my first day of new school was when the bad dreams began. But these, as I was to learn, were more than mere nightmares. They were in fact night *terrors*, and they would continue to haunt me for what I am now convinced will be the rest of my life. It's actually a recognized medical condition, night terrors, known also as *pavor nocturnus*, so I can't be accused of exaggeration. It's a parasomnia disorder characterized, so the doctor told me, by extreme terror and the temporary inability to regain full consciousness. In other words, I always knew when I was in the middle of one of these episodes, but was helpless to escape it.

I no longer recall the finer points of that very first dream, but it was the most frightening thing I'd ever experienced, and I woke up resolved to do everything I could never to experience it again. And the symptoms I experienced that first night set the standard for what became a regular occurrence. My limbs would twitch, then begin to thrash. I would whimper, cry, scream. The dreams themselves could have been lifted from any horror movie you've ever seen. A being would watch me from the corner of the room, a horribly distorted thing with lifelessly pale-grey skin covering its jutting bones, its elongated face carrying a melted expression of wretched agony. Sometimes, it would approach me with a stealth and patience that curdled my blood – so much so that by the time we were standing face-to-face I would have worked myself up into such a frenzy that, as future girlfriends would attest, it would seem as though I was suffering from an unconscious epileptic fit.

In later years, doctors would provide me with the perfect remedy for banishing them. Just relax, they'd tell me. The more you panic, the more likely you are to suffer from them. Wonderful advice, so very sage. Thing is, I never chose not to relax, just as I never elected to panic in my sleep. The anxiety set in then, as it still does today, for abundant good reason. And starting a new school in an alien land, so far as I was concerned, was enough to imbue me with sheer white terror.

I knew that school was going to be an ordeal. How could it not be? A tanned South African with twanging vowels was never going to go down very well in a place like North Motherwell. I was *different*, the very worst thing any teenager could be in a place like this. I had already been working hard on the accent, attempting to stem the elasticity of my Afrikaner vowels and toughening up the consonants with spit in my throat until I sounded like my father when he was drunk, but my sisters insisted I would fool no one. I'd stick out like a sore thumb, they'd mock. I'd be beaten to shit because of it.

I arrived at my modern comprehensive looking fit and healthy, my eyes shining from a diet in which nothing came frozen or deep-fried; palpably foreign, uninvited and unwanted. Every school, of course, has its fair share of bullies, but this one was full of them. If they were searching for a new target three quarters of the way through the school year, then they didn't have to look far. I was delivered to them on a plate, and the first dead arm came even before registration was taken.

'Welcome tae Scotland, ye cunt.'

Even without opening my mouth I had managed to rile my classmates. For reasons that probably had a lot to do with money, my parents hadn't sorted me out with a proper uniform for that first day. Instead, mistakenly convinced that I was using initiative, I wore a Motherwell FC tracksuit – but so contrary was your average Motherwellian that hardly any of the fuckers in my year, or in the three years above, were Motherwell fans. The tracksuit got me heckled. The walk from registration to assembly got me another dead arm, and then somebody smacked his schoolbag into my head. At break time I cowered in the corner trying to look inconspicuous, but my friendlessness could not be disguised.

'So where're you from, arsehole?' This from someone considerably taller than me. At eyelevel with me was his Adam's apple, which protruded from his neck like a conker.

'Here,' I tried. 'North Motherwell. Well, ma dad's fae Paisley.'

'Not with that accent yer not.'

And suddenly I was on the ground, having been tripped and thrown, while his mates stood around me, laughing. By lunchtime I'd been the target of half a dozen other blows. I was laughed at, spat at, smacked and kicked. I tried my best to ignore it, to inwardly rise above it, convinced that if I could do so then they wouldn't be able to hurt me.

I was wrong. It hurt like hell.

My father, who had already warned me that Scottish schools were rough and that things would be hard before they got easy, was of the opinion that a little playground fighting was no bad thing. 'You're a Bain, and Bains don't lose fights,' he told me. 'Never run, and never let them see you cry. Someone hits you, you hit them back harder. They'll soon stop. Besides, fights are character-building.' On the fifth day, I decided to take his advice. When somebody picked on me in the playground at break time, I hit back – a harmless shove to the shoulder, granted, but the intent was there. For a moment my attacker looked stunned, appalled. Then he looked amused, and punched me square in the face. I crumpled. A pattern emerged. The very fact that I was starting to stand up to people somehow made me even more of a target, a flash little fucker from fuck knows where who needed to be taken down a peg or two, and introduced to local custom. I got black eyes. I lost the occasional tooth.

A couple of the more persistent bullies stood out. One was

called Michael Ballantyne, big, strong and dumb, his eyes too close together, his mouth misaligned in a cruel underbite. He is hopefully dead and buried now. It was Michael Ballantyne who had given me my very first dead arm, and then came back relentlessly for more. He was there at the school gates every morning and every afternoon, white shirt untucked, skinny tie askew, a sneer on his ugly potato face. But he knew how to fight; and when I went at him with a retaliatory punch one day he spun seamlessly out of its path and suddenly had me by the arm, which he twisted one way as my body twisted the other. I screamed in agony. 'Please,' I begged. I howled. '*Please.*' He said something to me in response, but these were heavy words doled out in an impenetrable accent. I understood none of them. I asked him again to let go. He laughed. I thought again of my father. What would he do? I made a fist with my free hand. Catching him off guard, I spun out of the hold and cracked him on the side of the face with my knuckles. The dumb fuck never knew what hit him. He was down. I'd hurt him. Onlookers dared to point and laugh, mocking him and praising, from a safe distance, the new boy's reckless bravery. He gave me a wide berth after that; but, as I was soon to find out, he had simply passed the baton on to somebody else. Steven Ballantyne, his older brother.

Steven Ballantyne was taller and leaner than Michael, and more dangerously reckless with it, a lunatic who knew he had no hope of redemption. Steven had nothing to lose, certainly nothing so concrete as a future, and so his attacks, when they came, always had the potential to be properly dangerous. He routinely targeted half the kids at school, and was known to have broken the bones of several, one of whom, if rumours were to be believed, was still in traction three months after an attack with a crowbar. He now chose to target me for daring to stand up to his brother.

'Ye've crossed the line, pal,' he said, grabbing me in a headlock in the playground one morning. 'And ahm gannae have tae teach yer pretty sister a lesson. Michelle, isn't it?'

Steven was in Michelle's class, which meant he'd have ample opportunity to target her. I felt sick at the prospect. He tossed me to the ground, then, and I stayed down, sick with worry. Days later, he had picked her out of the playground scrum at the final bell, then stealthily followed her. Just before reaching the school gates, he acted, suddenly breaking out into a run and pushing her over. He didn't push her very hard, and she only fell to her knees, but this became a daily occurrence, and my fifteen-year-old sister, in her black uniform skirt and white socks, had perpetually bloody knees, which scabbed over and then broke again with each new attack. The more this went on, the more crazy with anger she became. She screamed at him and threatened to kill him, but he just laughed back. Once she slapped him, and Steven Ballantyne didn't hesitate. He grabbed her by the neck with his large right hand, his bitten fingernails squeezing into her flesh.

'Careful,' he whispered, and suddenly she believed him capable of so much worse. There was nothing she could do. She was the only girl in school who could be recognized by her knees alone.

I couldn't let him get away with this, so one afternoon I attacked him before he could attack her. I came up to him from behind and took him out in a flying, rugby-style tackle. He landed hard on the pavement, his chin taking the force of the impact. He roared, then rolled over, got up, and kicked the shit out of me. Bruised ribs, the doctor said later. They'd heal in time, *but be careful*.

When they finally did heal, I decided to try out for the school football team. Perhaps this would at last endear me to some of my other classmates, and put a stop to all the bullying. It was almost the end of the school year, after all: I was no longer, strictly speaking, a *new* boy.

Steven Ballantyne was on the school team. Not because he had any talent, but because he possessed the kind of brute strength that all teams ultimately need. Steven was the one who was brought on as a substitute when we were 3–0 down with a quarter of an hour to spare, when our psychotic PE teacher didn't want the shame of a 5–0 drubbing. He would then take out the legs of any attacker that dared come his way. If we were lucky we would even get a couple of goals back before his inevitable red card was issued.

I made the team, but our training sessions pitched us against one another, and Ballantyne refused to ever go easy on anyone. I had stud-marks up and down my legs, right up to the thighs. I had them in my back and, once, on my shoulder blade. Each one of them had come from him, and I was fast approaching my breaking point. In the bath one night, hoping to ease my bruised body, I resolved that the next time he attacked me, either on the pitch or in the playground, I'd bite a great fucking hole out of him.

I didn't have to wait long.

The following afternoon he was loitering as usual by the school gates. Today he was busy wrestling a bag away from a younger pupil, which he then threw to Michael, who launched it on to the nearest roof. The pupil burst into tears. They laughed loudly. They were still laughing as I walked past them.

'Bainy, ye cunt! How's the puncture marks?' He grabbed me in a headlock and forced my face against the steel fence. 'Wit the fuck are ye still doing here, anyway? Have ah no made it clear that yer no wanted in Motherwell? Fuck oaf back t'Australia, or wherever it is ye come fae.'

His bare arm was right there, inches from my mouth. This was the moment I had waited for. I bit him. I bit him hard, and I didn't let go. My ears filled with his screams as my mouth filled with his blood. He tried to shake me free, but I was a pit bull with lock-jaw, immovable. He thrashed and flailed and cried and shouted, but still I held on. A crowd had gathered around us by now, whipped up by the sight of blood and urging me on. Michael Ballantyne was nowhere to be seen. Eventually a teacher forced her way through the throng. It was Mrs Leonard, my English teacher. I liked Mrs Leonard, and I had convinced myself over the past six weeks that the feeling was mutual. Instead of shouting at us like any normal teacher would, she stooped to my level and whispered in my ear. She suggested, very quietly, that I should let him go now, and so I did. I spat Steven Ballantyne's flesh and blood to the ground, chicken skin and iron filings, and looked up at him looking back at me like I was a madman. His face was bright red, and riven with pain. And me? I was experiencing the pure, unfettered rush of the victorious, and I loved it.

After the summer holiday, the most unremarkable and boring of my life – there were no surfing opportunities in Motherwell, and the sun generated precious little heat – we moved out of my grandmother's tenement block. My father had managed, finally, to find us somewhere more permanent, a small cottage in Newarthill, a quiet neighbourhood on the other side of town. It was hardly Durban, but it wasn't Little Bosnia either. The house had four bedrooms, a decent-sized living room and a hot tap that worked. We were grateful.

In September the school corridors were no longer unfamiliar to me and not so relentlessly unfriendly, either. Steven Ballantyne had been kicked off the football team while under investigation for GBH on the field, allowing me the opportunity, at last, to shine. I began to forge friendships with my team-mates, which spilt over into the classroom; and, though I didn't yet socialize much, I was beginning to hold my head up high. Most of my evenings, meanwhile, were spent in my room, listening to music, writing stories and watching videos. I loved to lose myself in films: *Scarface*, *The Deer Hunter*, anything starring De Niro or Pacino or Jack Nicholson. I was in awe of actors; I loved observing someone losing himself so thoroughly in a role, pretending to be someone else. The whole concept of becoming someone else fascinated me. I'd have given anything to become someone else, to break free from the confines of my own character.

In South Africa I had been popular and confident, the class clown. I knew who I was just as sure as I knew that I belonged. But here in Scotland I was only ever a bundle of nerves, timid and cautious, clumsy and terrified in front of girls. School felt like a life sentence, with only brief bursts on the football field allowing me any kind of creative freedom. My night terrors came frequently now, three, four times a week. I woke up exhausted. My sisters were out all the time, my mother was working two jobs, while my father was travelling up and down the country, working all hours, and desperate to start making some proper money. No one was looking out for me.

But then somebody did. Mrs Leonard, my English teacher, clearly saw a need in me and took it upon herself to bring me out of my shell. Within the year she had started to single out my essays, telling the class just how full of vitality and enthusiasm they were. She was always on at me to read them out in front of everyone, but I lacked the confidence. I couldn't do it. Nevertheless, she encouraged me to enrol in the school's after-hours drama class, saying that it might just be the making of me.

I was tempted by the idea, if only to please Mrs Leonard, and for a while I committed myself to memorizing some of my favourite dialogue from some of my favourite films, then repeating these interactions endlessly before the bedroom mirror. 'You can't handle the truth!' I'd scream, Jack Nicholson to Tom Cruise in *A Few Good Men*. But the school plays tended to be more timid fare, things like *Grease* and *Oliver*, and I was far too self-conscious to appear in either.

I did want to endear myself to Mrs Leonard, though. She was like an angel, that woman, early thirties, sleek long blonde hair, with a trim figure of which she was justifiably proud. Her skirts were always just a little too tight, the zip gaping open a teasing centimetre to reveal the flesh of her hip. Her blouses gaped similarly at the chest, where the lace upholstery of her bra could be seen. Raise your hand to ask a question and she would come over directly and lean down in front of your open exercise book, the V of her neckline plunging so dangerously low that it was difficult to remember the question you had been poised to ask. The mischievous glint in her eye contact told you that here was someone who was sexually active, and that if you played your cards right with her, then, well … You never know. Stranger things had happened. She was a fantasy figure for all of us. And the preponderance of lace upholstery told us she knew it.

Mrs Leonard would often keep me behind after class on some or other pretence, aware that I was under stress and still intermittently bullied. Alone together, she sitting on top of her desk and facing me, we would talk about school, my studies, and of everything I had left behind in South Africa. I felt I could talk to her in a way I could talk to nobody else, and I soon learnt that if I looked emotional, my bottom lip quivering, then she would approach me with open arms, offering up an embrace. You don't fall into an embrace with a teacher when you are fifteen unless you happen to find her incredibly attractive. To me she was the perfect woman. She would give me special essay-writing assignments, and her subsequent excitement over their completion felt to me like being showered with her kisses. I was falling in love. More specifically, I wanted to fuck her brains out.

And perhaps I would have done had it not been for one particular parents' evening. My mother and I were doing the rounds of all the staff, most of whom were saying determinedly non-committal stuff ('Young Gavin is showing potential, if only he . . .' etc.). Mrs Leonard, however, was full of nothing but praise. She leant forward in her chair to tell my mother just how promising my work was, and how my clear love of writing; drama and art were subjects she thought I should pursue. My mother beamed back in response to the accolade but became quickly aware that much of it wasn't for her benefit at all, but for mine. Mrs Leonard was wearing her usual short skirt and, perched facing us as she was, her legs crossed provocatively, she left no one in any doubt that she was wearing not tights tonight but rather stockings and suspenders. At one point, she Sharon Stoned her legs, allowing me a glimpse all the way up her thighs, which were creamy and golden, and so soft I wanted to lick them. My mother watched me watch them, then transferred her aghast gaze to my teacher. My mother never was one for understatement. She erupted. She shot to her feet, stared Mrs Leonard up and down in disgust, and in no uncertain terms shouted her out before yanking me by the collar out of the classroom. She then dragged me through and out of the hall by my arm, half my year watching me go. I turned to look for Mrs Leonard as we left, but she too was leaving, in the other direction and just as hurriedly. Everyone was laughing at us, and I felt the hot fury of shame and anger that would boil for weeks and months after.

Mrs Leonard left the school shortly afterwards, for personal reasons. I dream of her still.

School was never quite that exciting again, but I did start to seriously pursue football. Within another year, I was one of the team's rising stars, and I managed to befriend one of the toughest kids in school, Paul Barker, whose patronage kept the bullies at bay. In return for his protection, I made him laugh and let him copy my English homework. I excelled on the pitch every Saturday morning, making goals and scoring them, and getting a name for myself. Soon, I was picked out for trials with the Scotland under-sixteens. My father, who never missed a match, was proud of me. But, a week before the trials took place, a particularly cruel fate intervened. I tripped down a set of stairs at school and fell awkwardly, breaking my ankle.

I was devastated, inconsolable, and spent weeks in a cast, under strict orders to rest the ankle completely. But rest and relaxation doesn't come easily to a teenager, and after just a few days I was going out of my mind with boredom. I couldn't sleep the day away because that would only invite the night terrors, and I couldn't stay awake and catch up on homework because all I could think about was what I was missing out on there on the pitch with my new friends, who were now busy making *other* new friends. And so I went to stay with my uncle Gordon. My ankle was feeling a little better by now, still bruised but mobile. A gentle stroll around a table could hardly hurt it. And snooker? Why not? My father's youngest brother had once been a champion snooker player, one of Scotland's best, and had even beaten the world's greatest player, Stephen Hendry, in an exhibition match. He was only too happy to take me under his wing and teach me everything he knew. I took to it with the same obsessive detail I did everything, and before I knew it we were practising for six hours every day. Snooker was never going to overtake football in my affections, but it was certainly going to make my recuperation period pass a whole lot easier. Within months, I was giving Gordon a run for his money. He was the finest teacher I ever had.

They say that ignorance is bliss, that fools have nobody to blame but themselves. And so it was that while I was going for that magical, if elusive, 147 break day after day, earning incrementally more respect from my uncle Gordon, I was actually doing serious damage to myself. What I didn't know then but do all too clearly now was that a snooker player has to put a lot of weight on one leg while measuring up his next shot, a process he repeats a thousand times during each match. The body can take this, of course, unless it is carrying an injury. Mine was. Day after day, from morning until night, I was putting all my weight on my left leg, which, although it felt fine to me, was still in the slow process of healing. When I went back to visit the physiotherapist after several months' absence, he couldn't quite believe what the x-ray was telling him. He asked me if I'd been keeping up the foot exercises as instructed, and I told him that I had. He asked me if I'd been kicking a football, which I'd been expressly ordered not to, and I replied, truthfully, that I hadn't.

'Well, I can't understand it, then. The bone looks more damaged now than it was when you first broke it.' He looked at me accusingly. 'You must have been doing *something* . . .'

I told him that I had been resting every day, doing nothing more strenuous than playing a bit of snooker with my uncle Gordon to pass the time. He held a hand up and I fell silent as he looked at me then the way I used to look at Michael and Steven Ballantyne, with bewildering contempt. He shook his head.

I was never going to become the next Ally McCoist.

It was around this time that the deaths started, first my uncle Robert (from a brain haemorrhage), then my grandfather (from cancer), not long after. This set the whole family reeling. We'd been very close to my grandfather, but he had been old, had had a good life. But Robert was still in his forties, and still far too young to have died. His funeral was a grim affair, and the whole family came together, bringing with it at least a flicker of optimism for proper reunion. If anything was to heal the rift between my father and Uncle Duncan, then this was surely to be it. It didn't. Duncan never made it to my uncle Robert's funeral. A fact that later sparked another row between my dad and Duncan at my grandfather's funeral in South Africa.

By now I no longer cared about sport at all, having switched allegiances once again. Sixteen years old, I realized that I could live without football, and without snooker and cricket, but that I couldn't live without music. Music was beginning to take me over, to define me. I had become obsessed with rock and rap, the angst of the former, the lyrical dexterity of the latter, and had started writing my own rhymes, many of them influenced by my favourite band, Rage Against the Machine, and full of invective for those in my life who deserved it most: the school bullies, my physiotherapist.

Despite being a school notable for its lack of talented individuals, we at Braidhurst High School nevertheless had to endure four, sometimes five talent shows a year, gala occasions in which every Tom, Dick and Rab stood up on stage to recite some or other shite. One year, I was encouraged to take part and, having turned down countless *Grease* and *Oliver*s, I knew that, though rigidly nervous, I was desperate to get up and have a thousand eyes all watching me in admiration. I said yes. I chose a song to perform, and committed it to memory. Nobody thought to ask what that song was until moments before going on stage. When they did, I was immediately ordered to come up with an alternative. No, said the headmaster furiously, I would not be permitted to give a rendition of Tupac Shakur's 'Strictly 4 My N.I.G.G.A.Z.' on the grounds of decency, and the likelihood that the title alone would cause offence. *Stupid boy*. I was given five minutes to come up with something else, or young Joanne Doran could read through her W. H. Auden again.

I ended up plumping for Coolio's 'Gangsta's Paradise', a rather tame 1995 middle-of-the-road hip-hop tune lifted from some cheap Hollywood movie starring Michelle Pfeiffer. I tweaked the lyrics, though – of course I did – and finished the song by segueing into 'Killing in the Name' by Rage Against the Machine, convinced that the impromptu battle cry of *'Fuck you, I won't do what you tell me'* would have the whole audience chanting right along with me, thereby elevating me into some kind of urban hero. But no one did. People in Motherwell weren't big on Rage Against the Machine.

I was discouraged from appearing at future talent shows, but that performance, in its own small way, successfully marked me out as someone different – a black sheep just possibly worthy of some kind of respect. I was still the school's square peg, the foreigner who now dressed exclusively in skateboard gear, but I was into my hip hop, and I had daring. I was cool, sort of.

What I should have realized, though, was that this would only bring me more attention of the ultimately negative kind. I got a lot of stick in the playground over the next few months for my talent-show turn, kids calling me a *wigger* or, worse, Vanilla Ice. But by now I had become impervious to criticism. Fuck them. It was water off a duck's back. At least, it mostly was. One lunchtime somebody approached me with the usual taunts. I gave him the finger and walked away. He followed, his baiting becoming louder. I tried my best to ignore him but he was start-ing to niggle. Then he said something about my mother. It was a facile comment, and it meant nothing to me really, not in the grand scheme of things, but I found myself turning on him anyway. I launched towards the fucker, and my fist caught him under the eye, splitting the skin wide open. It looked worse than it was, but the blood got a lot of attention. He fled, howling. Revenge, I knew, was inevitable.

I resigned myself to my fate. No point running away from something that was going to catch up with me eventually. As my father still so often said, it would make a man out of me yet. It happened quicker than expected – later that same day in fact – just minutes after I got the bus, and three streets from home. At first there were just a couple of them: the older brother of the one I had punched, and his wiry friend. For a few moments I was convinced that I could take them, but then more came into view behind them. *Fuck it, I'm not running*, I said to myself. The first punch was to my temple and it was as if someone had hit the mute button; the sound of the subsequent blows to the ribs was muffled. I doubled over before an uppercut sent me to the ground, the crowd kicking me in my stomach, my back, my solar plexus. The sound came back to me just before the stamping commenced, big feet coming down hard on my head. I heard a crack, I think everyone did, but the kicks just kept on coming. The pain lifted and floated away. I lost track of time.

At the hospital, the doctor told me that I had been lucky,

which I suppose was one way of looking at it. I had a fractured skull; but, though it was bad, he said, it could have been much worse. My father wanted blood, to get revenge on the mob who'd attacked me. My mother, ever the voice of reason, knew that a retaliation would only make things worse and she convinced my dad to let the police handle it. My mother was right, as usual. At school the attack had made headline news almost instantaneously. A counterattack was swiftly arranged by Paul Barker and, while I lay convalescing in bed, took place, meted out with a lot of aggression. There were casualties. A day later came the response to the counterattack. Just like that a gang war was started – one that I had inadvertently put into motion. The school playground became a battleground, and it soon spilt out into the neighbouring streets. It was written about in the local newspapers; the more violent attacks made the TV news. Over the next twelve months, five lads my age would be killed, either stamped or stabbed to death. Classrooms were full of boasts and battle cries.

Fearing for my life, my mother took the decision to remove me from school temporarily and send me back to South Africa and comparative safety. *Let's let things settle down, shall we?* Although exams were looming, I was happy to go. Couldn't wait, in fact, to board that plane and put thousands of miles between me and Scotland. Durban was just as I'd left it, an adventure playground full of sunshine and smiling faces. I was staying with some old family friends in a grand house whose guest quarters alone were bigger than our place back in Newarthill. Parties were arranged in my honour. I surfed at the weekends, played football every afternoon until the twinge in my ankle came back. I dated girls, got drunk, lost my virginity. After one fantastically chaotic evening, I

even spent the night in jail, but I far preferred this sort of character building to the sort that awaited me back in Motherwell. I
remained in South Africa for three months. They were the happi-
est of my young life.

When I was finally forced to return home, my exams now
imminent, I kept my head down. I studied hard because by now
I could see light at the end of the tunnel. Not long to go, and I'd
be free of all this, free to do as I chose. I sat my A levels, and
knew I'd passed all five. After that, the world was my oyster, but
my father wanted me to experience some hard graft before the
cushion of college. He put me to work on various building sites,
which at least taught me one thing: I was not cut out for proper
work. No discipline. Ordered to give his boss's office a fresh coat
of paint one morning, I sat in the corner and inhaled the pot's
toxic fumes instead, simply to see what kind of rush they would
give me. While still high, I painted everything within reach: tools,
engines, even the windows. Another day, I inadvertently set fire to
myself having played with the wrong kind of chemicals. And
every weekend, drunk and out on the town, I'd end up fighting,
being incapable now of walking away from any argument when I
could settle it with my forehead instead. Many nights I ended up
with blood all over me, and not always my own. I was my father's
son. But then something unexpected happened. Autumn came,
and I left home. And I became my own man.

Two

There were no tears when I departed Motherwell. The two and a half hours that separated it from Dundee, to where I was now headed to study art, felt like a distance to be measured in millennia, as if at last I'd left the Dark Ages for the modern world. There were fewer Neanderthals here, and the girls were prettier. It was incrementally warmer. And I knew that college was going to be as different from school as Dundee was from Motherwell. Just walking through its imposing gate for the interview had taught me this. Here I would be permitted, at last, to be myself. I was not sure quite who I was these days, but I was looking forward to finding out.

No night terrors haunted me the night before the first day, and for that I was grateful. Though I left the skateboard at home, I was dressed in skate threads like Vans and Zoo York, and I felt good, confident, as if on the cusp of something new. The art college in Dundee was full of posturing kids making statements, and I was no exception. Down the halls I passed goths and punks, indie kids and Bjorkettes. It felt exhilarating. I arrived at my room a little late – it was already mostly full – and this was clearly going to be like no class I'd ever attended before. There were no desks; rather there were easels, paints pots and discarded fruit bowls whose contents had been used for line study but now sat half-eaten on cupboard tops and in wastepaper baskets. My fellow students were of all shapes and sizes, half of them straight out of the pages of hairstyle magazines, the others straight out of tattoo parlours. In Motherwell they'd have had their heads kicked in for daring to go out in anything other than the uniform track-suit and trainers, but here everyone went out of their way to look as individually odd as possible. There were panda eyes and strange clothing, black lipstick and vicious fringes. And there in the corner, though I didn't know it quite yet, sat my future: Bill, the imminent Silibil to my Brains, and the man who would help change everything in my life completely.

How best to describe Billy Boyd? Bill was beautiful, a hand-some fucker who knew it, tall and broad and also dressed head to toe in imported American skate gear, with a pair of box-fresh Chuck Taylor's on his feet. He had punk-rock hair, his fingernails were Marilyn Manson black, and he was wearing eyeliner. I'd never seen eyeliner on a man before. It suited him. He sat astride his stool, nodding his head to the music pumping out of his headphones. He exuded self-satisfaction and natural confidence. Instinctively I liked him. He watched me walking over, his eyes seeming to draw me towards him.

'Over here, dude,' was the first thing he said to me, pulling out the stool beside him and encouraging me to sit.

'Missed much?' I said and by his reply I knew we'd get along.

'Nah, just some colostomy bags trying to teach us how to hold a paintbrush.'

Within minutes we were laughing and joking about music, skateboarding and comedy. I felt instantly that I could be honest with him in a way I never had with anyone before. It was as if, platonically, we were made for one another. He told me he was from Arbroath, a place that, he insisted, made Motherwell resemble Barbados. He confided that Dundee was as much an escape route for him as it had been for me. He needed to get out; his life depended on it. We talked about our favourite films, and quoted lines back and forth at one another. We had so much in common, as if we were the other's mirror image. But then, as I was to learn, Bill perpetuated this sensation in everybody new he met, a bond that everybody believed he shared with them alone, *Bill and me against the world*. He was good at complicity. By the time the tutor came in, an easy smile on her face as she laughed and joked with us, Bill and I were already inextricably linked.

Much of his confidence, I came to learn, was sexual. Bill's face was his passport, his demeanour a Get Out of Jail Free card. Everyone loved him. Even as they hated him, they loved him. He knew this, and played on it endlessly. Had he been born and raised in Los Angeles, he'd have had counselling for sexual addiction by now. But in Scotland he was simply an incorrigible old shagger, and proud of it. He'd fucked his way around Arbroath, going through not only his own girlfriends but also those of his closest friends. Occasionally he'd also bedded the *mothers* of his closest friends, and had a penchant for ugly girls as well because, well, why not? He could pull at a hundred paces, requiring no opening line because his smile was his opening line. Girls were drawn helplessly to him, like flies to shit. He dominated every room he was in. He made things happen.

He was the single most impressive person I'd ever met.

Within twenty-four hours of our first meeting, Bill almost ran me over in his Ford Escort – accidentally, I like to think. This was a pastime of Bill's, buying clapped-out old motors for never more than three figures, and then driving them with wanton abandon into an early grave. Each time, he had every good intention of doing them up, as status symbols in which he could later preen and race, but he never once saw it through. The majority of Bill's great schemes stalled at the starting post. On this particular morning, I heard the Escort's tubercular cough before I saw it approaching fast from behind, 2Pac's 'California Love' blaring from the window. I turned around to see it bearing down on me as it mounted the kerb. Instinctively, I jumped into the middle of the road, for safety.

'What the *fuck?*'

Bill beamed at me, his arm affecting a lorry-driver's pose on the window's rusty frame.

'What's up, bitch? Get in quick, this thing isn't insured.'

The engine strained, the chassis clattered back down on to Tarmac, and we were off, foot to the floor, touching the heady heights of thirty-five miles an hour in under twenty seconds, great bursts of smoke emanating from all points beneath us. We got out a minute later when we reached the staff car park, Bill having filched a parking permit somehow.

When I met him Bill was in a punk band. They'd play any dive that would take them within a fifteen-mile radius, and a great many did. I'd go and see his band whenever they played, while together we would frequent every rock and hip-hop club in the greater Dundee area, driving under the influence while tearing up the city streets. Bill had this gun, a replica, that shot pellets. Late at night we'd rumble down deserted streets shooting street signs, traffic lights, and scaring the slumbering homeless. We got stopped by the police so many times they began to know us by name. Not once did they check the glove compartment; a small mercy. But they did get him for driving without a licence, without due care and attention, without insurance, MOT or a tax disc, and confiscated the disabled parking permit he'd managed to obtain and refused to give it back.

We also met *a lot* of girls. Before Bill came along, sex had never really been high on my agenda. I'd always suffered from a succession of rather singular obsessions to which I'd devoted myself exclusively. Whether it was football, cricket, snooker or music, I would always follow it to the cost of everything else, and this included my private life. I'd always liked girls, but had never quite possessed the confidence to approach them. They looked through me, I was sure, as if I were glass. But with Bill they were everywhere, and we were spoilt for choice. And, even though he always got the lion's share, there were always more than enough pretty girls to go around. I was to prove his perfect comedy foil, the ideal sparring partner. We worked well as a team, each of us aware of our differing yet complementary strengths. I was his equal. Bill had never had an equal before.

His band was called Dead Foetus, and he was its only style – of that there was little doubt. You couldn't take your eyes off him, even in the rehearsal room. But then you couldn't remember any of his songs afterwards, either, and this was something I realized about them early on: they were never going to go anywhere. I told Bill so. To my surprise, he agreed.

The reason we clicked so well, I think, was that I was the first person to ever stand up to him. Everyone else he knew simply wanted to ride on his coattails, to bathe in the rays of his colossal ego. But there was no discipline to him. He never thought anything through, never once stopped to consider the consequences of his actions. He was on his way to crashing and burning, yes, but the journey would be a thrilling one.

What occurred to me was that I could harness Bill's essence and make something special of it. With his ego and my drive, we could accomplish something *together*. He would bring his brawn, his exquisite simplicity (Silly Bill, we called him) and me my brain, and we could leave Motherwell and Arbroath, even Dundee and Scotland itself, far behind us.

Bill's grandfather, once an aspiring musician himself, had a home studio – a humble affair that sat in the corner of his nicotine-yellow spare room – that he allowed us to use whenever we liked. After I had convinced Bill to ditch Dead Foetus, which he did without a moment's hesitation, we'd hole up in there trying to make some kind of mutant hybrid of punk and rap shot through with an overflow of teenage enthusiasm we didn't quite yet know how to limit. It was an educational time, and quickly highlighted just how disparate our personalities and work ethics were. Bill, I learnt, didn't much want to engage in the actual creation of a track, the nuts and bolts of it. He wanted only to grab the microphone and rap all over it, to imprint his characters so forcefully on to a song that you'd be forced to applaud its genius while laughing at its hilarity. It fell to me, consequently, to be the technical head, the engine room. It was me who built up each of our beats, who created the hook of any song we did. I went to sleep humming rhythms, which I'd commit to tape immediately upon waking. I would record the beats, and the samples, and arrange the tracks before putting my vocals on top, leaving spaces for Bill to do his thing later. Only then, when a track was finally ready for him, did I have his full attention. And what he came up with was effortlessly brilliant every time. I couldn't have done it without him.

Over the next few months we streamlined our influences in the hope of coming up with something that was definably *us*. Ultimately we were gravitating away from heavy metal and more into rap, specifically the Pharcyde, Cypress Hill and Method Man, but (we hoped) with our own unique twist. It was the dawning of the twenty-first century and our benchmark was Eminem, whose early splenetic brilliance we desperately wanted to match. Not only was he the best white rapper we could think of, but he was also a lyrical genius, and funny with it. As were we. And so we sang about sex and masturbation, drink and bad behaviour. We were eighteen years old, and we were irresistible.

Long before we started getting any proper gigs, we would perform anywhere we could: impromptu sessions in the skate park, the college canteen, old-man pubs in town and alongside any busker who would tolerate us. Occasionally we'd work under the name B-Production, though we were mostly still performing as ourselves. Either way, we never had any trouble whipping up an appreciative crowd, drawn to the performance itself as much as to the music we were playing. We were clever and funny, and our audiences themselves became part of the show. We flirted with girls and joked with guys, all the while trying to outdo one another with lyrical putdowns and deadpan disses. People cheered and applauded; girls would pass us their phone numbers. Pretty soon half of Dundee's student population were talking about us. Now we would roam the halls and corridors of our campus, skateboards under arm and feet, and were regularly stopped by students keen to know when we were next performing. Not wanting to disappoint, we made a daily occurrence of it: every lunchtime, the college canteen, a fresh new battle rap, all welcome. Battle raps are lyrical duels that have helped hone the skill of every self-respecting US rap superstar you'd care to mention; they require mastery of the art of making up lyrics on the spot, the vast majority of which will be sarcastic asides and withering critiques. A good battle rap can be hysterical, and we became *very* good at battle raps. We could spin them out for hours. Our audiences loved them, and soon we were all missing classes as a result. One afternoon in the college canteen went like this:

> Ladies beware of Bill, you don't know where his hand's been, plus I saw you buying Vaseline and *Playgirl* magazine. You're not a guy; you're a female drag queen, in a toilet with George Michael is where he was last seen. I saw you listening to Hanson, dancing, you're outta fashion and you're softer than Elton John in the Playboy mansion.

To which Bill responded:

> Don't listen to Gav – half of you girls know I'm actually straight; he's acting fake, I don't exaggerate his penis is so small he needs tweezers to masturbate. You're like a school kid on Saturday, you got no class today, and your rhymes are past their date and stale like this pasta bake.

A food fight followed and of course I was pulled into the head's office.

The head was a small, compact man with thinning hair who liked to walk the halls with his hands behind his back, resembling the kind of relic you'd expect to see in places likes Eton rather than at forward-thinking hubs of modernist creativity like ours.

I watched him take me in, frowning at my low-slung jeans, my trainers. 'Look here, young man . . .' he began.

I had riled him, and this brought with it a thrilling, if eternally teenage, sense of satisfaction. I liked the sensation of rubbing people up the wrong way. This would reach its apogee a few years later when, by then signed to a major record label and on the brink of major mainstream success, I suggested that one of our songs worthy of consideration for single release was the one entitled 'Cunt'. Rubbing people up the wrong way would ultimately work against me, of course, but I couldn't help it. I liked getting their goat. It made me *memorable*, and memorable was all I ever wanted to be.

Pretty soon, college took an inevitable back seat, predominantly now because our time revolved almost exclusively around our music. We came alive at night, playing small bars and clubs, getting drunk with local promoters, distributing the occasional demo tape and personally handing out hundreds of flyers. The bookings soon piled up, and we played chaotic shows to a smattering of mostly impressed and never less than roundly entertained onlookers. In truth, we still had little idea of what we were really doing at this point, a mixture of self-written raps and Rage Against the Machine covers along with anything that came to mind while actually on the stage, but whatever we did we did it with the delirious enthusiasm of the loudest Americans you've ever met, complete with American accents (which at this stage were entirely instinctive rather than contrived). We were the Beastie Boys and the *Jackass* crew and Joe Pesci in *Goodfellas* rolled into one. In every performance we did we were thrillingly unpredictable, following no script but our own often inebriated logic. Our shows became mini events, the kind that people spoke about for days afterwards. In a small but appreciative circle at least, we were infamous. And that, for the time being, would do nicely.

After one particularly frenzied show that involved so much dissing of the crowd that it almost resulted in a mass brawl, the promoter approached us.

'What the fuck are you guys playing at?' he said. 'You're Scottish, right?' We nodded, confused. 'Then why the hell are you singing as if you're Americans? Listen, if you're Scottish, be proud of it. And whatever you do, don't pretend to be someone else, least not when what you are doing is rap music, got it?'

We took offence at this slight, naturally we did, but the man had a point. Until then we hadn't even fully considered what it was we were doing. Rapping in an American accent had never been a calculated move; it had just come naturally to us, perhaps because rap is ultimately an American game – not an English one, and certainly not a Scottish one. But later that night we decided that the promoter was right. Our raps *were* Americanized, and this was wrong. From then on, we started performing songs in our own accent, thick and stodgy and brilliantly idiosyncratic. It gave us an edge, certainly, and a unique selling point, too. Besides, swearing sounded so much better in a Scottish brogue than it did in American drawl, and our songs were *full* of swearing.

The bookings increased, and we started landing proper paying gigs three, four times a month. I was writing more songs but, for one reason or another, Bill never quite found the time to rehearse them all, and so our set-list was limited to the same half-cocked songs, performed over and over again. It was fun, and our confidence was coming on in leaps and bounds, but I still felt we were missing one key component, something to make everything snap into place perfectly. Enter Oskar.

A few words about Oskar. Broad, muscular and fiercely intelligent, Oskar Kirkwood was the only person I knew who could talk about both Bruce Lee's legacy *and* the writings of Stephen Hawking with equal passion and knowledge. A fellow art student, skateboarder and martial-arts enthusiast, but a much better one than the two of us combined, Oskar was a genius, always destined for good things in life, and I endeavoured to take full advantage of his talents. An impressive wordsmith with a natural ability, he was the perfect addition to our still mostly nameless act.

Unlike Bill, Oskar was a stickler for detail, and suddenly I had a true sparring partner in the studio. He was with me every step of the way, keen to learn exactly how to turn a good idea into something great. He fizzed with ideas and energy and suggestions, and we bounced off one another endlessly. He even managed to spur Bill's fascination, and for a while at least we would be holed up in that small room together, fine tuning our cannons and mastering our freestyling. Bored one night we devised a battle-rap game where each player followed the verbal freeflow of his predecessor while rhyming and creating storylines on the spot using the obscure words, phrases or topics thrown at him. What we were doing was the rap equivalent of improvisational comedy, with increasingly leftfield verbal riffs that could go on for hours at a time. We called it Porcupine. With extra points for punchlines and comical or dramatic delivery, the eventual winner would be the one who could manage to use the word 'porcupine' within context, and each of us would of course do everything possible to steer the flow *away* from any kind of rodenty context. We became quite obsessive with the game; like bodybuilders lifting weights, we were exercising our lyrical muscles until they bulged. To watch us at Porcupine was like watching world-class table-tennis players running one another ragged around the table. And this was the key to our appeal: we were becoming an unmissable spectator sport.

The first performance we staged as a three-piece was incredible. We managed to land a gig at the Reading Rooms. It paid nothing, but if we impressed enough people on the night, we wouldn't have to pay for any drinks afterwards. Good enough. We spread the word beforehand, friends inviting friends, and the place was rammed, everyone crammed into this small space to see *us*. Moments before we went on stage, we stood outside the back of the venue looking at one another in open bewilderment. We were filled with terror, proper hand-trembling terror, as if on a rollercoaster carriage that had slowly scaled to its highest peak, and now sat squeaking on the brink of that inevitable plunge. Bill and Oskar looked like they wanted to get off. So did I – and yet, in truth, I don't think I had ever felt more prepared for anything in my life. This was it, and the nerves were wonderful; they felt like rocket fuel. I bounced on the balls of my feet, a boxer before a fight. We opened another beer each, our fifth – because frankly no matter how confident we felt, there was no way we were going up there sober.

The stage was tiny and the sound awful, but we killed it that night. It may as well have been Wembley. We played just six songs, early versions of 'The Underground' and 'The Movement' among them, and the crowd roared as if they were already firm favourites. We freestyled continually, turning each song into something else in the heat of the moment, bouncing off the cheers that were flowing our way like waves, each roar encouraging us to be funnier, ruder and more shocking still. We ripped one another, we ripped the crowd. And it all prompted so much laughter, *howls* of laughter, and uproarious applause. That half hour fast forwarded by in the blink of an eye, too much too soon, but it was magical, every second of it. Afterwards, they said we were amazing, as good as Eminem. No, wait – we were *better* than Eminem. *You should be superstars*, they said. The gig was all anybody spoke of over the next few days. *You guys should really do something with your music*. We were told this time and again.

How could we disappoint?

I stopped attending classes after that. I couldn't spare the time. Instead, I now concentrated every minute of every day on our music, on getting us out there and getting us noticed. I was hyped up and kinetic, the sensation a constant cocaine-rush of forward momentum. We were on to something here, and I wouldn't let the moment pass. We needed now to fund the project properly. Bill helped run a skate store called Ozzy's, and I ended up in a strip joint.

There are way worse places to work than a strip joint. The call centre, for example, where I was employed for four weeks immediately prior to the strip joint, was much worse, selling insurance for a television company eight hours a day, with just fifteen precious minutes for lunch.

'Hello sir/madam.' A bright, singsong voice, ideally the kind of voice someone would be happy to keep listening to, a voice you can trust. 'A quick question for you: do you currently have insurance on your satellite dish? No, you say? Just as well I called, then.' Forced jollity now, perhaps even a *ha ha*, should the occasion require. 'I'd certainly recommend you taking insurance out, sir/madam, and, as it happens, we are at the moment having a special offer on . . .' Click. '*Hello?*'

We were set a target by bosses who had clearly spent too much time in their windowless basement offices. Five sales a day. Pay was commission-based, so sales were crucial if we wanted to eat, to pay the rent. On a good day, I'd manage three or four, no more. Consequently I'd go home hungry. But pretty soon the survival instinct took over, and I found a way of . . . Not stealing, no, but *liberating* other people's sales. You needed to have only the barest idea of how the intra-computer system worked here, and I did. Child's play. Before long, I was logging twenty-four, twenty-five sales in a single afternoon. I was making good money now, and I'd have continued to do so had the bosses not discovered my scam and unceremoniously fired me. Working at the call centre did allow me to buy my first pro beat machine and sampler, the Dr Dre-endorsed Akai MPC1000. I got it second-hand and it still set me back £300 but it was worth every penny. It was by far the best toy I ever owned and even naked women couldn't lure me away from it. Well, that was until I got my next job, in a strip joint.

My role here was barman, my duties no more gruelling than weaving my way around the small tables, at which were huddled fat men in cheap suits, mostly, each of them with a leering smile on their face and at least one hand in a pocket. My job was to collect their empties and matily encourage them to order more drinks. The strippers were nice if often sad young women my age, either with children at home to feed or college fees to pay. Rather awkwardly, I already knew a few of those from the latter camp, girls I would see by day in the canteen at college. They'd kindly request that I didn't watch them while they worked – it made them uncomfortable to know there were familiar eyes in the audience – and I'd tell them I wouldn't. Usually I kept to my word.

If I was ever tempted by any of the other girls up there on that tiny, beer-sticky stage every night, I never acted on it. There was a reason for this. I had fallen in love. Her name was Alison, and she was a fellow art student and a friend of Oskar's. You could tell Alison was an artist. It was something she exuded from every pore, like perfume. She looked cool and clever; her dress sense alone told you just how creative she could be on a budget. She was kooky with it, Diane Keaton in *Annie Hall* but better put together, and with much more sex appeal. By this point the band's momentum was slowly building, but in Alison I had finally met someone to tempt me away from my singular obsession. Oskar was happy, so he said in that relaxed manner of his, to simply watch young love bloom. But Bill barely noticed. He had diversions of his own.

'Listen, dude,' he said to me one night in the Student Union bar, grinning inanely but with new pain in his eyes. 'I'm addicted to vagina, and it's getting me into trouble.'

Several of his girlfriends' boyfriends were out to get him. Bill would never be a one-woman man, at least not yet. But Alison, for me, was all I ever wanted, the perfect girlfriend: strong and supportive, gorgeous and sexy. We were inseparable. We would go through a lot together over the next five years, all manner of highs and lows – we had the most amazing sex, and a lot of fun, but spent far too much time apart (Alison always refused to join me when I moved down South). But ours was a one-way relationship; I realize that now. *I* was never there for *her*, but was invariably wrapped up in my own preoccupations, which ultimately always took precedent over everything. For years she was patient with me, a saint, an angel, but then it all got too much. She couldn't take my moods any more, nor the distance between us, and she would eventually break up with me over the telephone one sad and bitter night. By then, she said, she no longer recognized me: I had become someone else, the *joke* Bill and I had started having morphed into something fundamentally

45

wrong – perhaps, she suggested, even psychotic. She slammed the phone down and left me sitting there devastated, thousands of miles away from being able to go round to her house and reason with her. Alison had a habit of never being wrong, about anything. She was not wrong at the very beginning of our relationship, and she was not wrong at the end either. If only I'd had the good sense to listen to her.

All of Dundee was talking about the band now, and comparing us to Eminem. At least that's how it felt to us. Our small club shows were always selling out, and we'd even been given our own resident hip-hop night at the Doghouse. This was encouraging because by now, in early 2001, Eminem was already on his way to becoming the most powerful and popular performer on the planet. The packaging may have been unlikely – a white man in, ostensibly, a black man's world – but it had proved to be particularly seductive to a global mainstream audience. He was a marketing department's dream. George W. Bush had called him 'the most dangerous threat to American children since polio'. This was the kind of endorsement most artists could only ever dream of.

And so when people said that our rhymes were as clever as his, we became increasingly convinced that these people were right. Perhaps we should act on it?

Each night now followed a familiar pattern. Whenever I finally returned home from wherever I'd been, the last thing I thought of doing was going to bed. Sleep was a waste of valuable time. Instead, I sat in front of the computer in my room. I'd lay down some beats for more tracks, or else improve upon old ones just for the sake of it, because what else is an insomniac to do? On one particular night, Oskar and I got back late from a drinking session, stumbling through the door and laughing intensely about absolutely nothing. He fell instantly asleep on the sofa in the front room, and Bill was ten minutes away from bursting through the front door complaining loudly of a sore cock but an unforgettable fuck. I went to my room where I aimlessly surfed the net, looking at details of record companies I had already looked up many times before and browsing the current hip-hop scene in London, convinced that we were ready, now, to take this to the next stage. I then came across an online advert that spoke to me the way that God, I imagine, speaks to the devout. *Are you the next Eminem?* I read. Polydor Records had done what record companies always do: they'd seen a cash cow dominating the charts, a one-of-a-kind music sensation whose style was rich for aping. They now wanted their own Eminem, presumably a watered-down version they could mould for an instant, no-brainer chart hit. I'd no desire to be anyone's puppet, but I couldn't help thinking about this nevertheless. If the record company took a look at us, then surely they'd realize that they had stumbled on to something truly special. How could they possibly not?

The advert pulsed before my eyes. Clearly it had been placed there, in lurid neon on my computer screen, especially for me to find. I hadn't come across this by mere accident. No. Fate had called upon me, and I was ready.

I rushed next door and woke Oskar up. Bill came in loudly, a hand resting protectively over his crotch. I beckoned them both to follow me, silently, not wanting to ruin the moment with words. My room was still dark, still lit only by that electric glow. I pointed.

'What?' Bill barked.

'Shh.' I pointed again.

Their heads leant forward. They began to read.

Are you the next Eminem?

'Oh.'

'And you're thinking . . .?'

We had, as they say in films, a plan.

Three

Because of the speed limit on British motorways, and because the bus was already well past its sell-by date, a rusting white piece of metal with wobbling hubcaps and an out-of-order toilet that necessitated too-frequent pit-stops, it took us thirteen hours to travel from Dundee to London. It could have been the longest and most tedious night of our lives, but we used the time wisely, the three of us spread out across the last few back seats, playing Porcupine and honing, constantly honing our skills. If one of the most important requirements of rap is a level of self-belief that can, to the outsider, sometimes beggar belief, then we were already on our way to hip-hop immortality. You'd not met three guys more aware of their talents than we were.

As the sun started to creep up on the horizon, we finally merged on to the M25. The outer edges of London became visible to us now, its building-block beauty dotted with half-built skyscrapers, scaffolding and cranes, like one big building site. The place seemed huge, stretching out for as far as the eye could see, and seemed bigger still as the bus began to navigate its inner-city streets. It took us a further two hours to reach Victoria, the bus having now been reduced to a crawl in early-morning traffic. We were exhausted and yet also wide awake, desperate to arrive. At the coach station we got off and rushed for the nearest toilets. It was in here that we betrayed our underlying nerves about the day ahead, each of us disappearing into a separate cubicle where we privately contemplated the gooseflesh of our bare knees while our sphincters rippled and foghorned.

The typical newcomer to London wants to do all the tourist traps: Buckingham Palace and Madame Tussaud's, a couple of bridges and some of the bigger museums, an Aberdeen Steak House, a Pearly King or Queen or two. But not us. Though none of us had ever been to London before, and though we were still several hours early, we headed straight for our destination; first the Victoria Line to Green Park, then the Piccadilly to Covent Garden, a quick McMuffin and coffee en route, then arriving at Pineapple Studios just shy of nine a.m. To our considerable surprise, we weren't the only ones.

What we saw came as a shock. Not only were there several hundred people also three full hours early, but those assembled resembled not so much the cream of Britain's underground hip-hop crop but rather some kind of Victorian freak show. We walked the length of the line in stunned silence. This was all chaff, no wheat, an ugly motley crew of oddities whose overriding collective characteristic was surely delusion. Were we really supposed to take our position behind these people? Were we supposed to politely *converse* with them? Here at least, the next Eminem came in all different shapes and sizes, all colours and of either sex. I'd never seen so much poorly administered peroxide in all my life, nor such comical sneering of lips. Several heads were partially hidden behind backwards-facing baseball caps, others behind giant headphones, mouths silently articulating the phrase *My name is, my name is . . .* over and over again. Others came in twos and threes, and were attempting to battle rap like this wasn't Covent Garden at all but 8 Mile itself. These, though, were battle raps of the like I had never heard before, great big clunking things, raps for beginners, raps that rhymed *shit* with *hit* and *spit*, and then *shit* again, simply because they'd run out of words.

We walked to the end of the queue, Bill grinning impishly to himself, confident that this was no competition now – this was a walkover, the outcome a foregone conclusion. But Oskar and I felt the rumblings of something more ominous afoot: that just by being here we were effectively admitting that we, too, were something of a mockery. To join this bunch was to taint everything about us, perhaps irrevocably. But then we could hardly leave now, having travelled so far. We took our places, and spent the next three hours refusing to be drawn into conversation with any of these comic chancers. As the shops opened and the shoppers began to arrive, tourists descended into the area in their droves. Many of them stopped to take photographs of us, the Italians and the Japanese oddly thrilled by our very presence, and all keen to go home with shots of acne-ridden scowls and middle fingers raised firmly aloft.

Time passed like treacle, but eventually the hour arrived, midday, and the doors opened. We trickled in slowly, and I silently measured every inch that took me closer to my destiny. The A&Rs would be blown away, everyone else dismissed. We were the new Eminem, and more.

Another hour passed before we finally made it into the building itself, and then a further forty-five minutes before we snaked our way up the concrete stairs and to the first-floor audition room. Yoga and aerobics classes were taking place in several other rooms in the building, and we spent much of the waiting time peering through the windows. 'I love Lycra,' Bill grunted. Every new step took another five minutes, the delay a torture now, until finally there were the double doors, stuck on which was an A4 piece of paper that read 'POLYDOR AUDITIONS'. And then we were in.

It was a medium-sized room, with floor-to-ceiling mirrors filling the far end. I watched our reflections walk up to a gaffer-taped X on the kind of shiny wooden floor that reminded me of the school gym. In front of us were three desks pushed together, behind which sat three A&Rs – two men and one woman. They didn't say hello, but gave us a fleeting politicians' glance, at once smug and demeaning. I heard a clearing of throats that didn't come from any of the A&Rs. It was only when I turned to look that I realized there was an audience, a group of maybe twenty young guys who had been invited to hang around after their own auditions. I was relieved to see very little peroxide in those congregated. Rather, these were mostly serious-looking black guys who gave off an air of arrogance and menace that I could immediately relate to. Suddenly, I began to take this competition seriously again. I nodded in their general direction. They nodded back.

'Ready?' One of the A&Rs had spoken to us. Somebody, a pawn, seated slightly to the left of him, stood up and approached us. I handed over the CD. Seconds later, she pressed Play and the song I'd been so tirelessly perfecting these past few weeks came over the speakers loud and clear. The heads in the audience started to bob up and down, shoulders rolling with the rhythm. In three minutes' time this would all be over. My plan was to relish every second. The song was 'The Movement', perhaps our best track to date, clever and witty and driven by a furious beat, Oskar's voice coming in over mine, segueing into Bill's and back again, all delivered at breakneck speed, a mile a minute. I chose not to look at the A&Rs but instead directly into the mirror, where I saw Oskar and Bill beside me lost to the moment, full of concentration. I was so very proud of them. It was then that I saw a snigger, followed by a smirk on the young male A&R's face. He exchanged a look with the female A&R, and a smile tugged at their mouths as if being pulled by a needle and thread. Then they began giggling to each other like naughty school children on crystal meth. *What the fuck?* I thought. We carried on, six more lines, seven, the heads in the crowd bobbing harder now, some of the guys cheering. It was all in vain, though, because any positive vibes were being systematically undermined by the panel's laughter, which was by now unambiguous, as if they'd just inhaled nitrous oxide. Oskar and Bill had noticed it too, and each of us was beginning to falter. The oldest judge, the one dressed in the most expensive shirt (pale blue and neatly ironed), his bland face hugging a tight goatee, put his hand up as if flagging down a taxi. The music was cut. We fell silent.

'Thanks,' he said, looking at Bill before scribbling something on to a piece of paper. 'Thank you.'

'We've not finished yet,' Bill said.

'That's fine, thanks all the same.'

Beside me, Oskar launched into an impromptu rap, the words thinly veiled to pick apart the A&Rs' idiocy. Their response was to laugh all the harder.

'Where are you guys from?' one of them asked.

We told them.

'A long way back, then.'

Fury came to me like it does a charging bull. I saw spots

before my eyes. The main judge was waving his hand at us dismissively, showing us the door we'd only just come through. Bill tried to interject, but the judge spoke over him, explaining that they had a great many more hopefuls to see. *Hopefuls.* I hung my head, numb, as we walked away. Some of the assembled crowd still cheered us. One of the guys jumped up and approached me, asked if he could buy some beats. We swapped numbers and in walked another wannabe, peroxide hair peeking out from beneath his baseball cap, dressed in a wifebeater and baggy tracksuit bottoms. I hung back because I wanted to watch. He didn't have a CD with him, but instead asked the A&Rs' pawn if she had 'My Name Is'. Soon he was performing a stuttering version of Eminem's signature tune in a bad broad mid-Atlantic accent. This time they didn't laugh, but nodded their heads in time to the song. At its conclusion one of them brought his hands together in applause.

Outside, the sun was blazing and Covent Garden was packed. We drifted as if in a dream towards the piazza, the hotdog sellers, the teenage Italian tourists with graffitied backpacks hanging from their shoulders and the painted ladies who worked for money by standing stock still on upturned beer crates. It was well past lunchtime, but we weren't hungry. The vibrancy of Covent Garden seemed like a mocking insult after what we'd been through, and so we fled. We took the tube east, towards Ilford, where we'd managed to arrange a bed for the night – the original idea having been to make a weekend of this, a celebration in honour of our successful audition. Now all we wanted to do was return home as soon as possible, and hide. Bill sat opposite me, defeated. I'd never seen Bill defeated before. He looked like a different man, his hubris humbled.

That night we didn't make it further than a local pub, where we sat around a small table ripping beer mats into a thousand pieces in lieu of making conversation. But each successive round strengthened my resolve not to let this dishearten us. Three fucking idiots were not going to end our dreams as easily as that. There must be opportunities here in London of all places. Oskar was trying to lift Bill's spirits. 'We'll make it work, dude, we'll prove them wrong,' he said. I suggested we return to our room, and upon our arrival Bill and Oskar immediately turned in for the night. I logged on and started to do some research. Perhaps fate would speak to me again, I thought, only this time more effectively. The hours passed, and by six o'clock in the morning I had a list of names and addresses, and a fresh sense of momentum. Overexcited and hopped on a mixture of coffee, pure adrenaline and an overdose of wishful thinking, I woke up Bill and Oskar, pulling their covers off and throwing their clothes at them. Pacing back and forth at the bottom of their beds, I briefed them on the day's mission and objectives like a sergeant jacked up on methamphetamine.

We didn't bother with breakfast, and headed straight out. Overnight, London had revived itself into a city of infinite possibility. The early-morning sun glinted on the glass-fronted office blocks, and the streets were filled with pinstriped suits and briefcases and the clack of a million different stilettos. We walked through the constant stream of office-bound workers with an exaggerated loping stroll, forcing everyone to afford us a wide berth. We smiled at every power-dressing woman who came our way. Many smiled back. This human rush hour was a thing to marvel at. So many people, all new faces, a great number of them gorgeous beyond belief. A young man here could easily get led astray. He could learn so much.

We made it to Kensal Green by ten o'clock. I had the *A–Z* in my hand now, and I strode on ahead, the lovestruck stragglers several paces behind me. Two wrong turns later, and we arrived at the offices of Britain's most respected hip-hop label, a company I'd spent much of the previous night reading up on. The main man there, Dave Smith, was the kind of bloke whose career was built on spotting raw underground talent. He had form, a solid reputation. He was someone who could open doors, someone who wouldn't laugh at us like those powder-puff-pedalling cheesemongers had done yesterday.

The heavy glass door was emphatically closed, and the buzzer panel showed us four bells, none of which were labelled. What to do now? A postman pushed us rudely aside, pressed a button and was swiftly buzzed in. I put a hand on his shoulder, grinned at him and told him that we were on our way up, that I'd take the post for him, save him a hike, yeah? Not a flicker of expression crossed his face, but he handed me the bundle and went on his way. I took the stairs two at a time, yesterday having been designated somebody else's nightmare, not ours. Bill and Oskar followed. At the front desk was a pretty young girl doing her nails. Bill had already predicted that every record company in London would have a front desk manned by a pretty young girl. He'd clearly done some research of his own. This one took us in with searching, slightly mistrustful eyes – no wonder, really, us being three exhausted-looking lads with the morning's post but who clearly were not the postman.

'Yes?'

'We're here to see Dave Smith.'

She looked to the diary open on her desk.

'And you have—?'

'Gavin. Gavin Bain.'

'No, I meant, do you have an appointment?'

'Aye, yes.' I hesitated. Oskar coughed. 'Actually, no. But we have travelled a long way to see him – Dundee, thirteen hours on a bus; you wouldn't believe the pain in my arse. Anyway.' I tried to stand taller. 'We're not leaving until you get Dave out, here, now.'

'*Yeah!*' said Bill beside me, grinning inanely and already envisaging, for all I knew, how he was going to bed this girl. 'He means it.' He leant forward, hand outstretched. 'Billy Boyd, at your service. And you are?'

Before he could fully immerse himself in the smile that spread helplessly across her face, a door opened at the end of the short corridor and a head emerged. I recognized it immediately from his online mugshot as being Dave Smith's. I took a step forward.

'Dave, dude! Over here.'

Warily, he approached us, looking to his receptionist and then back to us.

I spoke quickly, with charm and eloquence, I hoped, my eyes full of pleading. But not desperation, never that. It worked. Two minutes later we were ushered into his office, the three of us standing before him. He sat. He was about thirty years old, short and squat, with a patchy beard, and he was dressed as if he had travelled to work by skateboard. He picked up the telephone, pressed a button and said, 'Hold my calls.' Music to my ears.

He started by asking some questions: who we were, where we came from, and what we wanted. While I spoke he nodded, and didn't stop – not so much in response, it seemed to me, but as if nodding were a nervous tic he did every morning until that first cup of coffee. He reminded me of one of those plastic dogs you see in the backs of all those Volvos on the motorway: nod, nod,

nod. I wanted to reach over, clamp his head between my hands, and stop him.

'And you have a CD?'

Oskar handed it over, sweaty fingerprints smearing the plastic sleeve. Dave Smith put it on, then leant his elbows on his desk and made a steeple of his fingers. His head kept on nodding. Thirty seconds into the first song, he reached for the remote control and skipped on to the next one. Momentarily, I had those spots before my eyes again. The veins in both temples thumped. Another thirty seconds later and he skipped on to the next track. Then he ejected the CD. The finger steeple fell away and now he rested his chin on his brought-together fists.

'What *is* this?' he asked, as if genuinely perplexed. 'You sound like the rapping Proclaimers.'

Back when Steven Ballantyne would wait behind the school gates for me every afternoon, there to greet me with a punch to the head or a kick to the back of the knees that would send me sinking to the ground in front of everyone, my mind would launch itself into flights of necessary fantasy. I would get Steven Ballantyne one day, and deliver to him his comeuppance. I would tie him to a chair, cut off his ear and feed it into his mouth. I'd take a blowtorch to his genitals, a hammer to his toes. *This little piggy went to hospital, this little piggy to the morgue.* Or at the very least I'd take a great big fucking chunk out of him, just like I eventually did.

I experienced a similar sensation now. The words *rapping Proclaimers* were still swimming in slow motion from Dave Smith's mouth, his lips squirming on a stupid face. At first I thought my ears had deceived me. *The rapping Proclaimers?* Why would he say something like that unless he wanted a battering? I felt sick, like I could literally be sick, there and then, all over him. Beside me, Oskar's shoulders slumped. Bill sighed.

Gathering myself, I answered back. I told him to listen to the lyrics again, the skill with which we rapped, the monumental beat. Couldn't he spot a classic when he heard it? I'd been told, I said, that he was a man who knew talent when he saw it. Well, *hello*. My eyes felt fat in their sockets. My gaze bore into him like twin pistons. Dave Smith picked up the telephone, and said something to the pretty receptionist. When he'd replaced it, he looked at us blankly and thanked us for coming. Our meeting was over.

'Look, I'm sorry, but there's nothing I can do with *this*.' He handed the CD back. 'You've not seen MTV recently?'

He stood, then opened the door for us. Meekly, we filed out one by one. The pretty receptionist watched us go.

We said nothing to one another on the tube, nor at the McDonald's in Victoria Station over a damp cheeseburger and chips. And by the time we boarded the bus bound for Dundee, we were so sapped of strength and morale that we simply slumped into our respective seats and closed our eyes. Bill and Oskar slept, but sleeping was way, way beyond me. I plugged in my headphones and looked out of the window, the grey London streets receding into a blur, the toxic kebab shops, the crowded bus stops, those pregnant kerbside bins overflowing with filth and rubbish, all stink and stain. I hated the place. The lump in my throat was lodged hard. The motorway couldn't come quick enough. In my head, over the ignored music, I *shit, fuck* and *cunted* all the way home, muttering to myself like a lunatic with murderous intentions.

We arrived shortly before dawn, Dundee several degrees cooler than London and so much less impersonal. But it felt humbling to be back, tails between our legs. Friends would want to know how it went at the audition, and that was the sort of conversation I simply couldn't face. In the petrol stench of the forecourt, Oskar hugged me, 'Don't worry, dude. Fuck 'em, fuck 'em in their stupid, blocked fucking earholes,' he said and smiled. I couldn't help feeling that we'd given it our best shot, and our best shot had failed. Soon it would be time for Oskar to consider his own future – a future that would see him prosper in all sorts of media, including website start-ups, in pursuit of his fortune. Bill hugged me as well, but this was a different kind of hug, as if we were afraid to let go, because then we would be all on our own again – and neither Bill nor I liked to be alone.

We had college the next day, and I approached that prospect with dread. Word must have got around that our audition had been unsuccessful, because no one said anything to me about it at all, and everyone avoided eye contact. By the end of the day I could convince myself that it had never even happened, and life soon resumed its humdrum pattern. It felt strange to be back in class, and once again I was a square peg. I couldn't concentrate any more, couldn't apply myself. The headmaster's eyes followed me wherever I went. At home, Alison picked up the pieces and put me back together again. She encouraged me to put the music on hold, for the time being at least, and to get back to simply being a student again: class, the Student Union bar, clubs, and drinking to forget it all. I took her advice, but I forgot nothing. By day I felt haunted by the memory of London, and the night terrors had become so pronounced that I simply stopped sleeping. I felt anxious all the time, fearful of crowds, terrified of solitude. I developed a burning sensation in my stomach. Only whisky would mask the pain, and help to calm its rage.

Three weeks later Bill received a phone call. We were in the bar just outside our campus one lunchtime, the table covered in beer glasses and empty crisp packets. I could tell it was an important call because his face lost all its animation. Clamping his thumb over the mouthpiece, he relayed the nature of it. It was Polydor Records, specifically one of the A&Rs we'd met at Pineapple Studios.

'We'd like you to come back down to London,' they told him. 'We'd like to see you again. Congratulations.'

Bill jumped three feet in the air. A beer glass fell to the floor and rolled between my feet. Most of the other lunchtime drinkers simply ignored him. It was just Bill being Bill. When he stopped, he told me the news. My heart lifted. I felt it physically rise. He put the phone back to his ear.

And then his face fell.

'No, no,' the judge told him – and I could hear this for myself now, as Bill had put the call on speakerphone. 'Not the other two, we just want *you*.'

He got up then, and hurried to the far corner of the bar for privacy. I watched him place an index finger in the other ear in order to hear better.

Had I received that call instead of Bill, a call to tell me that they wanted just me, not my bandmates, my comrades, I wouldn't have hesitated. I'd have told them to fuck off, that we came as an act, a unit, a three-piece, didn't they understand that? Wasn't it blindingly obvious? And did they really think it would be that easy to split up a band whose chemistry you couldn't just conjure out of nothing?

I watched Bill shake his head. *Yes!* I thought. He looked offended, insulted, and as he walked back towards me I heard him tell them so. Then I heard him tell them he'd think about it. He hung up, sat down again and finished his beer. I looked at him, agog. He gave me the same smile he gave to girls the morning after the night before. He explained that they offered to cover his expenses to fly down and just go in for a chat, to talk over possibilities, some opportunities. He said that last word as if it had been delivered to him in italics: *opportunities*.

The next day, Bill was gone.

One of the many things that kept me spectacularly awake each night around this time was a particularly recurring fantasy: Bill's pinkly exposed neck, and my throbbing hands squeezing the sweet life out of it.

Two days later, my phone rang. It was him, shouting the odds, his voice livid over something or other; the old Bill back again. When he'd done with all the swearing, I was able to piece together what it was he was saying. Things had gone badly in London. He'd had a terrible time with Polydor, felt belittled, insulted. His brief dream was over, and relief puddled about me. I was thrilled.

'They were full of shit,' he told me an hour later, in person, getting very quickly drunk in the Student Union bar. 'Get this, Gav. They wanted me to change my image, my hair colour, to sing only their songs and do it – wait for it – in a fucking English accent. Can you believe it?'

They no longer wanted the next Eminem, it seemed, but rather another UK-garage MC if only because UK garage was, for the time being, popular in the clubs and successful in the charts. It was also far easier, presumably, to become just another garage MC than it was a great white hope of British hip-hop. They had a personality ready made for Bill, and they'd told him they wanted him to step into it, effectively to be their puppet to push and pull as they saw fit. They didn't say this quite so crudely, of course, but that is what Bill took from it. Bill had told them, he said, to fuck off, and I believed him. It had gone so sourly, he told me, that he tore up the return-flight ticket in front of them, in protest.

'I stuck it back together afterwards, of course,' he grinned. 'I was angry, but how else was I gonna get back home? I hate that fucking bus.' He got another round in, pints and tequila slammers, and then as he lifted his shot up he started smiling. 'So, we back on, then? All forgiven?'

We didn't actually pick things up again for at least a couple of months. Bill was busy running around town anyway, notching up more one-night conquests. He invited me out with him most evenings but I mostly declined, on the grounds of college work, Alison and the fact that I was working on more tunes. But the truth was that I hadn't forgiven him. He *had* gone down to London, without me and Oskar, and so ready to compromise our ideals. It stuck in my throat. If I'm honest, it also bothered me that they had chosen him instead of me. Was I really so delusional about my own talents? I couldn't have been, surely. There was that guy at Pineapple Studios who'd wanted to buy my beats, after all, and the fact that half of Dundee thought we – not just Bill – were incredible, the next big thing. But then I remembered Dave Smith, and *the rapping Proclaimers*, and I deflated all over again like an punctured blow-up doll.

Alison was starting to get on my nerves; everybody was. I could no longer handle people. I shut myself away in my room, in front of my computer, a pair of headphones clamped to my ears. I created beat after beat after beat, and downloaded every underground American rap track I could get hold of. I studied them, made notes, copied them, improved upon them. My rhymes got better and quicker, full of quick intelligence and quick-fire humour. The songs were blossoming, alive with frenetic peevish character. I was convinced they would be irresistible to everyone, that it was only a matter of time now. Alison kept on calling. I never picked up.

One night she banged on my door until I had no choice but to answer it. She looked so healthy and alert standing there, beautiful and bright in her flared, cut-up jeans and oversized jumper, her face held at a concerned angle. I squinted in her natural sunlight. She shook her head.

'Look at you,' she said.

I was wearing an old pair of boxer shorts, black socks, a torn T-shirt that I hadn't changed in a week, and my mother's bathrobe. My eyes were sore, red-rimmed, with bags underneath. I hadn't shaved, had long forgotten to shower. She told me that she was worried about me and she folded me up in her arms, convinced that all I needed was a little human touch. She was sweet, Alison, but she couldn't accept what it was that really drove me, nor that I would stop at nothing to get it. I allowed her to take me upstairs, where she removed all my clothes and then hers. She was naked before me now, and gorgeous, but it hardly registered. I was off in my own head, someplace else completely. I got it up, though, and so we fucked. I felt nothing. She was on top of me, and then we did it doggie-style. Then I was on top of her, the headboard directly in my line of vision. I went at her methodically. Beneath her back, the crispy, unwashed sheets were whispering *shh-shh-shh*. The headboard banged out a *rat-a-tat-tat*. I lost myself to the rhythm, immediately freestyling to it in my head, careful to maintain the speed of it, the shh-shh-shh, the rat-a-tat-tat.

'What the fuck are you doing?'

Alison pushed me off. She sat up, bringing her knees to her chest.

'This is ridiculous.'

I reached for a pen to quickly write down the rhyming couplet I'd just come up with, then turned to embrace her. I pleaded for understanding, and she looked into my face the way you would a puppy's that you had no choice but to have put down. She told me that I had to pursue my dream or else it would kill me. 'You owe it to yourself,' she said, 'whatever the cost.' She looked sad. I thanked her. We hugged tight. She cried, and perhaps I did too, a little. We resumed having sex. I came. She left.

I cut myself off from her for months after that. Her encouragement had given me fresh impetus. I came up with what was surely an inspirational idea, the idea of the century; and the moment I did, everything slotted into place – everything made sense. My potential doubled, trebled. Of this I was resolutely sure. I wrote and I rapped and I rhymed, writing five, six new songs a day, then re-recording all the old ones. It was a dark time but the most creative I had ever experienced. With one small flickering lamp barely lighting the room, I would lose myself in sampling ghostly violins and sweeping string sections from the likes of Bach and Mozart, over which I would lay obese basslines on top of disgusting beats that were literally too fat to fit through the speakers. I forgot to eat, and wouldn't even leave my room for the toilet, but instead peed into an empty Lucozade bottle. Intermittently my dad would visit, bringing me food. Most of the time I barely registered his presence and whenever I did notice him trying to make conversation, I would snipe at him, demanding he get out and close the door before the magic particles of creativity in the room's nauseating air were sucked out. Yes, I was a complete cunt. I would feel dreadful every time my father left. Similarly, my mother would ring me up and attempt to have normal conversations with her son, but I would be so deep in thought, freestyling to myself and trying to memorize drum patterns, that I just couldn't engage with her at all. In an argument with my parents about my future, I angrily told them that music meant more to me than anything or anyone. To show them how serious I was, I threatened to kill myself if I hadn't made a career out of music by my twenty-fifth birthday. They never doubted my determination again and, although I knew I was hurting them, I convinced myself that one day I would repay their patience, that I would show them I could be a success by doing things my own way. My way was working three or four days straight, oblivious to the passing of time, to the growling of my stomach and the growing stench in my room. On one of those occasions when I did fall asleep despite myself, my head fell flat against the keyboard and I awoke moments later to find that I'd just wiped seventy-two hours' worth of work, having forgotten to save it all beforehand. That's when I would punch and slap myself, cursing at my stupidity and screaming with frustration. But then the unbidden thought of a lyric would prompt a beat, and then another one, and just like that I was lost inside another seventy-two-hour marathon. Every once in a very long while I would slip on my unlaced trainers and head out to the corner shop and a sustaining Pot Noodle. The world was disorientating in its colourfulness on those short trips. Every sound piercing, as if someone had turned the volume to all the way up. I noticed how green the leaves on the trees were, how blue the sky was. I didn't look into the faces of the people I passed, feeling uncomfortable in their presence, the way they ambled, their lack of purpose. I couldn't wait to get back inside my room, to close the door and to fester, but mostly to create more and more, always more.

When I was ready, I called Bill and Oskar. Bill sounded shocked, but pleasantly surprised.

'Gav, man! Where the hell have you been?'

He rounded up the usual suspects and arranged a house party to celebrate Gavin Bain's belated return to the world. It was good to speak to Bill; I'd missed him. When I got there the place was packed with some of our closest friends. Brian came up and embraced me; he was a childhood friend of Bill's who had become a good friend of mine. Oskar was there, and it was great to see him. He told me that Bill had been lost without me. We drank and drank, and I listened to endless stories and countless tall tales about women and skateboarding and fighting. Then I told them I'd just discovered this insanely good rapper, an American, but brand new, so new and so underground that hardly anyone had even heard of him yet, certainly not over here. But I'd downloaded this, I said, holding up a CD. It was worth listening to. I pointed to the hi-fi. Could I?

It was called 'Shut Your Mouth', a funny song about sexual frustration delivered in the style of Eminem as Slim Shady, the lyrics concerning an accident-prone guy. It had a massive chorus, a monstrous beat and hilarious lyrics, unforgettable after the first listen. I turned the sound up loud, and watched for their reaction as calmly as possible from beneath my fringe. Almost instantly they were grinning, and nodding their heads in appreciation. By the time the chorus kicked in a third time, they were all singing along.

'That's incredible,' Brian said, and everyone agreed. I looked at Bill. Bill was beaming.

'Yes, well, that's me,' I told them.

At first they laughed. Then came the frowns. Jaws hit the floor in open admiration, and in that instant the nightmare of London was eradicated from my soul forever. I had been accepted again, my talent reconfirmed. Bill spoke first.

'Really? But that's . . . *Really?*'

'But you sound American, like really American . . .' said Brian.

Oskar cued up the song again, and everyone listened even closer this time. The hairs on the back of my neck stood up. Bill took me to one side.

'Is that really you? Man, that's leaps, that's *bounds* better than anything we were doing before. Seriously, Gavin, it's *incredible*. And your accent. It's faultless. Do it like that, and no one in London will laugh at us again because—' He stopped short, the penny dropping. He looked at me, and I nodded back at him. 'Are you suggesting . . .?'

'If no one takes us seriously as Scottish rappers,' I told him, 'then let them try it with a couple of Americans.'

His eyes became discs, full of wonder and excitement. I was 100 feet tall, my heart at a manic gallop, all those hours locked up in my room time well spent, for me, for *us*. I told him that if we were going to try again, then this was the only way forward: as Americans. I watched him fully ingest this. It took him no time.

'Of course, dude! No sweat!' And he laughed, a wonderful, wonderful sound.

'I mean it, though,' I said. 'If we're to pull this off, we'll have to do it faultlessly. We'll need to convince everyone we're Americans, and I mean *everyone*. It won't be easy.'

He put an arm around my shoulder and squeezed. 'We'll be fine, fine. We can do it. If anyone can, we can.'

Bill, Oskar and I separated ourselves from the rest of the party, our friends huddled round the hi-fi, singing along to 'Shut Your Mouth' and getting acquainted with the five other tracks on the CD. We sat on the floor near the kitchen with a couple of bottles of lager each and brought Oskar up to speed on the plan. Oskar had reservations. He told me that, while he loved the new music

I was making, he was just about to graduate from college and would be advanced into his second year at Glasgow University. 'Become American. I don't know, man, sounds a bit loco . . .' I told him that the last thing I wanted us to be was fake, an act built on pretence, but that if the record industry was going to laugh us out of town simply because we had the wrong accent, then what option was left to us except to adopt the *right* one? My mind was racing now. I told him that this need not define us for ever. We'd sign a deal, have a hit single, then reveal ourselves to the world – a broadsheet exclusive, a TV chat show – and be hailed maverick heroes. It was far-fetched and ridiculous, I said, but it was our best bet, perhaps our only one.

'Or do you just want to walk away from it now?' I asked them.

Bill grinned, and clinked his beer bottle with mine. 'Never.'

Oskar took a deep breath; and just as I thought he was ready to smile and raise his beer to ours, he dropped the bomb and it came like a kick to the balls.

'I'm sorry, Gav, I can't do it. I mean, come on, who are we kidding here? You two were made for this and you should both go for it. I'm just going to do my own thing for a while, you know, as a hobby, for fun.'

My plan involved becoming something we were not and that just wasn't Oskar. He knew who he was. Bill and I, on the other hand, were still searching, searching for some sort of validation in life. We were chasing our future, convinced that it was in music. What future would we have if no one was going to give us a chance because of where we were from? Oskar downed his drink and hugged me and Bill before heading back into the party. We looked at each other in shock. I hadn't even considered going through this without Oskar. 'He's right, Gav,' Bill said, clinking his beer with mine again. 'We were made for this.'

I told Bill that we would need money if we were going to base ourselves in London, and that because of our student debt we would need to spend at least the next year working flat out if we had any serious hope of funding this trip. Could he be that patient?

His face fell. 'A year? Fuck that. I'm sure we can think of something to get us there quicker.'

He was drunk, his eyes unfocused, his words slurred.

'Like what?'

He frowned and scratched his chin. Brian came romping over, a big grin on his face. He had another six-pack with him, and he passed them round. A plan was hatching on Bill's face, his eyebrows unable to sit still.

'Easy,' he said. 'We'll rob a Securicor van.'

'Great idea!' I said.

Bill frowned again. 'Um, I was joking, Gav.'

I wasn't.

Brian did a comedy double-take.

'What did I miss?' he said.

I scouted the van's route for a full two weeks before I reported back to Bill, timing its progress through Dundee's city centre down to the last second. Despite the prevalence of traffic, it stuck to its tight schedule like a Japanese bullet train. I was impressed. At four o'clock, it left its headquarters bound for the shopping centre. For three days in a row I sat outside its HQ on the outskirts of the city and watched two men – the driver and guard, both bulked up in blue nylon and polyester and Doc Marten boots – lumber into the van with an air of officious ceremony, then watched them head off, never once dawdling. The next three days, I waited outside the shopping centre for their arrival, which came, each time, at between four thirty-three and four thirty-six. The driver stayed where he was, but the guard, wearing a protective crash helmet with a visor for his eyes, got out, an industrial heavy plastic case in either hand, and made his way into the centre. His first stop was Boots, at which he spent no more than six minutes. Then it was on to WHSmith, then Argos. At no later than eleven minutes past five he exited the shopping centre, which at this time was filled with early-evening shoppers, families and errant schoolchildren. By five thirteen he was back depositing the cases, now full of money, in a hatch at the back of the van. The cases were never attached to his wrist by handcuff as I'd anticipated, such extra caution clearly being more the stuff of movies than of real life. He was a big man, but middle-aged with it. His nose told me that he liked a drink, and he didn't look as if he prided his job over his continued health and safety. Once he was back in the passenger seat, he and the driver drove off, reaching the bank by five fifty-eight – a minute past six at the latest, if the traffic was particularly heavy. Then it was back to the depot by six thirty. By the time he left, de-uniformed and noticeably slovenly in appearance, in BHS jeans and cheap jumper, cigarette dangling from his mouth and striding with purpose towards his first pint (Stella) and his first packet of crisps (salt and vinegar), he was virtually unrecognizable: older now, less robust and much more couldn't-give-a-shit. In other words, he didn't unduly concern me. I could, if necessary, take him.

I began to report back to Bill at the DCA (Dundee's contemporary-arts centre), where no one would recognize us at the bar and I could have Bill's full attention. He would earnestly listen as I went over my notes, my calculations, my suggested margins for error and our viable means for getaway. I could never get rid of the feeling that he wasn't taking this quite as seriously as I was. He insisted otherwise, of course, and to prove this assured me that ultimately it was a petty crime, that no one would get hurt, and that our chances of getting away with it were high. But then a girl would walk by, and in that instant I would lose him. It is only with hindsight that I realize how catastrophically stupid we were to even consider something like this, but so desperate was I to make my mark in music that I was willing to consider anything that expedited the process. Robbing a Securicor van would undeniably do that.

'You still have your gun, right?'

Bill, still following the jet-stream of the girl who had just passed in front of our table, peered at me, momentarily confused.

'What? Oh, that. Yes. I need new pellets, though.'

After a further week of staking the Securicor van's progress alone, I insisted that Bill accompany me, and each afternoon we followed it as best we could as it made its way through the town centre. Bill's latest Fiesta was hardly the ideal getaway vehicle, but this one had yet to be registered (he had bought it for cash) and so it was easily dumped. The plan was to abandon the car within a couple of streets, then simply slip on to the nearest bus and melt into the rush-hour throng.

We went through the plan of action time and again.

Taking the guard unawares, I easily knock him to the ground just as he comes out of the shopping centre. Then I grab the cases, which have fallen to the ground during the attack, and make it back to Bill in the awaiting Fiesta in no more than seven seconds. Bill puts his foot to the floor, and we are gone. And I don't even have to use Bill's gun to persuade the guard. Bill keeps the windows down, I hurl the case in the back and jump into the passenger seat like I am a fucking modern-day Bo

Duke – at which point Bill tears off to safety, not a single second wasted.

Well, that's how it happened in my head anyway.

'Bill, Bill . . . You got it?'

'No problem: windows down, I got it.' This uttered with such a lack of concern I didn't know whether to envy or hate him.

'Still planning your big heist, then?'

Brian, joining us outside the DCA at the tail end of one of our final Securicor discussions, was convinced we weren't serious about it, that this was just one of Gavin's fantasies. He ribbed me about it constantly, safe in the knowledge that I would never do anything quite so reckless.

I felt peculiar when the big day came, a little like the sensation I'd feel before a big football match, a combination of nerves and excitement and rolling anticipation. I slept badly, eventually waking from the worst night terror I'd had in months, but after my shower I felt entirely committed to what was about to occur, and all for the greater good of Silibil N' Brains, our now-official name, and the name with which we would surely find success. Nobody would get hurt today. The gun fired only pellets. The security guard was older than me. We'd get away.

I ate no breakfast and no lunch and instead worked on some music, which kept me calm. Mid-afternoon, I got dressed in sweatpants and hooded top. I placed the gun in my waistband. It felt cold against my skin. My hands were wet with sweat. I had a surfeit of energy, and jogged all the way to the shopping centre an hour early simply because I couldn't spend another moment at home. I browsed the shops, bought myself a doughnut, then went outside and assumed position. Bill was nowhere. I called him on his mobile, but got voicemail. I left a message.

'I'm at the tennis courts, Bill,' I said. 'Where are you? It's five o'clock. We've got a game. You're not chickening out, are you?'

The words sounded so bogus coming out of my mouth, as if lifted from a cheap Hollywood script, but it was all I had. Ten minutes to go, and the Fiesta was still nowhere to be seen. Through traffic came the Securicor van. It parked up and the guard emerged, an empty black case in either hand. I sat on a nearby wall watching him go. He looked as bored as ever. Shoppers teemed past. Schoolchildren dressed much as I was goofed around at the entrance of the forecourt, jumping on to one another's shoulders and using their bags as footballs.

I checked my watch again. Seven minutes past five. Four minutes. I checked the traffic, desperate now to see the Fiesta. Ten past five. The Securicor guard emerged from the shopping centre, a full minute earlier than he ever had before. The sound of a car mounting the kerb too fast now reached my ears, a squeal followed by a thud. Bill. At last. The guard was halfway towards the van. I leant forward on my toes. I had fifteen seconds. I looked at the van again, reading for the first time what was written on it: *SmartWater anti-robbery system in use. 100% conviction rate.* How had I not seen that before? Too late now. I began to run at the guard.

A sudden pressure on my neck, and I was pulled back sharply, the crook of an arm pushing into my Adam's apple. *I'm being mugged*, was my first thought. I turned to my assailant, ready to fight. It was Brian, a look of furious determination on his face.

'It's for your own good, dude,' he said, and brought me level with the pavement.

I fought to break free, but his grip was stronger than mine. I glanced up. The Securicor guard had disappeared, the van now merging into traffic. I felt white-hot rage. Brian dragged me to the car, where Bill was sat smiling sheepishly. Oskar was in the back seat. He looked gravely disappointed in me. I slumped, and Brian let me go. Minutes later we were on the move. For a few seconds nobody spoke. Then Oskar did.

'Are you insane?' He turned to face me. 'You, the arch criminal? For fuck sake, Gav. What were you thinking?'

Brian swivelled in the front seat. 'We thought you were joking, man, but then Bill told us yesterday that you were serious. We couldn't let you go through with it. Gav, we just saved you from twenty years in prison. Be grateful.'

In the rear-view mirror Bill's eyes met mine. 'He's right.'

I leant forward and cuffed him on the back of his head. Bill spun the steering wheel towards the kerb, slammed on the brakes and turned to retaliate. All four of us were shouting now. A knock on the window brought us up short. We saw a wedding band, sausage fingers, and the starched heavy blue of a uniform. Bill turned around and wound the window down. A policeman lowered himself to our level. He looked at each of us slowly in turn.

'A problem here, boys?'

Bill grinned. 'Nah, no problem, officer. Just a domestic.'

'You do realize you are illegally parked, don't you? Licence and registration, please.' He leant back to take in a proper view of the Fiesta, which was heavily corroded by rust.

As Bill attempted to charm the officer in a manner not too dissimilar to the way he charmed half of Dundee's female population, I sank back into my seat, defeated. Brian and Oskar were still giving me admonishing looks, but they didn't realize what this meant to me. Nobody did.

A couple of weeks later, once I'd had the chance to calm down, Oskar insisted I come out for a drink, where we would all bury the hatchet and laugh about it. After some resistance, I agreed. When I got to the bar, Bill was his typically gregarious self and acting as if the incident had meant nothing to him – which it very likely hadn't. He embraced me as a long lost friend. We spent hours drinking that evening, and though the mood was convivial I couldn't shake off my private brooding. I watched him career about the place, pint in one hand, a new woman in the other, so uncomplicatedly content with the most trivial of things. How had I ended up with him? How had he become so intrinsic a part of my future? This was not the face of a man who cared whatsoever about our joint destiny. All Bill wanted was another drink, another fuck. He was the least complicated man I'd ever had the misfortune to meet. I watched him now as he once again recounted the story of how we were ridiculed out of Pineapple Studios in London, as if it was something to laugh about. His mouth was moving at a mile a minute, saliva gathering at the corners. Everybody laughed right along with him simply because that was what you did with Bill: you had a good time, a laugh. Anger rose within me like mercury. Very carefully, I placed my empty beer glass back down on to its coaster. Then I went for him.

It wasn't a pretty fight, and it unsettled nobody. Instead, it was more of a drunken wrestle, and we quickly tumbled outside into the streets. Bill was holding on to me with both of his arms, not allowing me the space to properly deck him, to get him on to the ground and beat the shit out of him. As we were rolling on the pavement, I could hear him laughing. I began to lash out wildly.

It was Oskar who came outside to split us up. I caught the expression on his face immediately, and knew that something was wrong. His mobile phone was sitting lifeless in his left hand,

and the blood had drained from his features. I let go of Bill and rolled away. We lay there, side by side, staring up at our friend.

'Ozzy, what the fuck? Who died, man?' Bill said.

His answer was like a knife to the ribcage.

'Brian's dead.'

Brian, who hadn't yet joined us in Dundee that night, was with other friends back in Arbroath where, if I knew Brian at all, he was well on his way to getting joyfully wasted. Bill looked up at Oskar, waiting to have the joke explained. But he was all too evidently serious. His face was pale. I got up quickly.

'*What?*'

'An accident. He's dead. Brian is dead.'

An hour earlier, outside a pub called the Cairnie in Arbroath, across from Brian's house, he had been messing around with a friend of his just yards from his front door, play fighting in perhaps a similar way to Bill and I just now. But Brian had fallen awkwardly, with his friend landing on his neck and crushing his voice box. In the time it took him to die – mere minutes, really – his friend chose not to call an ambulance, or for any kind of help. Instead, he gave himself over entirely to panic. He ran. He fled the scene leaving Brian choking slowly but fatally on his own blood.

Brian had always been one of our most vocal supporters. The last time we spoke, he told me he loved my latest music and supported the decision to go to London. We had planned to hook up for drinks but every time he called I was too busy making beats. Hell, I had even turned down his invite to stay at his place that weekend, to listen to music, skateboard and get drunk. And now he was gone. He was only twenty-two years old.

This was too much to take in. Bill and I looked at one another in horror, fists still curled but beginning to go slack. There were no words for a situation like this, no words at all. We simply walked away in separate directions, Oskar rooted to the spot and watching us go. I walked all night that night, numb to everything around me. I arrived home as the sun was coming up. For the first time in weeks I didn't turn on my computer. I sat on my bed and hugged my knees. I saw my room as if I were a stranger to it, a tiny universe filled with all the paraphernalia I had thought would lead to my eventual escape. The walls needed painting. The plaster was peeling everywhere. I got up and tore as much of it off as I could with madly grappling hands. This revealed the woodwork underneath, much of it rotten.

Brian's funeral was the following week. Hundreds turned up, pretty much all the skaters he knew from the surrounding areas. Every last one of us still stunned to silence by such a senseless tragedy. The sound of so many people crying throughout the service was obscene somehow. I saw Brian's family up at the front of the church and I knew that I had to avoid them, that under no circumstances could I face these poor people. What could I possibly say to make it any better? Oskar stood mutely beside me. As we filed out at the end, Bill approached us. Oskar left us to it, as I knew he would. Bill nodded at me. We hadn't exchanged a word since that night, and it felt strange seeing him again. We walked out past Brian's grave and made our way to the tree where he had taken his last breath. From my jacket pocket I pulled out a piece of paper, on which was a poem I had written for Bri. To my surprise Bill had prepared one too; we looked at each other and smiled. I guess it was the process of nailing them to the tree, above all the flowers that had been laid down for him, that triggered the tears again. I had never seen Bill cry or show anything that resembled that kind of emotion.

'We have to do this,' he said, his voice a whisper. 'It's our destiny now. We've got to get out of this place, Gav. We've got to make something of ourselves.'

We made up our minds. We were leaving.

Four

The weeks before we departed were fuelled, for me, with the most delicious sense of purpose. Suddenly everything was coming together, and quickly. Each night in the DCA, where we knew we wouldn't be disturbed by anyone, we occupied a corner table and talked tirelessly over our plan and how we saw it playing out. If we were going to be American now, then it would have to be wholeheartedly so. We would have to prepare for it with the precision of scientists. We were going to have to come up with plausible accents, and an authentic-sounding back-story that would require research.

'I've got family in California,' Bill offered.

'Where?'

'Some place called Hemet.'

'Where's that?'

'No idea.'

'Never mind, that'll do.'

I got us an appointment with a Scottish music-industry lawyer over in Glasgow, a smooth-looking guy in his mid-thirties wearing a pair of tortoiseshell glasses that pinched the end of his nose.

We sat on leather chairs in his leather-bound office, feeling like schoolchildren. 'How can I help you, gentlemen?' he asked. I cleared my throat, and asked him just how honest you had to be when signing a record contract. Could you, I suggested, pretend to be someone else? His eyes squinted at me over the tortoiseshell frames, bemused. 'But why would you want to pretend to be someone else?' he said. 'Not me, a . . . a friend. It's just for the sake of argument,' I told him. Still bemused, he said that it would not be a good idea to ever pretend to be somebody else, legally speaking, but instead to be ourselves. 'Yes,' I conceded, 'but what sort of repercussions would there be if we – I mean, if *someone* – were to give false information, and were later to be . . . unfortunately exposed?' I sensed he was becoming a little impatient now, but he endeavoured to explain that to give false information to something that required the signing of an official document could only result in legal action. 'A contract, you understand, is binding.' He was grave now. 'I suggest you tell your friends to go over the small print and then prepare for the worst, because the worst will come.'

This was not what I wanted to hear but, hell, I wasn't going to let a little thing like the law hold us back now.

Back in Dundee, Bill and I spent every evening together in my flat, locked in my bedroom, channel hopping until we found something appropriately American to watch: American films, American chat shows and so on, our aim to expose ourselves as much as possible to the American accent, which we would then study in great detail. I was confident that this wouldn't prove difficult for either of us. If actors could adopt different accents, so could we. Besides, I'd already gone from South African to Scottish, so it didn't seem too big a leap to become Californian now instead. And Bill already had the broad characteristics of a stereotypical American, so he too would be fine. We watched all sorts of programmes, and repeated everything that was said. After a while, we decided to focus on particular people, actors like Michael J. Fox and Matthew Perry, both of whom had, to our ears, fairly region-less, but pleasing accents, and spoke in broadly recognized American*ese*. I liked the way the words sat in their mouths and came out clean, easily discernible, easily understandable, and easily mimic*able*. We watched *Back to the Future* until we could recite the dialogue right along with Marty McFly, and countless episodes of *Friends*, which E4 seemed so willing to foist upon us all hours of the day and night. We tested one another exhaustively. I was Michael J. Fox, Bill Matthew Perry, and we would converse about the weather, about girls, sport, our favourite beer, the beaches in California, and why we would like to assassinate George W. Bush. We asked each other questions, taunted one another, then sang songs and rapped lyrics. We coughed in American accents, sneezed in them and said 'Bless you', or rather '*Gesundheit*'. We were meticulous in our preparation, so much more than we ever had been at school or college. And we were disciplined, too, never letting anything slip. If one of us messed up, the other would immediately flag it up. We were merciless. Soon, our dedication began to pay off. We were speaking in our American accents at all times. Even when I masturbated, the dirty voice in my head, the one narrating the fantasy, would be an American voiceover. It was no longer 'aye', it was 'sure'. It was never 'mate' or 'man', but always 'dude'. We tried them out on Oskar. He thought we were insane, but he was impressed.

Now all we needed were personas, because we were never going to get away with this by simply affecting accents alone. No, we were going to become *other people*. Correction: Bill was effectively going to become an extension of himself, so voluble was his natural character already. But *I* was going to become another person. I was going to shelve the neurotic, obsessive, insomniac Gavin Bain, and become a larger-than-life Brains McLoud. I could hardly wait to meet him.

I already knew who I was going to be. Jim Carrey. Brains McLoud was going to become Jim Carrey, loud and gregarious, perennially over the top, his face in constant gurn and stretch. I could be funny and zany and wilful, completely unpredictable. I'd have superhuman confidence. Bill would be my mirror image, and together we'd be a couple of uncontrollable livewires. Everyone would want a piece of us. Our whole shtick as Silibil N' Brains was, to all intents and purposes, to lampoon rap, much as Eminem had with his Slim Shady character. Though we believed, in a very real sense, in our gift for dextrous, multilayered and *clever* rapping, we were not above laughing at ourselves, or anybody else. This was why Jim Carrey was so perfect for the both of us. My old English teacher, Mrs Leonard, had always said I had acting potential. My success in this role would prove her right, that I was an acting natural.

I'd spent weeks and months previous to this scouring band websites and online information posts from record-company A&Rs about what it was, precisely, that record companies looked for when signing a new act. I read all the industry handbooks, *How to Get Signed* and *A Guide to the Music Industry* and the rest. The titles alone suggested that these books were not aimed at guiding artists towards a long successful career. I may as well be reading *How to get Fucked in the Ass by Businessmen*. But at least it let me into the mind of the enemy. I learnt that the music itself was never enough. In fact, reading between the lines I could tell that music and talent weren't really the most important things. You needed to be sellable, a commodity, attractive to a mainstream audience. Everything I read convinced me that this is what was required, not just to be heard but to prove a point and break the mould. We were going to turn Silibil N' Brains into personalities that burst off the page just as surely as the music burst from the speakers. We were going down to London, and we were going to take over the world. I had never been more sure of anything in my life.

A week before we left we re-recorded every track in our arsenal, but this time in our American accents. Everything else went unchanged. The results were beautiful and supple, every track flowing now so much more naturally. By becoming pseudo-Americans, we were sounding like fully authentic rappers, the best unsigned hip-hop duo in the world. London wouldn't know what had hit it.

It could be argued, of course, that we never needed to 'be' Americans at all, that we could have remained entirely Scottish in ourselves and simply *rapped* in the appropriate accent. But while virtually every other Scottish music act you'd care to mention – with the exception of the Proclaimers and, more recently, The View, Glasvegas and Biffy Clyro – has invariably done just that, singing in a mid-Atlantic accent that gives little indication of a rough upbringing in, say, Dunfermline, rap is the one musical genre in which this approach just wouldn't cut it. Its entire ethos is built on its grim urban reality: music from the hood delivered by people from the hood to people from the hood. Its success, at least at grass-roots level, is dependent on its believability. And so, while me and Bill felt every bit as justified as either Eminem (white working class) or Kanye West (black middle class) in pursuing a career in hip-hop, the record-buying public wouldn't agree. We'd already been told this in no uncertain terms back at Pineapple Studios and with Dave Smith, where we had been viewed as nothing more than a novelty. Rap, as far as they were concerned, was *preferably* black but *definitely* American. We couldn't be one, but we could certainly be the other, a pair of cheeky Californian skateboarders who, like so many Americans these days now that rap had gone mainstream, wished they'd been born in the hood. Under Bill's tutelage, we dressed if not quite to impress then certainly to dazzle. His idea was to swap the dark, khaki camouflage of the underground hip-hop scene for the blinding, luminous colours of commercial rap and R&B. This look, we told ourselves, would be for the stage, industry events and meetings only. The thought of dressing like this all the time was too terrifying to contemplate; the last thing we wanted was to be defined by it. No, this was to be temporary, to get us noticed, make us memorable. Bill encouraged me to let my hair grow out, while he dyed his in multiple colours but mostly blonde. We experimented with facial hair, and accessorized with wristbands and trucker caps, our eyes hidden behind wraparound sunglasses. We looked brilliant, ridiculous, a million dollars. We looked like pop stars.

'We look like Ali G's kid brothers,' I said, staring back at our new reflections.

'It's perfect.'

No one would question our motives now, no one would laugh in our faces. Deep down I knew this to be a shameful state of affairs, little more than blinkered, prejudiced bullshit from an ignorant industry, but if we weren't able to subvert the system from outside it, then we would do our best to do so from *within*, by lying to them and having them buy that lie, no questions asked.

I stayed with Alison on my final night in Dundee. We made love one last time and lay in bed, facing each other. Neither of us slept but just lay there staring into one another's eyes, as if silently communicating our mutual fear that London would be the beginning of the end of us.

I met Bill in the centre of town, it was five a.m. and while the rest of Dundee slept, we made our escape. Walking down the still, sleeping street, beneath the yellow glow of a street lamp, we stopped to look back once. Then we faced each other and knocked knuckles.

'Yo.'

'Yo.'

'Let's get out of here, yeah?'

We spent the first half of the journey fantasizing, running over best-case scenarios, while completely ignoring the possibility of failure. What if it worked? What if we actually managed to pull it off? We were brimming with a rabid excitement at the very idea – convinced that we would be an instantaneous success in London, then return victorious, our real story revealed, our names conveniently cleared, game on. We would be heroes to family and country alike.

Much of the journey proved to be a real bonding experience, reminding me why Bill and I had been such good friends all along: we were the perfect team, so ideally suited, so complimentary. Just being around him could make me feel better about myself. Over several hours, we refuelled our ties exponentially, and with each new beer felt even more full of the most searing confidence.

But then, one by one, as the beer soured in our mouths, so did our collective mood. What if we never got signed? What if we crashed and burnt? Or, worse, what if we got signed but were then exposed as what we really were? What then? Our reputation in tatters, our friendship lost. The vilification of friends and family. Recriminations, lawsuits, worse.

'Nah, we'll be fine,' said Bill.

Failure was not an option.

But then why consider failure when we had already succeeded, in one small but significant way? Just outside Birmingham, I told Bill that I had recently been listening to Radio 1. They had been running a new music competition, unsigned talent, all genres. I didn't think twice. The moment we'd re-recorded our material, I whacked a demo tape of one song, 'Shut Your Mouth', right over. The response was almost instantaneous. They loved it. And so even as we were sitting on the bus on the way down to the capital, 'Shut Your Mouth' was being played on national daytime radio, and would continue to be every day that week. The night before our journey to London, I'd checked my emails. A Sony A&R guy had heard the song on the radio the day before. At that point I'd had no idea it had already been played. (If I had, I'd have been glued to the radio all day.) But apparently 'Shut Your Mouth' was even now having the desired effect. We were being talked about, discussed, the subject of hype. The A&R was impressed. He wanted me to make contact. If we were ever passing through London on our travels, he wrote, then I should be sure to look him up. I emailed back, affecting a casual, laidback *Californian* tone, and told him that, actually, we were in London right now. When was good for him? I couldn't wait to log on again to see if he'd replied.

I relayed all this to Bill now, fully anticipating a row as I hadn't cleared it with him beforehand. I'd said nothing because I had wanted to test the waters without an audience. Perhaps I was terrified of a negative response. I wasn't terrified any more.

But Bill wasn't furious at all. Instead, his face cracked into a massive smile.

'Shit, that's fantastic.' He hugged me. He hugged me hard and whooped. The driver's beady eye watched us suspiciously in his rear-view.

We spent the rest of the journey locked again into our mutual goal, talking over everything in minute detail. When Bill focuses he can be brilliant, and right then he was totally zoned in. The bus was full now, with new passengers boarded from Birmingham. Bill spotted a couple of girls a few seats up from us. 'Our first guinea pigs,' he whispered. We shuffled up the aisle on our knees and faced them with impish smiles: these were the first girls we'd ever tried to pull as Americans. They were all over us in an instant. They loved our accents, they said, and wanted to know where we came from. We told them our entire history, and they bought every word. Of course they did. By the time we pulled into London, we had their numbers. They told us they were planning a holiday to California later that year. We promised to hook up. *Call us*, we said, making phones out of our fingers and holding them up to our ears. We kissed them on the cheeks, twice, because that was how we had been told the Europeans did it, right? They giggled deliriously.

We were Yanks now, officially. This was going to be too easy.

Sometimes I think my sister Michelle was forever trying to escape me. It was she who left Motherwell first, relocating to Dundee, but I was soon hot on her trail, and when I won a place at the city's art college it was in her spare bedroom that I ended up. A couple of years on, she had left Scotland altogether for London, a small studio flat in Walthamstow. Until Bill and I arrived, she was living alone. Not any more. She kindly offered us space on her floor for the first few nights, a week or two at most, until we got ourselves settled. But we'd arrived in London with just £350 between us, so I needed her to be patient. She was. Before long, without any of us fully acknowledging it, her floor became our permanent address. She was a wonderful host, Michelle. The fridge was always full of beer and milk; and as long as we cleared up after ourselves and contributed a little to bills, she would continue to tolerate us.

Though we never got to hear 'Shut Your Mouth' being played on Radio 1, a great many others did, and within a week the exposure had landed us our first booking. We'd been added to the bill at a Central London venue called Sound, amid the fast-food joints and cinemas of Leicester Square. The booking came via email; a new-talent booker had heard the track and got our email address from the competition website. They loved the track and invited us down. They'd be thrilled to have us.

It was a cold March night, and we were hunkered down into our parkas as we arrived at the club, a pair of Californians shivering in the nasty British wintertime. Sound was a subterranean hovel invisible from ground level except for a featureless door outside of which stood a bodyguard the size of an ox. We told him we were on the guest-list. He scoured his clipboard for our names as our breath clouded in front of us, then stood aside. Downstairs it was packed, full of wannabe pop stars but of a clearly much higher calibre than at Pineapple Studios, young, beautiful and talented, and each of them here to watch their peers, sound out the competition. If anything, it felt like a stage school that had spilt over into the evening. All anyone was talking about in the cramped backstage quarters – a couple of dressing rooms and a single toilet – was the audition they went to yesterday, the one they were preparing for tomorrow, how their agent had let them down again, and didn't we all hate our agents? Someone was walking around stark naked, asking everyone if they'd seen the bag in which she had her stage dress. I'd not seen a girl walk stark naked around a backstage area before. She was slim and limber, her ribcage prominent. Nobody paid her any mind, as if this was simply what people did at such occasions, but Bill and I, so far from home, just gawped. She found her bag, and slid a sparkly dress up her hips and over her knickerless pelvic bone. She glanced up and caught us looking. Even Bill was speechless.

'Hello,' she said.

Bill quickly recovered. He complimented her on her birthday suit. 'The best I've seen all year,' he said.

'Oh!' she exclaimed, now pulling the dress up over her breasts. 'You're Canadian! I've got family in Ontario!'

We felt palpably more comfortable once we were out on the safety of the stage, which we treated as our own personal playground, sneering at everyone in the crowd, making up raps on the spot about the girls we most fancied and those we comprehensively didn't. Amid the sparkly professionalism of the rest of the acts here, the majority of which played straight-ahead pop music with an emphasis on cinematic ballads, we were a glorious anomaly. We couldn't help but shine. 'Hard to Smile' brought the house down, 'Accident Prone' went over even better, and 'Shut Your Mouth' received cries of instant recognition. We were allotted just twenty minutes but played for thirty, freestyling between songs, unravelling existing songs as we performed them, taking them off into different directions, with new lyrics, call-and-response choruses, and full audience participation. We were brilliant, on fire; they loved us. At the end of the final song, we didn't disappear backstage but jumped straight out into the crowd and headed for the bar. People were whooping and cheering at our cheek, our chutzpah, rushing over to give us high fives, and their cards. I counted four, maybe five people saying *'Call me'* over the din. One of them was Robbie Bruce, the Sony A&R guy who had contacted me previously via email. I'd feared from his name alone that he might just be Scottish. A quick word with him that night confirmed my fears.

We tumbled out of Sound at well past midnight, drunk and celebratory. Silibil N' Brains, in all its incarnations, had gone down a storm all across Dundee, but to do so well here in London, the place of our previous shame, was something else altogether. This was significant. The response tonight proved that we weren't delusional, that we were surely something special, and that Brains – not Gavin Bain – was the person I was born to be. We ran through Soho's sodium streets screaming, shouting and whooping, scaring the prostitutes and the tramps, and flinging ourselves at the windows of Chinese restaurants, behind which hung lobster-red ducks from merciless hooks. Chinese chefs stood implacably with large chopping knives in their hands and gazed out at us without expression, while late-night revellers crossed the street to avoid us. We had never felt so thrillingly alive.

Two days later came our first real test. Robbie Bruce was as Scottish as a deep-fried Mars Bar. The few record-company types I'd met previously had convinced me that not all humans were so very far developed from apes, but Bruce was shrewd and canny and all too alert. I wished he were Australian, Scandinavian; anything but Scottish.

Our eleven a.m. meeting with him did not prompt a good and

restful sleep the night before. I was exhausted, pent-up, my eyes raw. Relaxation was beyond me. Bruce's office was smaller than I would have liked. There was not enough room to breathe, and I felt self-consciously bright in my ghetto outfit that had sent my bank account deep into the red but that was ultimately worth every penny. He leant over his desk and shook our hands, and the silence that followed – a silence that lasted no more than a second, two at most – stretched on interminably. *Calm down*, I told myself, willing Bill to do the same. *Just calm the fuck down. Don't blow it now, before we're even properly out of the gate.* I could feel flop-sweat breaking out all over me. The hair under my cap was soaked through; there were puddles under my arms. Any sympathy I hoped Robbie Bruce would have for such fresh-faced and inexperienced talent was nowhere to be found. Instead, with his beady eyes and pinched expression, this was a man who was all-purpose, a suffer-no-fools type. We were sunk.

Beside me, Bill overcompensated. 'Good to be here, baby, good to be here.' I cringed.

Bruce, to his credit and my merciful relief, suddenly looked happy that we were there. He leant towards us, arms resting on his desk.

'So, what part of the States are you guys from?'

Fuck, here goes.

We told him.

'Ah, OK. I thought I detected a bit of Canadian in there, but what do I know?' He laughed with what I took to be suspicion. A sliver of sweat inched down my back towards my arse crack.

'Yeah, well, we've travelled around a bit,' said Bill. Before Bruce could ask any further questions, Bill threw one back at him. 'And you?'

'Glasgow,' he said.

'Aye?' was Bill's response. He laughed loudly. So too did Bruce. We all did. And then, quite suddenly, the laughter stopped. Bruce showed little interest in playing the CD we had handed to him, at least not in front of us. Mostly, he seemed intent on getting more back-story. It was only as the questions came, and kept on coming, that I realized just how many holes remained in our concocted biographies. Why were we in London right now? Were we signed, in any capacity, back in America? Did we have representation, any management, either over there or over here? Why would we be seeking a deal in the UK rather than back home? What kind of visas were we travelling under?

This was awful; it was torture. We had in no way prepared for an interrogation on this level, and as I endeavoured to answer his questions as much as Silibil N' Brains – a pair of stoner skateboarders, after all – were prepared to do, I convinced myself that he was on to us, our accents letting us down at the first hurdle, our story with more holes than a hooker's stockings. My answers came back at him with a casual shrug. I told him that we were on a European vacation, had been bumming around the world, in fact, pretty much ever since Dubya had been re-elected in '04. Our visas had expired a long time ago, but we were hippies, dude, what the hell? I told him that we had ended up in the UK by a kind of osmosis, drawn here by its emergent skate scene, and that we really dug his country's music ('Britpop, right? Too cool . . .') and felt the UK deserved some fresh and untapped talent such as us. This wasn't so strange a concept. Las Vegas's the Killers were busy establishing themselves in the UK long before they ever thought about doing so back in their native America. Well, hey, we wanted to do much the same, except in rap.

Robbie Bruce took this all in with what seemed like a keen interest. He made a few notes, then picked up our CD, first to peruse the track-listing, then simply to hold tightly in his left hand and use it to punctuate his sentences. He was clearly taking us seriously, and this was good. Bill told a couple of crude jokes, and he laughed. He offered us tea, coffee, water, and laughed again when Bill suggested Krug, some coke and a couple of hookers.

And then suddenly, with no talk of a contract, our signatures, nothing, he stood abruptly and thanked us. He extended his hand, and said that it had been a pleasure. He wanted to play the CD to people in his office, he explained, to gauge their reaction. He would be back in touch with us soon. Suddenly I began to doubt everything.

'I'll call you,' he said.

Robbie Bruce never did call, but the truth was we barely noticed. We had some serious homework to do on our back-story. It came together with satisfying ease.

Hey, hi. The name's Brains, Brains McLoud. This here is Silibil. Say hello, Sili. We're from California, a real small town you've probably never heard of, goes by the name of Hemet. It's a small place, Hemet. If you ended up there on holiday you'd have to conclude you went there by mistake. Nothing happens in Hemet, it's just your regular cookie-cutter neighbourhood made up of real nice families with real nice children, and with real nice cars in the drive. People have nice lawns here, nice white picket fences. If you trespass, we'll shoot you. Armed response, you know? Dad works in insurance, he's something big behind a desk. He could sell you life insurance, vacation cover, or perhaps help with the upgrading of your Cadillac when it gets totalled by a drunk Hispanic. Mom? Mom is a housewife.

She helps out at the local church, and with the neighbourhood's old folk. If you want the truth of it, she is probably fucking the guy next door as well, but let's not go there, shall we?

OK, yes, let's. Behind the cookie-cutter regularity of our lovely little hamlet called Hemet, the place is a hotbed of sex and drink and drugs and adultery. No one ever talks about it, is all. Come to Hemet, and all you'll see is good, solid, Republican American folk. Kenny G's the music of choice round here, the soundtrack to all our Sunday evenings. Which means that this is one totally suffocating place, full of secrets and sin. You seen *Twin Peaks*, right?

OK, so in among all this surface uniformity, you've got Silibil N' Brains. Me and Sili bonded early in high school. We had the same likes: skateboards, rock music, rap, alienation. And we had the same dislikes: fraternity assholes, sorority bitches. People who used the acronym BFF. Sports jocks. Anyone who drove a Toyota Prius. We were Hemet's disaffected youth, and we liked to fuck with people. After Columbine, me and Bill took to calling one another Eric Harris and Dylan Klebold, in honour of the murderers, just to freak everybody out. It worked. It got us a week's suspension and some psychological evaluation. We were never invited to prom night. We weren't missed.

Soon as we could, we left the place and moved out to Huntington Beach. You been there? It's a great place for skateboarding, for picking up chicks. It's real popular. You can vacation there quite happily. We found us a duplex, some part-time jobs, and we got majorly into the skate scene, the bong scene. The kids there came tattooed, and the bands came regularly. Rage Against the Machine at Surf

City Saloon back in '93, a totally secret show, was an awesome night, dude. Never forget it.

Then it was rap, rap in a real big way, Eminem's '96 debut, Infinite, anything Tupac did before he died, and a whole lot of the stuff that followed after. That's one prolific dead fucker. Biggie Smalls and, further back, NWA and Wu Tang Clan. Me and Silibil started making our own raps back in '98, '99, nothing serious, just slacker fun, all part of the scene while we were hanging out on the local campus doing drugs and doing girls, spring break, beer and beaver, souvenir STDs.

We started performing, local bars and dives mostly, but pretty soon we started getting us a following, kids telling us that we were good, as good as Eminem – better, even. But we never really pursued anything just because, well, that was never what we were about. We were just having a good time, you know?

Then we did the whole beatnik thing, riding trains across our great country and into New York, then jet fuelling it across the Atlantic, rocking up in Paris, France, some place in Italy, then down on into London, England. Played a few more shows, met a whole load of girls. And the compliments? They just kept on a-coming. We liked the compliments. Great opportunities to play live in London, dude, and so we just kind of settled here.

So, yeah, that's pretty much why we're here now, in your office. Excuse me for saying so, sir, but you don't look like the kind of guy who looks a gift horse in the mouth. That's what you Brits like to say, right – a gift horse in the mouth? What you are looking at right now is the best damn unsigned rap act in the world. Hello. Pleased to

meet you. We are Silibil N' Brains, and we are at your
service!

A couple of weeks later, after bombarding promoters with emails,
I got us added at the last minute to the bill at Madame JoJo's, a
claustrophobic nightclub in the heart of Soho popular with pre-
op transsexuals and drag artists in feather boas. Having seen the
standard at Sound, we knew we had to up the ante here considerably, because, while Sound was full of pop star wannabes, this
bill's emphasis was strictly R&B and urban. Backstage was packed
with super-serious guys with scowls on their faces, knocking
knuckles and calling one another *blood*. The gathered crowd, we
quickly learnt, was crammed with A&Rs. What happened tonight
could count. The sense of discipline around us was like nothing
we'd ever seen, ambition streamlined. All anyone in this room
was thinking was: *I'm going to get famous, and quick. And it
could all start tonight.* The competition lent the atmosphere a
harsh, almost brittle air, and I had never felt more at home. These
were my people, each as obsessive as me.

Bill and I had by now got our act down to a fine art. We'd
spoken exclusively in American accents for weeks now. Michelle
thought us crazy, but she couldn't help but be amused, and
wanted nightly updates on our latest exploits. This, I hoped,
would be the most exciting yet. Before our performance we
indulged in a couple of beers and kept to ourselves, pacing back
and forth in a little corner of the backstage area. In a carrier bag
I refused to let go of I had a bra, a wig and a long kitchen knife.
Looking around at everyone else here, most of them still scowl-
ing and mooching and taking themselves terribly seriously, I
knew that we couldn't help *but* make an impact. They may not
necessarily have liked us out there, but I would ensure that they

wouldn't forget us. Bill looked at me, and gestured at the tension visible in every face we watched. We drank it down, and fortified ourselves. A girl came backstage and shouted out our name. We were on.

The walk from the backstage area to the stage itself was no more than ten feet, but as we placed one foot in front of the other, Bill leading, me close behind, we became transformed into the Dumb and Dumber roadshow. Bill, now suddenly full of life, broke out into a mad dash. Fumbling in the carrier bag, I made chase, the kitchen knife tight in my grip and held aloft. He screamed. I screamed. The audience stood in unified horror for an exquisitely pregnant moment before the penny dropped. Then, cautiously at first, and then more easily, they began to laugh. We went straight into a song called 'Stalker', a parody of a love song in which two men murder the girl they stalk. I'd always read from online blogs that London crowds were the hardest to impress, but this was like playing the Doghouse back in Dundee on Hogmanay. The crowd were in the palm of our hands, cheering loudly, fists pumping. As soon as the song had finished, we launched into some freestyling, turning our attentions, as was our habit, on to the crowd. There were some sexy young women in the front row, so I started singing Madonna's 'Like a Virgin', which I changed to 'I Like Virgins'. This prompted a mass singalong. After the next song, a towering 'Headcases', Bill started to diss a guy standing just in front of the speakers, picking apart his dress sense, his executive glasses, his hairstyle. He took it well, laughing along with everybody else despite the colour flooding his cheeks. I put the bra on, and halfway through 'Shut Your Mouth' Bill approached me and slowly slid the straps down my shoulders before unclipping it and tossing it into the crowd, the crowd grappling for it as if it were a bouquet at a wedding. We performed six songs in total, obliterating all those dull R&B and garage acts before us with our colour and sheer energy. People were calling for more. I stage dived, then peacock-strutted to the bar, where I thumped my fist down and demanded some beer. We were *mobbed*.

You guys were amazing! We were told this again and again, from every direction. I know, I responded. I know. *So, where are you from?* I told them, Bill followed through, both of us by now so expert at this that we were finishing one another's sentences, completing the other's jokes. *Call me, let's do lunch. The future's bright for you two, I'm serious. Let's meet.* We shrugged as if we couldn't care less. *You're not going back to America any time soon, are you?* 'Chill,' I told them, 'take it easy. We'll be hanging around here for a good while yet.'

Just a short while ago, we were the rapping Proclaimers, a laughing stock. Now look. We were the hottest new act in the country.

I love it when a plan comes together.

The next day started early. I had barely slept the night before, and got out of bed completely wired at five a.m. Bill staggered into the kitchen an hour later, naked but for underpants and oblivious to his morning glory. He was hungover, but then so was I. We'd had a lot of drinks at Madame JoJo's after our triumphant perform-ance, and we hadn't paid for a single one of them. When you're this talented, you rarely need to.

'Do we have a meeting today,' Bill croaked, 'or did I just dream it?' He grinned. 'Fucking fantastic dream.'

I showed him the card: Ray Stone, Island Records. In Biro alongside his name was scrawled a time: ten thirty.

Ray Stone, a large man with a character to match, had come

backstage as we were gathering our bags and getting ready to leave. He'd introduced himself to us by showing me his card. I'd read it, looked up at him, and nodded.

'Whereabouts in the States are you guys from, then?' he asked, and the manner in which he said it, or perhaps the manner in which I heard it, made me feel as if it wasn't a question so much as it was an accusation. Was he calling our bluff? I paused, I think, for a beat too long.

'California,' I told him. 'Hemet, California.'

'And Huntington Beach,' Bill added.

'We moved,' I said, in perhaps unnecessary explanation, suddenly hot under the collar.

Ray Stone smiled. 'I make things happen for dope cats like you.'

Dope cats?

He snatched his card from my hand and scribbled something on it, before handing it back.

'See you tomorrow morning.'

We breakfasted and dressed, and within half an hour we were on the first of three tube trains that would take us across London in rush hour to our meeting, and very probably our destiny. We didn't speak much en route, each of us alone with our thoughts. We were dressed again for success: XL basketball vests, low-slung jeans, box-fresh And1's. We may have been penniless, but, after Bill had blagged boxes full of free clothes from fashion-industry contacts he'd made while working in the skate store in Dundee, we looked a million dollars.

I'd have expected a major record company to be situated in the heart of the city behind an imposing glass front with revolving doors and security guards, but Island was located at the far end of a pretty green square in a part of London so posh you half expected people to refer to one another here as 'squire'. As we padded down well-scrubbed pavements, we passed a succession of manicured yummy mummies negotiating heavy 4×4 prams, and trailing dogs and nannies.

We arrived fifteen minutes early. The girl behind the reception desk fulfilled our expectations perfectly: she was achingly beautiful. We told her we were here to see Ray Stone. Bill reached over to shake her hand. She giggled. We signed in and were told to take a seat: Ray Stone would be with us shortly. We sprawled across a leather sofa in front of a large plasma screen. MTV was on, playing – what else? – an Eminem video. This was no coincidence; this was cosmic.

A recognizable pop star wandered through the lobby area, not one we particularly admired but whose life we certainly craved. He nodded hello to us. Bill stood up and saluted him. He frowned and hurried off. Ray Stone kept us waiting a good half hour, but I'd have been happy to wait an eternity in reception. I liked the atmosphere of the place, the music, the beautiful women, the attendant pop stars and, above all, the exquisite sense of anticipation.

'Ray will see you now.'

We looked up to see the beautiful receptionist addressing us. Before her desk, Bill fell deliberately and gallantly to one knee. 'Darling, will you marry me?' he asked.

'Let's see how your meeting goes first, shall we?' she responded.

Bill grinned. 'Hey, I like your style.'

She showed us into a boardroom empty of people. It was dominated by a large oval table around which were gathered several leather-backed executive chairs. A rubber plant sat in one

corner, with an enormous music system opposite. The windows
gave out on to a small concrete garden. On the walls were silver,
gold and platinum discs for U2, Grace Jones, Bob Marley.

We were still gazing at Bob Marley's dreadlocks when the door
opened behind us. Ray Stone came in and greeted us warmly.
Behind him trailed five others, four men, one woman. He introduced us to them all, and then more people dribbled in from
adjoining offices, from press, promotions and marketing depart-
ments. We were shaking hands and waving to everyone,
desperate to avoid one another's eyes if only because we didn't
want to catch the fear in them. Underneath our bravado was
freezing-cold fear.

Ray Stone told those congregated how good we had been the
night before, and we loudly agreed, telling everyone they should
have been there. 'And why weren't you?' Bill demanded to general chuckles. The momentum was already so strong here, so
much more positive than with Robbie Bruce at Sony, that I anticipated an instant overflow of admiration, that the assembled
would start cheering once our music came flooding through the
speakers. Ray, however, had other ideas. Amid all the commotion
I noticed him handing a CD to one of his assistants. He hushed
the room and told him to throw on the beats they'd received from
a producer on their books. 'You have got to hear this,' Ray said,
addressing the room. Bill and I glanced at each other and gulped
in anticipation.

'All right, guys, go for it,' he said, as the beat came through the
sound system.

'Uh, what, freestyle?' Bill asked politely, buying us precious
thinking time.

'Yeah, you know that thing you did last night, in between
songs.'

'Er, yeah, cool,' I said, trying to hide the nerves, fearing every-one would hear my voice shake. Bill went first, apprehensively, not sure of just how controversial we could be.

Hey yo, remained glued 'cause Sili's the new Babe Ruth and
I'm about to blaze the roof like forest fires in Australia do.
The sabre tooth, I make it hot like Beruit . . .

'No, no, no . . .' Ray said, pausing the beat. 'I mean the thing where you went around the crowd dissing them – that was hilar-ious.' He nodded in the direction of his co-workers, which we interpreted as our licence to *get ill*. I looked at Bill and he shrugged back at me, as if to say, *Fuck it, let's murder these clowns*. I picked up where he left off, just as I would in a game of Porcupine.

OK, it may be rude but I'm one crazy dude who's picturing
every lady in the room naked, nude or wearing bathing
suits, sitting there lazing with my face in yer boobs, feeding
like I was a baby back in nineteen-eight-two . . . [Bill then
interrupted while approaching one of the women in the
room] And I'm feeling that after this meeting I may be walking away with you . . . [He put his arm around the girl before
moving on the next victim] Oh no check this bro's Converse,
all burst, must of stole them from a hobo after he walked the
earth, brown slacks and the wrong shirt, nearing thirty but
clearly dressed by his mom for work . . .

They were laughing now; they were ours, and our confidence grew with every line. Pretty soon we were bouncing around the room with the energy levels of athletes on steroids, the laughter music to our ears. Our performance lasted five minutes. It felt like more. I could have gone on – we both could – but Ray Stone raised a hand.

'Thanks, guys,' he said.

Ray also thanked everyone for coming in, which must have been a signal, because people started to get up, chair legs dragging on the soft carpeting beneath. Some came over to shake our hands, and those who did were promptly swallowed up in a bear hug from Bill. 'I'll miss you, man, I'll miss you. Write me, yeah?'

There were just three of us left in the boardroom. Ray Stone asked us more questions about representation, the Musicians' Union, PRS. He told us that we should really think about securing management before moving forward. I liked those words, 'moving forward'. Before he saw us out, he took our numbers.

When we left, Bill telling the beautiful receptionist that the meeting had gone so well that he was off now to look for an engagement ring, the midwinter day was bright and warm, vibrant and full of opportunity. London, I decided, was a magical place where dreams came true. I loved it. At the tube station we raced one another up and down the platform, screaming off all our pent-up adrenalin until a guard came over and asked us to stop. We were upsetting our fellow passengers.

Ray Stone was true to his word. He did call us back – several times, in fact, over the next few weeks. He lined up gigs for us, and we were brought in to perform before more of his colleagues as well as a succession of potential managers. I couldn't quite understand why he didn't want to just go ahead and sign us there and then, but I guess I was still naïve to the industry and its convoluted workings. From what I've learnt since, even people at Ray Stone's level are reluctant to stick their necks out, just in case their sure things turn out to be a flop. Had someone signed us and we weren't an overnight sensation with our very first single, they could have been out of a job. Consequently, no one in the industry was ever prepared to make a decision alone. They acted as a pack, and would only show interest when the rest of the pack did, at which point everybody would clamber for our signatures in an excitable rush. Sheep. Until then, we would be forced to stew. No one had the courage of their singular convictions, no one. It was pitiful.

That said, Stone continued to prove a vocal supporter. We had by now met a handful of music-industry managers, all of whom had made positive noises about us, but none of whom had so far come up with a concrete offer to represent us. Music-industry managers, I was quick to learn, were a little like boxers' managers: you wouldn't want to meet them down an alley after dark. A lot of them wore jewellery, but badly. Some of them had ponytails. They each had the waxy look common to all middle-aged men with a propensity for excess. To them, we and others like us were the new Persil, the new Ford Focus – nothing more than a product to sell. They cared little about the finer details, it seemed. They just looked at the packaging: two good-looking, over-confident young men adept at grabbing the attentions of an audience with ready cash in their pockets. Many of them appeared to be convinced that we could sell records, lots of records. One suggested he could set us up in a Central London penthouse with all mod cons. Another pledged to hook us up with some of the finest hip-hop talent America had to offer, but when I asked him to offer up some names he started stuttering. Another asked us whether we'd ever considered doing ballads, cover versions. We trusted none of them, and liked them even less.

Then Ray Stone recommended us to Jonathan Shalit, of Shalit Global. I had of course heard of Jonathan Shalit, who was one of the biggest music managers in London, having signed many chart-topping acts. Ray Stone said that Shalit was worth seeing, and so, in particular, was his second-in-command, a younger guy known only by his initials, J. D.

'You'll like J. D.,' he predicted. 'He's on your wavelength.'

'Really?' Bill said, deadpan.

Despite our reservations about seeing a man more tested in pop opera than he was rap, we took the meeting. Ray Stone was right. We warmed to J. D. instantly. He was a nice guy – ultimately as full of shit as everyone else in the industry, of course, but there was something underneath that veneer. He seemed decent, someone we could trust. A huge music fanatic, he was also an obsessive rap fan. At last here was someone we could relate to, perhaps even work with. The first thing he said to us was, 'I get you guys,' and for a moment I thought he meant that he knew we weren't really American at all. But he knew no such thing. This was simply his way of saying that he liked our music, he respected our songs, even those about virgins and grannies. We respected his respect, and told him so. To prove it, we knocked knuckles. Then another set of knuckles came our way, hungry for contact. Jonathan Shalit's. He had arrived late to the meeting but came in now like a proverbial ray of sunshine, with a wobbly smile on his face and a smoky laugh in his throat. I looked him up and down and the first thing I thought of was Penguin from Batman. Small in height and large in stature, he was dressed like a vaudevillian pimp, lots of shimmering silk, plenty of car-dealer bling. But you couldn't fault the man's natural-born enthusiasm. His eyes appeared to jiggle in their sockets as he spoke; and, though it felt likely that he'd only ever resort to listening to our music if a gun was held to his head, he insisted he loved it, just loved it, and that when he heard it he could see dollar signs materialize before his eyes. This sounded fine by us. He said that he wanted to represent us not so that he could turn us into stars, but simply because we deserved a manager as good as him.

Bill looked at me. An imperceptible nod of the head passed between us. We liked the guy. It was hard not to.

It turned out that J. D. knew the rap scene well, and the ideas he was mentioning to us in terms of positioning and marketing sounded both plausible and promising.

Nothing official happened immediately, but over the next month or so we hung out with J. D. a lot, going to clubs, getting smashed and doing things that at the time felt incredible (if illicit, and always illegal) but that would come back to haunt us the morning after like a shameless taunt. In other words, fun. A bond was forming. He would tell us that Shalit was poised to make us an offer soon, that he was extending his feelers throughout the industry and that the general response was beyond positive. Our name was out there, creating a buzz, and we were making friends, flirting with industry types, learning names and acquiring insider knowledge, knowledge that we would later use to make us seem so much more connected than we really were. The key to being a good liar is to be a great listener. We were fantastic listeners.

It was only a matter of time now, Shalit said. Thank Christ for that, because we were by now past skint. That was another good reason for hanging out with J. D. so much: he paid for everything.

Like it was yesterday I still remember the morning Shalit called to make it official. It will live in a part of my mind as the moment our lives changed, for better or for worse, for ever.

It was early, barely ten o'clock, and I was still asleep. My phone was vibrating on the floor beside me. I grabbed clumsily for it, then croaked *Hello*, and immediately had to hold it away from my ear as Shalit gave me his singsong greeting in the kind of voice I always thought could have landed him a job as a breakfast DJ. He told me that he wanted to become our manager, that he would help set us up in a house befitting emergent rap stars, and would also cover all our expenses while we worked on our music. He would then set about landing us what would undoubtedly be the record deal of the year. All he needed now was for us to come in and give him our signatures. When could we be there?

I sat up in bed and rubbed the sleep from my eyes. Michelle, I knew, needed her flat back, some space. And Bill and I needed *more* space. The timing, then, was perfect. I asked him, in my most cocky American manner, to talk money.

'Well,' he began, 'in addition to all your expenses paid . . . £30,000 up front.'

I looked across the floor to where Bill was still fast asleep. I stretched my leg and toed him awake. He looked at me grumpily. I threw a shoe at him, mouthed the name *Shalit* and he came quickly to life, shuffling over to sit right next to me, cocking an ear towards the phone.

Had Shalit really just offered us £30,000? This was more than I could ever have dreamt possible. He didn't hear me swallow, and for this I was silently grateful. Nor did he have any idea quite how dry my mouth went.

'Hey, man,' I drawled, 'we don't get out of bed for anything less than £70,000.'

I had no idea what I was saying. Bill looked as if he was about to batter me. I snapped my phone shut, killing the conversation dead.

Since our arrival in London Bill and I had had an unspoken agreement: that no matter how physical our arguments got, we would never throw punches at each other's faces because our faces were our fortune. Anywhere else, yes, but never the face. This was why he now had me in a headlock instead, and was trying to grind the top of my head into the floorboards of Michelle's studio flat. Were she here right now, she'd scream at us to stop acting like children. But Michelle was at work; we could fight all we wanted.

'What the *fuck* are you playing at?' He was livid, a fat vein throbbing down the middle of his forehead. 'You're turning down £30,000! Are you insane? We're broke!' He was standing over me now, holding a bedside lamp above his head and threatening to bring it down on top of me. 'You, fucking idiot, I'm going to kill you.'

The phone rang again. I clambered around Bill's legs to answer it. Shalit.

He sounded terse but resolved. 'OK,' he said. '£70,000 it is.'

I dropped the phone, Bill the lamp. We embraced and jumped all over Michelle's sofabed until we fell over the side in a heap, sending various items of furniture flying. Tears were streaming from my eyes. Our laughter was shrill, disbelieving.

'*Hello* . . .?' Shalit called, his voice now a tiny dismembered thing emanating from a lost corner of the room.

Five

The Dairy in Brixton was our first professional studio. Three hundred pounds a day, all covered by our newly-in-place management team. It was a great place, small but cosy as a womb, and J. D. had set us up with a young engineer who was basically at our beck and call day and night, whenever creativity struck. We were professional musicians now, on the payroll. We would turn up mid-morning and often not leave until dawn. The sofa room was our HQ. It was where the TV was, where we would watch everything from MTV to late-night porn. We set up the Xbox in there for when we needed a little break from all the feverish productivity. In the kitchen was a fridge that we'd filled with Jack Daniel's and beer, sandwiches and, for me, biltong, which reminds me of my South African youth.

Producers from New York, Los Angeles and Stockholm began sending us tracks to write to, but I was one step ahead of all of them, having already created countless new beats myself, all of which seemed far better than any of those on offer via the professional channels. Words were swarming around our heads all the time now, and in the studio they came pouring out into the microphone and were then committed to tape. We were knocking out a track a day. We completed 'Tongue Kung Fu', 'Let's Get it On' and 'I've Drunk Too Much'. We tweaked 'Stalker' and came up with two of our most important tracks, 'I Play with Myself' and 'Losers' – which sounded like the world's greatest anthem, a stone-cold subversive classic.

It was an extremely creative time and when we weren't in the Dairy recording we were competing in every battle-rap competition we could find. This way we figured we could build a name for ourselves in the underground scene as lyricists, while still recording mainstream hits. We were winning these competitions, and easily. However, a few competitions down the line we had overstayed our welcome. In one final I was even booed for no other reason than – and get this – being a Yank. My success in London's battle-rap scene came to an abrupt end one night at the Oh! Bar in Camden town. It's fair to say that things got a little out of hand. It was all going well until the final, where, on the spur of the moment, and without thinking twice, I used the breasts of a girl in the front row, or should I say lack thereof, to describe how small my opponent's chances were of winning. The girl, who clearly had no sense of humour, began spitting in my direction and I don't just mean little drops of saliva – no, no, this charming young thing was hawking up large, slimy, back-of-the-throat wads of phlegm and firing them at me like tennis balls. I returned the sentiment, and her boyfriend and his crew rushed the stage. A brawl ensued and my cousins Warren and Byron (who were by now living in London) jumped to my rescue; Bill was at the other end of the bar working his way towards us, swinging wildly, roaring like Begbie from *Trainspotting*, appearing to be having the time of his life. Then there was a sound I had never heard before, at least not in real life. Two heart-stopping bangs that sent everyone to the floor.

Gunshots. I froze on the deck, head ringing, trying to figure out what had just happened. Play dead . . . No, fuck, bad idea – get up. Run. Now everyone was rushing the exits. Warren dragged me by the collar to my feet and within seconds we were outside gallop- ing past Bill and Byron who had sprinted for Mornington Crescent tube station. The incident really shook us all up and I for one couldn't get the sound of the gunshots out of my head for weeks to come. It was a very close call, an unnecessary brush with death that reminded us where we were, the dungeon, where gun crime was rising by the day. And hip-hop here in London, not to all but to the vast majority of street kids, was not just about the music, the art of rhyme or making beats. It was about acting tough, being a gangster, hustling, selling drugs and making money by perpetuat- ing American gangster-rap stereotypes. Bill and I were here to make music, to entertain and have fun. We had no interest in being shot in the chest, no matter how much kudos death by gunshot received.

So back to the studio, where we were so convinced of our genius that the knowledge of it acted as an aphrodisiac. I could get an erection by just gazing at myself in the reflection of the microphone-booth windows, and Bill – Bill was in his something else, a caricature of rampant ego whose personality filled every inch of the studio until it was all you could see hear smell touch taste. J. D. loved everything he was hearing. We were *worthy*. Rap stars have long been the world's most arrogant people. Rock stars, in comparison, are wallflowers. Rock stars never usually need to name-check themselves so constantly in song, but rap- pers, who have previously been so marginalized and underappreciated, rarely do anything else. We name-checked ourselves endlessly. We'd earned the right to, as if it was the aural equivalent of having our names in lights. *Everyone* would be name-checking us before long. We were going to be superstars.

Meanwhile, J. D. was working tirelessly on our behalf, lining up showcase after showcase, and a string of late-night, unannounced club appearances for us. We would play to record-company sheep by day and to urban youth by night. They were all the same to us – an appreciative crowd – and each time we killed it, we nailed it to the mast: Silibil N' Brains, the future of music. The Eminem comparisons came thick and fast from everyone, a daily occurrence now and everywhere we went we were asked to *do that thing we do, the freestyle thing*. We were playing Porcupine, or a version of it, almost every day. One girl said that we were so entertaining that we should have our own TV show as well. We liked this idea *a lot*. We were living the dream, and we wanted to boast about it. We wanted to go back home and have a parade thrown in our honour. But of course we couldn't, and this was where we came up against the problem that was to define us, that would in time be the undoing of us.

Silibil N' Brains may well have had a natural gift and talent to die for, but our whole appeal was built upon a lie, a scam. We were a couple of Scots pretending to be something we weren't: American. Being American was why we were here, of course, and it was a pretence that we maintained round the clock, even when just in one another's company, and with a discipline that would have surprised everyone who knew us. But then we had to, because the moment we exposed ourselves for what we truly were – or, worse, the moment somebody else did so for us – would be the moment everything ended. Shalit, I knew, would go mental, all his money invested in something that never really was. Record-company interest would fall away instantaneously. We'd be laughed out of town. We'd be sued. And so we had to maintain our lie at all costs. We were going to have to live our new lives as if our old ones had never even existed in the first place. This was *our* secret.

Until we decided to share it, that is. To protect a lie of this magnitude, we felt we needed to enlist the help of at least our closest friends. And we needed people around us we could trust. That way, if it all went wrong, at least we wouldn't be alone. And so we had Oskar, we had my cousins Warren and Byron, and a couple of South African mates, now settled in London. When we got them all together and briefed them on what we were doing, every response was the same: jaws hit the floor.

'You're *what*?' they said.

'And they believe you?' they said.

'But what happens when you get found out?' they said.

'You know, the moment you have your first hit single,' Warren explained slowly, as if talking to halfwits, 'will be the moment half of Dundee gets on the phone to the tabloids to tell them you're not from California at all. What then?'

'Hey, dude,' said Bill, punching him on the arm. 'Accentuate the positive. The important thing here is this: we're going to become fucking *superstars*!'

We committed those we told to utmost secrecy, to be broken upon the threat of death. I told Alison, my increasingly distant girlfriend. Alison wasn't amused and could see only an unhappy ending. She promised to keep quiet and wished me luck. Could we trust the others? We'd have to wait and see.

My cousin Byron *loved* it, decided it was too good a lark for him to miss out on. He would frequently crash at our new place in London over the next twelve months. We appointed him our sometime DJ and gave him the title of Stretch Jnr, our mixologist. He would film everything we did for public consumption. YouTube was in its infancy back then, but it was ripe for mining, for generating an online campaign that would get the buzz J. D. talked so lovingly of properly up and running, perhaps even on a global scale. With £70,000 in our pockets we were cash rich, and London suddenly became our playground, with so many opportunities to party, to drown out Alison's many concerns and warnings, to court notoriety and become infamous. Nothing was stopping us. We were going to have the time of our lives, and all of it would be immortalized on film, proof that we were always looking towards the bigger picture: to the gatefold special-edition CD of our debut album, now including for a limited time only a DVD on *The Making of Silibil N' Brains*. J. D. thought this a perspicacious idea. *Perspicacious*! How about that?

Shalit funded our move into our new place in Arnos Grove, at the arse end of the Piccadilly Line just two stops from the total oblivion of Cockfosters, a suburban neighbourhood thrumming with the exotic overspill of London's mulch. Our place was big and roomy and detached, three bedrooms, two bathrooms, a huge kitchen-cum-living room and a sprawling, unkempt garden. We christened it Eagle's Nest, decorated it to our liking and set about trashing the place methodically over the coming weeks and months by making it party central, bringing back all sorts of people, from the industry, from bars and clubs, even from the last bus home, sometimes, all of us here to drink and smoke and fuck the night away. We filled the fridge with booze, and bought a corkboard upon which we pinned flyers from the local pizza, Chinese and Indian take-aways, along with the mobile numbers of those dealers who were prepared to serve us this far out of the centre of town. Michelle was relieved to see us leave her studio flat at last, but she became a regular face at our parties. She had an open invitation to visit as often as she liked. It was the very least I could do.

'Good news, guys. It looks like we're about to get a firm offer on the table.'

Back then there was rarely a call from Shalit that didn't contain good news for us. This one was better than most.

'I'm sending a car round for you. Be ready.'

Two hours later we were in a studio complex under London Bridge performing a six-song set before a couple of high-ranking record-company executives, the kind who wore sunglasses indoors. This was the boldest test of our mettle yet. They were American, associates of Shalit's who happened to be in town and couldn't possibly pass up Shalit's promise of America's greatest unsigned hip-hop act in merry old England. They bought our accents straight off, and they loved our back-story.

'OK, let's see what you can do.' Dave Clansey was a heavyset fifty-year-old with silver hair, a trim goatee and what was clearly a year-round tan. He had the air of a man who dabbed eau-de-Cologne behind each ear each morning and who ordered his cocaine by the kilo. His associate beside him, Michael Feldstein, was completely unreadable behind his shades, tall and thin and possibly older, dressed in bleached denim and leather and a pair of tassled moccasins, no socks. His shins, revealed to us as he perched on a high stool, were entirely hairless.

We gave them 'Let's Get Naked' and 'I Play with Myself', a song about masturbation and the sexual shortcomings of Silibil N' Brains, which we delivered with such an aggressive flourish that Shalit, bless him, was on his feet for the entire performance, clapping along like the drunken uncle at a wedding disco well past midnight.

'Impressive, guys, impressive.' Dave Clansey liked us. 'But one thing I don't get. What the hell are you doing here, in London, with music like this? You should be back home, surely?'

I opened my mouth to explain, but Dave Clansey was still talking and wasn't the kind of man who liked being interrupted. He told us that he wanted to take us back to America, back *home*, now, immediately, tomorrow if possible, where he would begin the process of signing us to Sony US. On native soil Silibil N' Brains would make much more sense and have a far greater impact than we ever would over here, where the charts were dominated by boy bands and floppy-fringed indie acts. The UK market, he told us, was small fry. We could come visit a ways down the line, but only once we'd conquered America.

Shalit was practically vibrating with excitement. So, bizarrely, was Bill.

'He's right,' Bill announced to me, before turning back to Dave Clansey and pumping hands with him. 'You're right, Dave. I'm getting tired of all these limey sons of bitches anyway – no offence, Mr Shalit, sir.'

Dave Clansey laughed. Michael Feldstein crossed his arms across his chest, and nodded once.

'When can you leave?'

Bill checked his watch. Now Shalit laughed.

Dave Clansey explained that during the next few days he would sort out our travel arrangements. Bill's request for a private jet was noted, he said, but would ultimately be rejected. 'You'll have to make do with business class, I'm afraid. The private jets can come later, but I like your style, buddy.' We high-fived these men old enough to be our fathers, and they left.

Afterwards, Shalit took us to a nearby bar to toast our success. As he and Bill continued to celebrate, with talk of further celebrations

on the Sunset Strip with the likes of Paris Hilton and her sister
Nicky, I watched my partner in crime with a growing sense of dis-
orientation. What part of his brain wasn't functioning properly here?
How lost was he in all this? I was grateful when Shalit told us he
had another appointment to attend. He hugged us and made his
exit. Alone now, I turned to Bill, glowering.

'What?' he asked.

'What do you mean, *what*? What the hell were you playing at
back there? We can't go to America, Bill.'

I endeavoured to explain it to him, the way a parent tells his
young child that Father Christmas isn't real after all. I told him that
we couldn't go *back* to America because we'd never been to
America in the first place. We were not from California, but were
from Scotland. Remember? We held British passports. Were we to
travel to America, we'd need to get visas – and even if visas were
granted we would not be permitted to stay in the States for more
than three months. Could he see now that this presented a certain
problem?

His face fell as I spoke, and even in this light I could see
colour flushing his cheeks.

'Shit, sorry, man. What can I say? I just got caught up in the
moment.' He was crestfallen. 'But hey, that was fucking exciting,
huh? They thought we were geniuses!'

We finished our drinks, and ordered some more. An hour later,
sufficiently emboldened, I felt myself ready to face what was
bound to be an exquisitely awkward telephone conversation with
our manager. I found a quiet corner of the bar, and dialled.

'Hi Jonathan. It's Gavin. I think we'll pass, thanks.'

His voice boomed. '*What?*'

'I think we'll pass on Dave Clansey's offer.'

'Why on earth would you do that?'

I swallowed. 'I'm not sure. I just wasn't, you know, *feeling* him.'

'Feeling him . . .?'

Bill grabbed the phone.

'Yeah, and he kinda looked at me funny.'

'Funny? Funny how?'

Bill addressed me. 'Think he could be gay, Gav?'

I took the phone back again. 'Yeah, definitely gay. I think he was coming on to me, too.'

'What on *earth* are you two talking about?'

Bill snatched the phone, and made a loud crackling noise into the mouthpiece. 'Oops, tunnel,' he said, and hung up.

We stood there, panting through open mouths.

Bill whistled. 'Oof. Close one.' Then immediately he brightened, and brought his hands together. 'Whose round is it?'

A week later, divine intervention. Sony UK wanted us.

It was only with hindsight that I realized just how fatal it was that the day we signed to them happened to fall on Friday the 13th. I'm surprised I didn't make more of it, for I am a man of many neuroses, but I didn't, not at all. In the darker days that were perhaps inevitably to follow, the days of pill prescriptions, of Alison leaving me, the drug-swamped nights and suicidal mornings after, it hit me time and again, a convenient fact upon which to lay all the blame. Sometimes, in my more delusional moments, I like to think that if only we'd signed on the 12th, a common or garden Thursday, things would have turned out differently. Or a Monday, a Tuesday or Wednesday. But no, it was a Friday, Friday the 13th of February 2004, the worst day in any calendar, in any year. Early that morning, during breakfast, the toaster backfired, a lightning fork of electricity bursting from its innards and very nearly flooring Bill. Mere coincidence? I think not.

I had been desperate to sleep the night before, all the more so when I could hear Bill flat out and snoring loudly. We'd been sensible and stayed in, an evening in front of the television while skirting around the issue of tomorrow as if tomorrow wasn't really happening at all, both of us fearful that the instant we started to discuss it properly would be the instant it revealed itself as nothing more than conjured-up fantasy. It's all very well living in a dream, but when the dream starts to come true things get weird. I was in bed by midnight, ramrod straight beneath the duvet and staring up into the black ceiling above. Blissful silence enveloped me for one complete minute. Then came cacophony.

First it was Bill in the next room, snoring so loudly that the noise passed through the dividing wall and flooded my ear canals like a tsunami. Then came the clock on the bedside table, a tiny tick-ticking drum rhythm to Bill's strident horn section. Two a.m. and I was still horribly awake, by now panicking that a sleepless night would be all too evident in my ruined eyes at the signing which was now just – what? – just ten short hours away. I got up and padded into the kitchen to retrieve a face pack from the back of the fridge, a present from my mother who knew all too well what my nights were like. Back in bed, I arranged its slimy plastic sacs over my eyes, and soon they were cucumber cool. Minutes later, I tossed it on to the floor, abruptly convinced that the cold would bring out crows' feet. Who, at twenty-three years old, can afford to have crows' feet?

Outside, cats were fighting, their strangled meows stretching until they snapped and broke, then started over. And was that really a moth on the light bulb above my head, a moth in the middle of freezing February?

Straight Outta Scotland

Time did eventually pass, after a fashion, because suddenly it was seven o'clock in the morning. I must have gotten at least a couple of hours of fitful sleep. I showered but deliberately didn't shave, not today – today I wanted definition – then went into the kitchen where Bill, recovering from the exploding toaster, was busy wolfing down a buttered slice of bread he would later vomit right back up again. It was interesting to see my overconfident friend so obviously nervous. He looked at me, my clean-shaven friend, my accomplice, but he chose not to speak. I drank a glass of milk down in one gulp. Then we went upstairs to our separate bedrooms, where we dressed for the most important day of our lives.

We weren't used to Arnos Grove at eight o'clock in the morning, if only because we were mostly still asleep at that time, or else only beginning to think about going to bed. But its streets were full of bleak expressions, rushing city-bound suits on the way to the tube station. We stood out, Bill and I, like golden sunshine streaming biblically through storm clouds. You could say we had made an effort in the wardrobe department, dressing for success like the pair of wiggers we were (or, more specifically, like a pair of American rappers so very far from home). Bill *yo*'d everyone who caught his eye, and took great amusement from the fact that nobody responded.

'You Brits,' he said to no one in particular. 'So uptight.'

We were done up in loose-fitting layers, everything oversized, our chests ablaze in red and yellow basketball vests, our jeans low, boxers on proud display, imported skateboard sneakers on our feet. We were Silibil N' Brains, pimp-rolling down the high street, past internet cafés, past exhausted second-hand-clothes outlets and gangly schoolchildren, on our way to the tube station, and unstoppable. Or at least we would have been had Bill not been frequently forced to stop, hands on knees, to puke up again. When we reached the station we found a human traffic jam, everyone trying to force themselves through the gates at the same time. A guard pleaded for calm, and organized us through two at a time like a British Transport Noah. The tube train was empty when it pulled up, but full by the time it departed. We stood strap-hanging in a central carriage surrounded by pinstripes and pencil skirts. There was no space to move. A woman had her face practically in Bill's armpit.

'Don't worry, lady,' he assured her. 'Old Spice. You're safe.'

Six tube stops later, and Bill was starting to sweat. The more I watched his face contort in a barely suppressed panic, the more I felt it necessary to remain calm for the both of us. He checked his watch, then checked it again. I felt terribly protective of him.

'We're going to be late, Gav.'

'Chill,' I told him. 'We'll be fine.'

But by Caledonian Road it was clear that we *were* going to be late. The unscheduled stops between stations didn't help, and as one stretched from ten to fifteen minutes, with no announcement from the bastard driver, and with the carriage lights flickering on and off, I suddenly remembered I was claustrophobic.

I could no longer breathe, my lungs parched and painful. Panic came.

'If this train doesn't move *now*, I swear I'm going to fucking lose it. Bill, I can't breathe, I . . .'

Bill looked down at me wryly. '*Chill*,' he said.

I saw that he too was starting to pale.

'Christ, you're not going to be sick again, are you?' I said.

And just like that, in a tube train so tightly packed that nobody had an inch to spare, there suddenly formed a generous space

around us, passengers forcing themselves back on to one another
and away from us.

Bill grinned. 'That's better, guys. Sure do appreciate it.'

The train farted, lurched forward, juddered to a halt and then
moved on. By the time we were finally ascending the escalators at
Leicester Square, we were properly late. But we didn't care. Our
nerves had evaporated and we had *become* our characters. We
were as cavalier as fuck now, all attitude, all colour, and that loping
pimp-roll. This would happen to me countless times over the next
few months. It would feel as if I had pulled a mask over me, a mask
that banished Gavin Bain to the eaves and allowed me to become
Brains McLoud entirely. It was tremendously empowering. Right
now, we had the focus of trained athletes, and if you knew what
was about to take place, how we were going to *play* this record
company like a fluid move on the basketball court, you'd have
been impressed. We worked our way through the grey streets of
Soho, and met up with Shalit and J. D. at the prearranged corner,
Shalit making a big gesture of checking his watch, then wagging a
nagging finger at us. We grinned back at him – *don't sweat it,
man* – and then we all set off together, filling the width of the
narrow pavement like a quartet of mismatched Reservoir Dogs.

It quickly became clear, however, that I wasn't fully Brains
McLoud just yet, and as we walked on the world seemed to tilt on
its axis. I couldn't see straight, and fear, as pure as vodka, started
to rise from my stomach. My footsteps dragged, and as our management team strode ahead, I fell purposefully back, pulling Bill
with me.

'Our story,' I said to him. 'We need to go over our story one
more time, just in case.'

But now it was Bill's turn to calm me down. He smiled at me,
a smile full of warmth and perhaps even love. We were in this

together, a partnership, a team. We'd fooled everyone already, and we would fool Sony today. We were the masters of our own destiny.

A moment before we caught up with Shalit and J. D., Bill spoke.

'Look, it's just another game of Porcupine. If anything gets tricky up there for either of us,' he whispered, 'then the other just cuts in, changes the subject and *recovers*, right? Lead and recover, baby, lead and recover.'

Recover. It was to prove the day's most valuable word.

Turning into Great Marlborough Street, we fell into step with Shalit and J. D. Shalit, resplendent in an electric-blue suit with silver lining and fire-engine-red socks, was all purpose, all business; he'd done this before, many times, and was a man in his element. His eyes were tiny and focused behind his rimless glasses, and he stared straight ahead, unwavering. J. D. was more on our level, dressed down in a cool pair of jeans and T-shirt beneath a big fat puffa jacket, schoolboy excitement alive in his face. While he and Bill reminisced about a night out we'd all had recently, I felt a frog lurch up into in my throat. My mouth was like the desert.

We arrived to find the familiar revolving doors, and shiny white linoleum stretching all the way to a high front desk behind which sat not the habitual beautiful girl but rather a stone-faced security guard, his cheeks pocked with acne scars. I swallowed. Here we were; this was it. We were going to go through with this now, come what may. We signed in, pinned our passes to our chests and walked forward. No turning back.

The lift was smaller than any claustrophobe could have been happy with, but by now I had managed to fully flip my inner switch, and all panic – OK, *most* panic – was effortlessly overridden by sheer adrenalin and something I felt was suspiciously close to pure joy. I was Brains McLoud, my trusted Silibil at my side. The lift pinged.

'Ready?' Shalit asked. J. D. offered us his knuckles. My reflection in the lift's mirror beamed back at me. The doors opened and out we bounded, Beavis & Butthead, Bill & Ted and Ren & Stimpy combined, performance in motion. We stepped out on to a floor full of people earnestly hunched over their computer monitors. We started shouting.

'Yo, yo. Hey dude! Yo.' Every head looked up, each face now smiling our way. 'Silibil N' Brains, in the motherfucking building.'

Strange how easy it is to slip into the exaggerated vernacular of your average American rapper, not least when your only real aim is to parody it mercilessly. To the people of the third floor of Sony Records, we were a slice of bright Californian sunshine come to brighten up their miserable winter's day. We were forty-five minutes late and boastful of it, strolling up to folk, high-fiving any outstretched hand that came our way, slapping people on the back of their heads, ruffling hair, joking with one, joking with all. If we were irritants, nobody let on, but then this was a record company, where people were paid to smile and praise *the talent*, irrespective of their private thoughts, their personal pains. By the time we reached the boardroom, everyone was on their feet, their ringing telephones left unanswered.

It wasn't a big boardroom, not a boardroom to entertain the likes of Mariah Carey, I fancied, but big enough; it would do. It filled up quicker than a church on doomsday once we entered it. I counted ten, fifteen people, all sandwiched in alongside one another, each of them wanting a piece of us. It felt like a party in a broom cupboard. I recognized many of the faces here, familiar from several of our shows and showcases. Luckily, there was no sign of Robbie Bruce, the A&R we had visited in this very building just a few months ago and who hadn't called us back – most probably, we thought, because he suspected foul play. A lot of the people present were those who had given me their cards after one of our gigs, full of grand promises; among them was Ruth Adams, the woman who would become our long-suffering A&R. She was a blonde and attractive thirtysomething, with a solid if understated confidence to her. I liked her. Unfortunately, she was married. The door opened again and somebody brought in a bucket of champagne, then another. Champagne is not really my drink – find me any guy from Dundee who'd ever drink it willingly – but right now I'd have killed for a glass.

An overfriendly hand draped itself on my left shoulder, soft and slender, the nails manicured and painted.

'Oh, hey. Hi.' I looked up and she blushed. I had no idea who she was, but she was female and attractive, which was a bonus. 'It's so great that you're, you know, like, here and everything,' she said. I gazed into her face, all eyes and teeth and hair down to *here*. 'Love your music,' she continued. 'You guys just crack me up, you're so funny . . .'

I didn't have time to respond because somebody else was interjecting. By the look of him, A&R department. Complete arsehole.

'Soooo,' he said, and there were a great many o's, all of them drawn out like elastic. 'J. D. tells me you and Silibil first met in San Diego, right? *Love* San Diego, man, fantastic place. Ever been to—'

The blood drained from my face until I could feel my toes swelling with it. It wasn't San Diego – *was it?* No, surely not. It was Hemet, Hemet, California, then Huntington Beach, right? My mind freewheeled while the A&R guy waffled interminably on. We *had* mentioned one of the Sans along the way in our back-story, if I wasn't mistaken: a skateboard competition. But that was San Francisco, not San Diego. Though I was sure of this, on such a momentous occasion it all became so much sand in my head. Recover, Brains, *recover*. I shouted over to Bill, to Silibil, and pointed out the many framed photos on the wall, of pop and rock royalty we'd grown up admiring, worshipping and ridiculing: Michael Jackson, Pearl Jam, Celine Dion. Bill saw the look on my face, and immediately started up a comedy rap about Michael Jackson getting it on with Celine Dion. I took over for the second verse, and a song unfolded so naturally that you'd have bet we'd previously rehearsed it. Crucially, it succeeded in drowning out any more of the bovine A&R's awkward questions, thus immediately giving me back the upper hand.

It was cool, everything was cool. We were on top of it. We were.

Small talk followed, and small talk was no effort at all. It helped pass the time. We got on to talking about our music and particularly our freestyling, battle rapping and this intriguing Porcupine rap game we had become known for. Our explanation of the word game prompted a little demonstration which clearly tickled them – there were oohs, ahs, laughter and compliments. After that came the Eminem comparisons and questions about what we thought of Eminem. Did we rate his music, his lyrics? Had we ever met him? Caught up in the pure momentum of things, I replied, 'Yeah sure. Christ, we go way back, I mean, I was probably closer to Proof, you know, his wing man, but yeah, we were real tight.' I don't know what the hell I was saying but, spurred on by the look of excitement in their eyes, as they stood there looking like kids in a candy store, I couldn't help but enjoy saying it, lost in my own little fantasy land where the nightmare of the Pineapple Studios never happened. The strange thing was that they bought it, straight off the bat. Then again, why wouldn't they? I was Brains McLoud, the closest they were going to get to the best and that's exactly what they believed they were about to sign.

Finally, a couple of executives came in, and you could tell their rank because of the strength of their aftershave and the deference shown them by everybody else. Like Dave Clansey and his silent sidekick, these were men in late middle age who wore their previous successes with hauteur. It was there in their eyes, their sly smiles, their light-catching cufflinks. If either of these two men had ever been present at any of our shows, then no one had had the foresight to introduce them to us.

One of them had the contract, and as I caught sight of it my hands began to shake so much that I thrust them in my pockets to squeeze whatever they found there. The attractive young woman with the manicured nails glanced over at me, so I brought them out again and folded them across my chest. I winked at her, showing teeth. She smiled back, and blushed again. I worried, for the briefest moment, that she could sense my fear, and the reasons behind it, but there was nothing suspicious in her look at all, just an overflow of warmth and, for all I knew, attraction. To everyone in this room, we appeared cloaked in a supernatural confidence. Silently, I prayed: *Please don't let anything go wrong here; don't let either of us slip out a careless 'aye'*. I didn't want us to be sunk, not yet, not here. I felt like I was on trial for murder.

The contract was spread out on the table before us. No blood-red wax seal, no crest of arms, nothing quite as regal as I had anticipated, just a few sheets of A4; but it was a beautiful thing nonetheless, and crammed with small print I had no intention of reading. Suddenly, Bill was by my side. I grabbed the pen when it came my way and signed it quickly, rashly. Shalit pointed out I'd signed the dateline by mistake. Bill laughed, took the pen from me, and did the same. Everybody laughed. People patted us on the back. There was the sound of popping, and a champagne cork puncturing the ceiling. When a glass came my way, I lunged for it.

By one-thirty in the afternoon of February 13th 2004, Silibil N' Brains were officially Sony recording artists. Plans were immediately drawn up for us to go into the studio the following week to record our first single. The budget for our first two singles was to be £50,000, and the mooted album budget would be upwards of £100,000, but the Sony suits were already talking a bigger picture: Europe, America, Asia and beyond. To break a band globally, they said, they would have to commit millions – and Sony assured us, with jocular smiles, that they would spend a million on us *at the very least*.

'You're going to be superstars, boys.'

I caught Bill's eyes, which were glazed from all the champagne. Astronomical figures, these. In the handful of months we'd been in London, we'd signed a management deal for £70,000, and now a recording contract whose signing-on fee alone was £50,000. We were rich beyond our wildest dreams, and it was only just beginning. A million was already being set aside for us. And then there'd be the profits from record sales, from concert tours, T-shirts, downloads, ringtones. They were right. We were going to be superstars.

The champagne didn't last long, and people were now drifting back to their desks, to check their mounting voicemails, and to counter the effects of the champagne with some coffee or perhaps complement it with cocaine, either or both, depending. Those who hung around wanted to get personal.

'I spent a summer once in Huntington Beach.'

These words came from someone from the marketing department. I knew this because I'd been introduced to him earlier. I couldn't remember his name now, but he was young and fresh-faced. He seemed likeable.

'Which street did you live on?'

Likeable he may have been, but the little fucker wasn't about to catch me out so easily, if that was his game. I'd Googled Huntington Beach so many times over the previous weeks that I knew its grid system like the back of my hand. I told him the street, and even the number, and then I told him the address of the skate store we worked in. He swallowed everything I said with naïve eagerness, and then wanted to know if we'd been to a particular club, a club I'd never come across during my research. *Shit.* Once again my mind clouded over and panic set in, Brains McLoud shrinking to nothing more relevant than belly-button fluff and leaving a trembling Gavin Bain in his place. What should I say to this guy? Yes, I knew the club, had been there many times? Or was he trying to catch me out, inventing it to see if I really was who I claimed I was before the ink was dry on the contract? My head span. Where was Bill? Where the *fuck* was Bill?

Across the room, as if in slow motion, a champagne glass slipped from a careless hand and fell to the floor, knocking the large table on its way down. It smashed into a thousand pieces. *Bill.* He apologized grandly to all – *Oops, butterfingers* – then grinned at me. I turned back to my young interrogator, remembering his name in the nick of time. 'Paul, right? So what does your job involve?' Having forgotten what we were just talking about before Silibil's interruption, he was happy to fill me in.

The perfect recovery. But the first chance I got I whispered in Bill's ear, 'Let's get the fuck out of here.'

The greatest day of our lives it may have been, but I'd had enough; I needed air. Shalit, seemingly sensing this, began to make departing noises, and we spent a quarter of an hour shaking hands and pumping fists, knocking knuckles and receiving yet more congratulations on a day already heavy with them. Then, mercifully, we were set free: the lift, the lobby, those rapidly revolving doors, and out into the cool crisp street, a sharp February wind whipping our cheeks and bringing us back to life.

Shalit congratulated us with genuine fondness. J. D. made a joke that this time next year we'd all be driving Bentleys. We embraced. Then they went that way, us the other. We fought to remain composed until we reached the junction with Poland Street. The very moment we disappeared up into it, I was on my knees, howling and laughing and screaming, my voice boiling inside my throat. I very nearly burst into tears. I was shaking all over. Bill dragged me to my feet, we staggered, then hugged wildly and screamed some more.

And now we were running, fuelled by deranged excitement, up on to Oxford Street, weaving in and out of the worker drones and daytime shoppers and the sneering truants, across traffic lights, dodging traffic. At Regent Street, we came to a pub we knew and went in. Up at the bar, panting hard but still laughing, we ordered up some shots, downed them in one, then ordered some more, each squat little glass lined up along the counter, glistening wet.

We had much to celebrate.

Time became a malleable thing. We lost all sense of it. I do remember this, though: a succession of Soho bars, including our favourite, the heavy-metal joint the Crobar. The stench of Jägermeister and the beer-drenched floors led you through the narrow interior of London's most famous rock bar, low-lit and jam-packed. It was messy, intoxicating, the perfect place to cele-brate. Beer and shots, no need for food, just beer and shots. We were loud and American, and every girl in every place flocked to us in the way that throughout history certain girls have always flocked to loud Americans. After Crobar we hit a club in Regent Street, and it was surely late by now, gone midnight at least, when something happened. Dialogue was exchanged with some guys who had come over, and suddenly we were being hailed as members of the *Jackass* crew. How? Did one of us look like Bam Margera? Well, we did now. 'You the guys from *Jackass*?' we were asked. 'Hell yeah, sure! Why not?' we barked back, and were promptly ushered into the VIP area with bottles of Alazay, the hip-hop drink of choice, set before us, gratis, and we were knock-ing them back, fondling more girls, laughing and shouting above the joyful din of the music while the strobe lights strobed, my head throbbed and then this . . . darkness.

The music, I came to understand, was at one remove from me now, through a wall, its dull heavy bass a febrile thing in the pit of my stomach. Some amount of time had passed, I couldn't say how much. I licked a sticky coating of alcohol from my teeth and opened my eyes. I could see nothing, but the smell was definitely lavatorial. I sat up, and realized why. I was in a toilet cubicle, a women's toilet cubicle if the overflowing receptacle in the corner was anything to go by. I peered into the bowl, reared back in horror, and quickly flushed. I stood up. *My head.* My head was pounding. *Kate sucks cock*, said the graffiti. *Size IS everything.* The watch on my wrist had gone. I checked my pocket. So too my wallet. I opened the door and made my way to the sinks, splashing cold water up into to my face, a terrible tremble in the back of either knee.

Back out on the club's floor, the place had emptied out considerably. There were just stragglers now. How long had I been in there? I couldn't see Bill. Where were the girls? A man appeared from nowhere, close up. I recognized him vaguely as one of the guys who had been plying us with free drinks. He looked bigger now, and markedly less friendly.

'Yo, man,' I said.

He pushed me. 'You ain't from *Jackass*,' he was telling me. 'Fucking liar. You owe me for them drinks.'

I was in no fit state for a fight, it's true, but that didn't stop me. I lamped him. Somehow I made it out into the street, and I was grateful because it gave me an opportunity to run. I saw one of the girls who had been at our table earlier. She flagged down a taxi, and let me jump in. '*Go go go!*' I screamed.

When it pulled up outside my house, I woke with a start, unaware I had even been asleep. The cab was empty. Where was the girl? This was a problem, for I had no money to pay the driver. I looked out of the window, as if for help, and there help lay in the unlikely form of Bill, apparently comatose on our front step.

'One minute,' I told the driver, then lurched towards my friend. I rooted around in his pockets and found his wallet, which was full of cash. I took three twenties, paid the man, then dragged Bill into the hall and left him there, breathing heavily, snot bubbles popping at either nostril. I went into the kitchen and retrieved a bottle of Jack Daniel's from the fridge, by now way beyond drunk but still thirsty for more. After a while, Bill stumbled into the kitchen like an extra from *Night of the Living Dead*, his face a map of fresh bruises. I poured him a drink and we clinked glasses, a touching moment between us that needed no words.

The stomach convulsions woke me rudely some time after that. Either that or it was Michelle, my poor, put-upon sister, thumping me hard on the back that roused me. When had she arrived or had she been here all the time? I came quickly awake now to find myself vomiting repeatedly, unable to stem the flow of bile that quickly covered the kitchen floor like a bloodstain, the horror of this fresh new situation throbbing in my painful eyes. Michelle called 999, and presumably an ambulance arrived, because there I was, in one, hurtling towards the nearest A&E at full pelt, sirens blaring.

Awful fuss they made of me in that hospital, and I remember none of it. I recall only a bed on wheels being moved at speed, strip lighting above, then an all encompassing, blinding bright light. Heaven?

Saturday 14 February, Valentine's Day, and I, Brains McLoud, temporary resident of Northeast London but American by birth and therefore of no responsibility to the NHS whatsoever, was nevertheless being kindly administered to by hospital staff, my stomach pumped and re-pumped until empty. I awoke to starched bed covers and bright clouds drifting by a small unwashed window behind my head. It was early afternoon. It hurt to move, and so I didn't. My innards felt as if they had been set on fire the night before, and now all that remained was blackened bits of charcoal floating somewhere between bone and bowel.

'Do you have any idea how much alcohol you consumed yesterday?'

I looked up and saw a nurse standing beside my bed. She had a stern look on her face that reminded me powerfully of school. I told her, with a heavy croak to my voice, that I remembered champagne at lunchtime, but could remember little after that. I tried to smile but it went unreciprocated.

'You were admitted this morning as an emergency.' She looked seriously pissed off, as if I had somehow personally let her down. 'Alcohol poisoning. Your stomach ulcer very nearly burst as a result of all the spirits you'd had. You'd have been in big trouble then. Surely your doctor has told you not to drink spirits on account of the ulcer?'

I'd had no idea of any stomach ulcer, and told her so. Before she moved on to the next bed and her next victim, she leant towards me, her voice a flat and dismissive monotone. 'You've been very lucky, young man.'

Events of the previous day came flooding back to me like the click-click-flash of a camera's shutter: the deal, the money, the bright prospects of an unimaginable future now within touching distance. She had a point, that nurse. I was very lucky indeed.

I breathed out slowly, and sank back into the mattress, suddenly desperately low. If last night had been the high, then this was now the crashing comedown, because even this early on in the game – and it was, in fact, a game; I realized this – I knew that the luck wouldn't last. Silibil N' Brains were living on borrowed time.

For a fleeting second, I tried to imagine the day our lies would catch up with us, and what would happen to us when they did. Would we be able to turn it round to our advantage, get all those we'd duped along the way laughing right along with us, admiring our derring-do and calling us clever dicks, maverick geniuses? But then I remembered the one clause in the contract that had stood out among all those meaningless paragraphs of print, the one that suggested that if we in any way attempted to deceive the record company in any manner that could prove harmful to our commercial value, then they would seek to recoup any losses forthwith – them, the biggest record company in the world, versus us, two likely lads from Scotland who'd gotten a little carried away. How on earth would an anxious neurotic like Gavin Bain deal with something like that?

I blinked, and the fear floated freely away.

I fell asleep on my hospital bed with a smile on my face because, right then, despite my sore head and my poor scorched stomach, I had the world at my feet. Look at me there in that ward full of the elderly and the infirm, the ordinary folk in their ordinary, unspectacular lives. I was the luckiest bastard in the world. I looked like an angel.

Six

We were back at the Dairy within a couple of days, and I was back on the Jack Daniel's even sooner. Drink was inescapable now. It helped lubricate everything; it made me feel creative. And for us, essentially million-pound recording artists, it felt *necessary*, an obligation. I knew at last why I had always been suffering from a burning stomach, but I now had prescription pills for that. If I mixed them with the drink, and got the quantities just right, I could feel skyscrapingly good.

Alison came to visit me while I was still in the first flush of our post-signing celebrations. I decided not to mention the alcohol overdose but instead focus on all that was good. I should have picked her up at the bus station with a huge bunch of flowers in my hand, but I didn't. Instead, I took her out for the night with the guys, to bars and clubs, and I spent a huge amount of money, more in one night than I'd have made in a month back home in Dundee, and I felt it important that Alison realize this: I had left Scotland for a reason. Most of the time Alison wore an expression that looked a bit like confusion. Here was her boyfriend in England's capital partying with pop stars, actors and other assorted C-list celebrities, the very people he had mocked in his old songs, and he was having fun. It seemed, to Alison anyway, that my reason for coming down to here had completely changed.

We had a wild night, but on the way home Alison gave me the most pitying look, with such sadness in her eyes it took the breath clean out of me.

'I don't believe it,' she whispered.

'What?'

'You spoke to me most of the night in an American accent . . .'

I shrugged my shoulders. *And?*

Her chest heaved. 'But why?'

I shrugged again. 'It's just who I am down here, Alison, that's all. Think of it as method acting, and don't let's make a big deal out of it, eh? It's a laugh, nothing more. *Chill.*'

She shook her head, and spoke in a voice so low I had to lean towards her to hear it. 'You look different. You act different. You've become . . . You've become a monster.'

I did my best to sideswipe this low blow, but it was hard. Couldn't she appreciate this new world opening up to me – to *us*, if only she permitted? Back at Eagle's Nest, I fetched us some more drinks and dropped my American accent, slipping back into Scottish. It felt jarring somehow, as if suddenly I was naked.

I couldn't help thinking now that her reassuring smile was forced, that she fundamentally wasn't enjoying herself here; there was all this luxury on tap and she couldn't care less. In the other room, a party of sorts was winding down, Bill having brought back his by now usual bunch of undesirables, people he'd picked up wherever he'd stopped off during the day. Most of them, in one way or another, were music related, club promoters and bookers, vampiric types who only came alive at night, and here they were puffing away, feet on my table and drinking my beer. I recognized several faces and gave a quick wave. Normally I'd have sat down alongside them, but the living room was thick with smoke and steamy squalor. I steered Alison away from it as quickly as possible. This was not the time to show her around the place. I took her upstairs. From behind Bill's door came the kind of noises I'd learnt to ignore of late. Alison gave me a disapproving look. I shrugged my shoulders and grinned.

In my room, I fired up the laptop and gave her the headphones to slip on. I cued up the latest tracks we'd been working on, which, with a little help from the studio engineer, were sounding incredible, and clicked Play. I sat alongside, listening to the music buzzing tinnily from the cans. I turned the sound up louder until she raised her hand to say *enough*. From the corner of my eye I then watched my girlfriend listening to me, to my heart and my soul. I was terrified, so desperate was I for her to like what she was hearing, to have her *approval*. The corners of her mouth began to curl in an unambiguous smile. She raised up her thumbs and, shouting over the music, said that she liked it. *She liked my songs*. For now, that was all I needed to hear. I relaxed.

The next morning I felt it wise to keep her away from Bill, because if she didn't approve of Brains McLoud then she certainly wouldn't of Silibil, the man she once knew simply as Billy Boyd but who now did debauchery for a living. I took her out for breakfast, and then into Central London and all the sights. We did some bridges and river walkways, an art exhibit or two; she could have done anything she wanted, all she had to do was ask. She told me she was tired. She wanted a coffee, a sit down. Nothing more.

Then my phone rang, or rather one of them. I had three

phones. Did I mention this earlier? It was complicated but, trust me, necessary. One to speak to the people back home – family, friends, allies; one to speak to industry types and associates down here; and the third full of fake numbers, which was useful when pulling small cons and industry blags. This phone's address book read like some kind of roll call: Simon Cowell, Simon Fuller, all sorts of other record-company executives, and the occasional actor.

Alison watched me juggle my phones, and groaned.

'What are you into here, Gav?'

She wasn't impressed. But the call was a genuine one: I had to dash back to the studio to oversee the remix of one of our songs. And so I left her there to make her own way around London, and later had some friends meet her and keep her busy until I'd finished, by which time it was well past midnight and our time together was almost up.

I think we were both relieved when the moment came for her to go back home. At Victoria Station we went through all the motions of boyfriend and girlfriend saddened that they now had to part. I embraced her stiff body and she promised to call. I told her I'd get her back down to London again for one of the big shows we had coming up, and that afterwards I could take her to a hotel, a proper posh five-star place. She smiled and said yes, of course, she'd love to. Her eyes told me otherwise. She boarded the bus, and I suddenly began feeling that it was a mistake to let her go. The bus pulled out of the forecourt in a great belch of fumes, leaving a dirty great oil slick in its wake, and in response to my wave she placed a cold hand on the window and pressed until her flesh went a ghostly white.

As soon as the bus disappeared out on to the road and beyond that I began to miss her desperately, my girlfriend of five years now virtually a stranger to me. I made my way home slowly, the lump in my throat refusing to ease.

Eagle's Nest was mercifully quiet when I arrived. Bill was sprawled in front of the television in the living room, elegantly wasted in yesterday's clothes, an exhausted grin on his face. He looked me up and down, tutted and shook his head.

'Cheer up, dude,' said my American friend. 'Might never happen.'

The record company were wasting little time. A few months after signing, we were lined up to appear on MTV alongside that season's other fresh new signings, Kasabian, Bloc Party and Natasha Bedingfield, between them a bunch of Oasis wannabes, indie art poseurs and a blonde pop starlet – none of whom, we were rightfully confident, were likely ever to get anywhere, and certainly nowhere near as far as us. As part of Brand Spanking New Music we would be on *TRL* – the most popular show on MTV.

Bill celebrated by getting royally drunk. 'We're going to be on television!' he'd say over and over again, no other care in the world. But I rapidly became convinced that the exposure would blow our cover overnight. How many homes in Dundee, I wondered, had a satellite dish? *Every single one of them*, surely. But how many of them watched MTV with any regularity, specifically *TRL*, which was on in the middle of the working day? In all probability, shitloads. Within minutes of our appearance, the phones at their Camden HQ would start ringing. *I've got news for you*, they'd say; the producer would stalk across the studio floor with murder in his eyes, and Bill and I would be forced to flee, out through the fire exit, down the stairs, across the canal and into the nearest taxi, then Heathrow, an aeroplane and gone. Trouble is, we weren't ready to disappear into the sunset just yet.

Bill was unconcerned. 'We'll be fine, Gav. Let's just enjoy it, yeah?'

The morning of the recording came. He burst into my room and woke me up, jumping up and down on my bed and singing his familiar refrain. 'We're going to be on TV! Whoo hoo!'

He had beer for breakfast, beer again in the car MTV had provided for us, and also in the green room before we went on to perform. I joined him. 'Dutch courage,' he insisted. Ten minutes before we were due to go on, first to face a grilling from *TRL*'s host Dave Berry, Bill's eyes had lost all focus. When I tried to talk to him, he stared at an imaginary spot just over my left shoulder.

'I'll be fine,' he predicted.

And then there we were on the shiny studio floor, bright television lights in our eyes, a studio audience cheering robotically in one corner, a microphone thrust under our chins.

'We're joined now in the studio by Silibil N' Brains, yeah, America's latest rap sensation.' Dave Berry, with his perfect tan, white teeth and the ingratiating manner of a Hare Krishna, turned to read from the autocue before turning back to us. He waited for the necessary raucous applause to die down. 'So, I've been hearing a lot about you guys, where are you actually from originally?' We were about to lie to the nation.

'Planet Zordon,' I said, and the crowd chuckled. Dave smiled.

'But how about really?'

He wasn't buying it, and so I rushed through our already exhausted back-story, Bill ad-libbing right alongside me. Once we had finished our shaky explanation there was an awkward pause, abruptly ended by a drunken belch from Bill followed by some crude slur pulling Dave Berry into another topic. I was amazed Bill was still standing, and as I watched him banter with the studio audience I thought to myself that, if he could stay on his feet long enough, we might be able to pull this off.

For the performance itself, Bill, no longer looking drunk now but seemingly fresh, alert and sober, was fizzing with enthusiasm. We did 'Losers', and bounded about the primary-colour-daubed studio floor as if it were a padded cell. The cameras had a hard time keeping up with us. We continued to joke with Dave Berry, the other presenter and the studio audience, and we didn't swear once. We were good boys. They loved us. The moment we cut for a break segment, the director and producer came bounding over. Hugs, kisses and the kind of by now familiar accolades that began, *You guys* . . . This was a drug to us, and we wanted it more and more, a compliment a day keeping the psychosis away. We gave the crowd a little example of us playing Porcupine, just to hear some more studio laughter, and the director went wild.

'That's amazing! Fantastic! Do that again when we go back on air, and do it into this camera here –' he pointed – 'because that, guys, was just wicked!' Next to him, a man in headphones held up the fingers of his left hand. 'In five, in four, in three . . .'

The cameras turned, and I freestyled as instructed.

They say violence sells, well how about this, I'll punch myself in the face with Porcupines wrapped around my fist, throw a grenade in the toilet before Silibil sits down on it. It ain't over till the fat lady sings but let's leave Dave's mom outta this . . .

The studio audience went wild all over again. Dave Berry couldn't help but laugh, and then apologized to his mother as the credits rolled.

'You guys are naturals, the camera loves you. Well done, thanks.'

The ON-AIR light was switched off, the show wrapped.

Afterwards we got the MTV car to drive us not home but instead straight into Soho, and to the Crobar. *TRL* had gone fantastically well; we deserved a toast. By eleven, we were messy, still in Soho, in another bar now, and facing down any punter who didn't like the cut of our jib, who thought us too loud, too American, too whatever. Friends had joined us, J. D. among them, others I'd never met before in my life but who I already loved like brothers, like sisters. We got back home by three o'clock that night, and Bill never even made it up the stairs, falling flat-out unconscious on the living-room sofa. I waded upstairs on heavy legs to my laptop where I Googled Silibil N' Brains. My blood instantly thinned as my worst fears materialized on the screen in front of me. Comments and threads on a Dundee hip-hop website. But viewable by anyone with an internet connection. This was bad.

Is that the same Billy Boyd I went to school with – in Arbroath?

Dave McIntosh, Forfar

I had a fight with Gavin Bain in a chip shop once. Wasn't in America, though. This was Dundee. Yer man's a Scot.

Lee Davis, Dundee

And so it had happened. Already. Earlier than I'd expected. I had anticipated that this moment would bring with it all-out panic, but instead I felt a strange sense of calm. We could simply give the money back and walk away. No harm done, surely. Yep, that's what we'd do. I looked for more comments, but there were none, just these two. I tried to hack into the system to see if I could delete them, but no joy, and so I just sat there, breathing slowly through my nose and out through my mouth, re-reading them time and again. I had indeed had a fight with Lee Davis in a chip shop once. Kicked the shit out of him, if I remembered correctly. Would again, happily.

I awoke a few hours later, still slumped in my chair, to the sound of my mobile ringing. I cleared my throat, and reached for it. The screen told me it was Shalit. MTV had contacted him already, then.

'They loved you!' he enthused. 'They want to go back on again soon. Not those other pop tarts, just you two. I've also had calls from Channel 4 and Endemol. They want to meet the pair of you. And so do I. I've got a proposal for you.' He cleared his throat. '*Multimedia*.'

He wanted to talk to us, he added, about fronting our own TV show.

Now how the hell did *that* happen?

We were used to the camera. For months now Byron had been filming us whenever he could, day and night, drunk and sober, asleep and awake. We were all over YouTube by now, and we'd watched the results endlessly. We looked terrific on TV, and we had loads of great ideas for our own show. Not once in talking over the prospects did we give Dave McIntosh from Forfar or Lee Davis from Dundee another thought. We were truly invincible now.

Our main idea was for a mutant combination of *Jackass* and *Dirty Sanchez*, in other words, a bunch of high-risk skateboard stunts combined with a music-related chat show, bands of the day coming on to see if they could hold their own against our guerrilla-style presenting. We put down pages and pages of ideas, most of them written in a mad spurt of frenetic creativity at three o'clock in the morning, and later presented them to management. Shalit and J. D. loved it. Sony got wind of it, and gave us their cautious backing on the proviso that music would now not suddenly take a back seat as a result. No way, we assured. We were true to our word. Though we spent our daylight hours producing enough material to record not just the pilot but an entire series, we spent every night working on the music, on my part to an obsessive degree. While Bill frequently catnapped, I never did. I couldn't. Instead I worked. I spoke to no one outside our tiny nucleus, maintaining no contact with my folks, my girlfriend, my friends back home. I lived entirely in the moment, in a constant hive of activity and creativity, convinced that everything I came up with was comedy gold, so sure that I was truly on my way now and that nothing could stop me, nothing *would* stop me, a tireless machine that just produced and produced and produced.

My stomach still howled with pain, all day and every night, but I drank the pain away and I popped any pills I could find. My favourites were the little red ones. Rocket fuel.

I'm not sure if there is a joke that starts with *How many TV executives does it take to change a light bulb?* But give me five minutes and I'm sure I can come up with a putdown of a punchline. Shalit had asked us to meet with three different teams of producers, all from nationally recognized production companies whose programmes clutter up BBC1 and Channel 4's peaktime schedules. Without fail, each of them appeared to love us: they loved our ideas, they said, and were going to green-light our project now, immediately, without delay. But then, nothing. One or two suggested we should write for others until we were celebrities in our own right, at which point we could draw the kind of audience a major production company required. How did we feel, they wondered, about becoming writers on somebody else's show instead of fronting our own? We'd be credited, of course, and paid handsomely, but nevertheless relegated to mere writers-for-hire.

'Is this guy serious?' Bill asked me in front of everyone, as the TV producers' cheeks began to colour. He turned to them. 'You serious?'

J. D. attempted to ameliorate. 'Take it as a compliment, no?'

'We just think,' one of the producers said, 'that you don't have the necessary screen experience just yet, and . . .'

'But how can we get screen experience without—'

'. . . But because your ideas are so good, so cutting edge,' he continued nervously, 'this could be your way in, because I really do think—'

Bill stood up with a theatrical flourish. 'Do you see this middle finger I am raising at you?' He asked them, at which point J. D. bustled us out while apologizing profusely, keen, I guess, that his clients' misbehaviour wouldn't reflect badly on Shalit Global.

Meanwhile, Sony had decided to hold off on the single release, opting instead to wait and see what happened with the TV show. But when the production companies failed to green-light anything, they decided it was because of the outlandish things about the songs and the bad language that filled them. We needed to be neutered, or at the very least diluted before being exposed to the general public. They suggested media training.

'It's about time,' our manager said.

'Did Eminem have media training?'

'That's beside the point. Give it a chance. Maybe you'll learn something.'

Our media training took place the following week in a small room inside Sony's headquarters. It lasted twenty-two minutes. I timed it. Our benevolent guide to the world of etiquette and good manners was a prim lady with her hair scraped back, in her late thirties, of average height, who dressed in sensible clothing in colours no louder than grey and black. We loped into the room like a couple of errant schoolchildren, and happily endured some exquisite misunderstanding as she attempted to shake hands while we preferred to slap and snap. In the end it looked as if we were playing some kind of children's pat-a-cake game. She bid us to sit down on two chairs alongside one another, while she sat opposite, legs joined together at the knee and ankle like Siamese twins.

'Right,' she began, hands clasped together, a kindly, almost religious smile on her face. 'We'll start with an interview situation. You'll face a great many interviews once your music is released, and it is important to know how to behave in them. OK, good. I'm going to ask you a series of questions now, and I shall record your responses, and then we will listen back to the results, yes?'

We just stared at her.

'Ready?'

Bill picked his nose. I shrugged.

She asked us a string of ploddingly obvious questions that she read from a piece of paper: our names, our ages, where we were from, our influences. What did we think of the British music scene? Did we like English girls? What were our aims, our ambitions? Did we have a favourite colour? Name six items we'd take to a desert island.

After a slow start, during which time it had been difficult to leave the surly schoolboy personas fully behind, we began to answer her questions fulsomely and, I was convinced, entertainingly. She nodded her head throughout, often making notes, sometimes throwing out a curt smile. As she concluded the interview, her smile flattened itself out and disappeared altogether.

'Now,' she said. 'I'm going to play the tape back. Shall we listen carefully?'

'Are we six?' I asked.

'I beg your pardon?'

'You're talking to us like children.'

Her cheeks flushed, and for a moment I felt sorry for her. Bill snorted. She continued. Our voices filled the room now, loud and customarily obnoxious. Our answers were funny and lively and entertaining. As we listened back to our recorded selves, I watched as the woman made marks on a piece of paper, little black vertical lines. She could hardly keep up with herself. Presently, she stopped the tape and addressed us.

'What I've been doing here is counting off all the times you swear during the conversation.' She turned the piece of paper around and showed us several paragraphs' worth of | | | | | | . 'Rather a lot, isn't it? I suggest you curb your language. We don't want to cause offence, especially not to the newspapers, some of which *loathe* bad language.'

Bill looked at me. 'Is she for fucking real?'

The woman ploughed on. She told us that we had a habit of cutting one another off in mid-sentence, that something we had spent months perfecting in freestyling was actually hampering our skills as conversationalists. 'Breathe after each separate point is made,' she suggested. And then she came to our accents.

'How do I put this? You seem – and I say this only because you are settled in London now, so far as I understand it – you seem to come across as rather *too* American, almost as if it were caricature. Perhaps you could play it down a little, what do you think?'

It was a long and dispiriting twenty-two minutes, and I found it monumentally disheartening. Despite having signed us very specifically for who we were, Sony were now trying to systematically eradicate those parts of our personality that had seemed initially to appeal to them most. We thanked the woman for her time, but silently vowed to ignore every single fucking thing she'd told us.

On the way down, we stopped off at the A&R department to catch up with Ruth. We still liked Ruth a lot. The fact that she wore a wedding band was, to Bill, like a red rag to a bull (he flirted shamelessly), but she knew the power she held over us and, to date, she had used it effectively.

She was all smiles when we popped our head in through her open door, rushing up to kiss our cheeks and tell us how great we were looking. It was only when we sat opposite her that I suddenly saw a new discomfort in her eyes. Pre-promotion for 'Play with Myself', which had been designated our debut single despite MTV's airing of 'Losers', was already gaining momentum. We were getting college-radio play, and the word from the street teams, she had previously reported, was good. But still something was up.

'So . . . How're things?'

The media training had already tested my patience for the day. I was clean out of it now. 'Cut to the chase,' I barked at her. 'Something is wrong. What?'

'Oh, nothing, nothing,' she said breezily. 'It's just . . . Well, we've had discussions – a meeting – and, well, it's your lyrics.'

'Which lyrics?'

'To "Play with Myself".'

'What of them?'

'They appear to be about, well, masturbation.'

'Aye,' Bill said derisively, the word slipping out of his mouth before he'd had a chance to check it and Americanize it. But if it jarred with her, she said nothing, gave nothing away. He continued. 'The song *is* called "Play with Myself", after all. Was that too subtle for you?'

'Yes, I know, I know, and it's a brilliant song, really just terrific. But it's got lyrics like *getting a woody like Geppetto*, which is presumably a reference to . . . to an erection, right? That won't get us Radio 1 daytime airplay, I'm afraid, and we need that if we are going to have a hit. And we are going to *need* a hit if they upstairs,' she indicated to the ceiling, 'are going to green-light the album. Maybe we could modify it . . .?'

A week later, Ruth reported back to us in a much better mood. She sounded bright and effusive on the phone. No decision had yet been made regarding the lyrical content of "Play with Myself", but they did have good news all the same: they'd remixed 'Losers', which had initially been thought of as our second single but which now, on reflection, having taken advice, etc., seemed in fact to be a much better *debut* single. Definitely.

This all came out in a rush, and I found it hard to keep up with what she was saying. Did she really say a *remix*? I'm not sure you can do a double-take on the telephone, but that's what I did now.

'What? You've remixed our song?'

'Come in and listen to it. It's *fantastic*.'

We were there within the hour, sitting in Ruth's office which, I now realized, was small and boxy, with walls that bore down on you if you looked at them too long. Her smile stretched from one side of her face to the other, and I thought for a moment she was slightly deranged. She slipped a CD excitedly into her hi-fi. 'You're going to love this,' she said.

It was possible, I suppose, that the appointed producer – we never caught his name, and he certainly never showed his face to us – could have been on crack at the time he worked on our song, or perhaps the entire A&R department had. Addiction can be a terrible thing. It can obliterate all parameters of good taste; I've seen it happen. As Ruth pressed Play and the recognizable opening strains of 'Losers' blared, it quickly transformed into something else entirely. Halfway through the first verse it segued into what was for us an entirely unexpected *timpani-drum solo*. It's worth saying again: *a timpani-drum solo*. This high-pitched noise instantly brought to mind someone vomiting all over a beach in Ibiza at five o'clock in the morning. It reminded me of . . . Something. Then I realized. It reminded me of a ringtone, a fucking mobile-phone ringtone. I watched Ruth dance in her seat. The timpani-drum solo now continued throughout the track, its abiding refrain. We sounded like idiots rapping over it, Tweedledum and Tweedle-fucking-dee. Then, not a moment too soon, it finished, the follow-through silence filling the room like a giant bubble. I had to physically restrain Bill from attacking the hi-fi. Instead, he spat on the floor. Ruth watched, aghast.

'You . . . You don't like it?'

'Release that,' Bill said, 'and die.'

We stormed out of the office, knocking down chairs and rubber plants on the way. I called Shalit, but got his voicemail. I screamed abuse into it until it cut me off. Bill grabbed my phone, ready to leave his own tirade, but dropped it to the ground, cracking its case cleanly down the middle.

'You daft fucking cunt.' I pushed him, bending to pick it up. He looked at me as if suddenly I were nothing more than shit on his shoe. We stalked to the tube station in fuming, furious silence.

The singles chart around that time, I remember, was full of new acts. Kasabian, Bloc Party and Natasha Bedingfield, those chancers who had appeared alongside us on MTV's Brand Spanking New just a few short months ago, all had Top 20 hits now, each of them experiencing that first flush of fame, on tour, on TV, in hearts and minds.

And Silibil N' Brains? Bill and I were having a fist fight with each other on the Piccadilly Line home. Who else did we have to take it out on?

Ten. It takes ten TV executives to change a light bulb: one to unscrew the bulb itself, the other nine to pass comment on which wattage it should be, and what colour, what shape, and whether to change the lampshade as well, and, if so, with what material – and then, before you know it, several dozen other executives will have entered the room, all of whom are carrying their own solid-concrete opinions, but none of whom are sufficiently confident to air them in case they get laughed at and shouted down. The bulb-changer himself then schedules a meeting to discuss the matter further at a later date.

After shooting a brief pilot funded by a small but well-respected independent music channel, none of the major TV companies decided to commission our show. They did, however, decide to use much of our ideas and material in some of their existing shows, although it was censored and not as funny, of course. Shalit was bewildered, but told us it was typical of the idiocy that permeates television on every level in this country. So we were now back to just being recording artists which, frankly, was fine by us.

But there was further trouble afoot. Sony were wounded by

our reaction to the remixed 'Losers'. They were sulking, wouldn't take our calls. The decision-making concerning what was to *be* our debut single, never mind when it would be released, was postponed. They'd discuss it more fully at a later date, and would be in touch. When these discussions finally took place, a cautious Shalit warned, we would need to show diplomacy, a willingness to collaborate. 'Be nice,' he said. I suggested we call Kofi Annan. It was a joke, but the truth was that this left us spinning. Where were our allies? Who did we have left to rely on? Not Sony, at least not now. No, just Shalit Global. Thank God for Shalit Global.

And then a bitter newsflash: J. D., our linchpin, our comrade, our brother in arms, had left the company for pastures new. The bastard. Shalit, when we scheduled an emergency meeting to discuss this with him, was his usual gregarious self.

'Boys,' he beamed, gathering up the young man who stood uneasily to his left in an avuncular hug, 'meet Del. The new J. D.'

Del, quite frankly, looked as if he were auditioning to become Silibil N' Brains' third wheel, an understudy. He was a couple of years older than us, handsome, and every bit as fashion conscious, shifting nervously on his feet while offering us a smile on full beam. Within seconds of our complicated handshake ritual, he was displaying the manic zeal of either a celebrity chef or a cocaine addict. We hit it off instantly.

Turning quickly to other business now, Shalit sat us down. His voice was grave.

'Pay attention, boys. There have been several changes at Sony.' He didn't go into too much explanation, but simply said that this was a record company after all, where such upheavals happened all the time. Nothing to worry about, he assured. He then provided us with a list of people we knew personally who were no longer employed there, either having been fired, made redundant, or else, in one case, having left for a rival company. Among them were some of our most vocal supporters. Ruth's job, for now at least, was intact, and for that we were relieved. But then ever since she had revealed to us her love of timpani-drum solos, she no longer had quite so much of our respect.

'Where does that leave us, then?' I asked.

Shalit insisted that it actually left us in a stronger position than ever. We were the main priority for Sony right now, he claimed, irrespective of whom precisely the company chose to employ, and once a debut single was finally decided upon, likewise its lyrical content, we would be ready to move forward. In many ways, he said, it was a good thing that we'd missed our window for the originally planned single-release date. This way, we could use the extra time to build even more momentum.

I interjected. 'What do you mean we've missed *our window?*'

He faltered for a second, but only that. Blink and you missed it; Bill did. If one of Shalit's requirements as our manager was to save us from all the ugly details, then he was very good at it. He explained that he'd attended a big conflab at Sony to discuss strategy. Several of our pluggers had suggested that were we to release a single now, at this early stage, as we had been about to do, then we would completely destroy any underground hip-hop credentials we'd ever hoped to obtain, and underground hip-hop credentials were paramount. 'These guys,' he explained, 'they know what they're talking about.' Meantime, he continued, we would go out on the road and notch up more nightclub appearances, more pirate radio-station guest spots. There would be more battle raps at high-profile venues, some key early press interviews. We needed to get the local hip-hop community on our side, no mean feat for a bunch of Yanks. The scene was different over here, Del said. 'You're not in Huntington Beach any more.

But don't worry, we're all on the same page, all raring to go. We just need to launch it properly, is all.' 'And we will,' Shalit interjected. 'We will make you superstars yet.'

Later that night, Alison called. It was the first time we'd spoken in weeks. I'd barely had time to think of her; she'd grown vague in my mind's eye. On the phone her voice was soft and bruised, like an old peach. I told her about the timpani-drum remix of 'Losers', the media training and the imminent tour of underground hip-hop clubs. Her responses were quiet and monosyllabic. Then she changed the subject.

'It's over.' No preamble, no attempt to soften the blow. Her words came like a punch. 'I'm sorry.'

The tour of the underground hip-hop clubs and pirate radio stations went well enough, quick and easy and never too far from home. Those who turned up were receptive enough, and our songs went over well, but it seemed to the both of us that something was missing. Infuriatingly, I couldn't quite put my finger on it, but it gnawed away at me day and night. We needed a fresh rethink, new impetus. The more time Bill and I spent in one another's company alone, the more arguments we had. Our levels of frustration had gone through the roof; we bickered endlessly, an old married couple in need of counselling. I desperately wanted us to become a streamlined creative machine, to live only for the music. All Bill wanted, so far as I could see it, was to have fun and get wasted. Things would come to a head soon, I knew it.

After the final date of the tour, a small club at which we played to no more than 100 people at something like two o'clock in the morning, we came back home with the formulations of a plan, about which we had spoken to no one but which we already knew we would implement no matter the fallout it caused. That night I fell into the most untroubled unconsciousness, a proper sleeping beauty.

In the kitchen the following morning, I buttered toast. Bill made coffee. Things were *civil* between us. It felt novel.

'You're sure about this?' I said.

'One hundred per cent.'

'Let's announce it, then.'

It was this: we became a punk-rock act, a five-piece punk-rock act.

We'd been putting out feelers for some time beforehand, sounding out friends and associates with a view to three of them joining the band and turning us into something special. We didn't have to look very far. Greg Keegan was a South African living in London whom we'd met through one of my closest South African friends. He was a terrific guitarist, and more importantly he had the look and attitude of someone born to play loud guitar in a punk-rock act. Gordon Donald and Colin Petrie were well-known faces on the music scene up in Perth. Colin was the maddest drummer Arbroath had ever produced and had played drums in PMX, one of our favourite bands back home, while Gordon worked in a snowboard store and was on the brink of becoming a pro snowboarder himself. He was also a brilliant bassist. Colin had been friends with Bill from years back, and I'd known him almost as long as I'd known Bill. We knew both of them would be perfect. We got together several times over a few weeks, playing our old songs in this new style, and everything felt right, as if Greg and Gordon and Colin were what we had been missing all along. They felt it too, and each wanted to become a part of Silibil N' Brains. One night Bill and I made the offer official, but with one key proviso.

'Can you keep a secret?'

We needed them to know the truth about us; because, while we could lie to the industry, we couldn't to our closest friends. They took it surprisingly well. In fact, they thought it hysterical, and were only too happy to play along. I was relieved and ecstatic. Things at last could move on.

Now all we had to do was convince everybody else.

To Shalit's horror, and Sony's raised eyebrows, it seemed a rash, unthought-through decision, but in fact it had been much more of an organic process, something that had been building and hatching in our minds for several weeks, possibly months. Bill and I had become increasingly uncomfortable with the way things were proceeding at the label, the ambivalence that had so swiftly followed on from the initial enthusiasm, their doubts over our lyrics, our underground credentials, our overall attitude. Maybe they were right. Maybe we needed to rethink everything. And so we did. We hadn't taken any notice of the stagnant rap scene for some time. The hip-hop charts consisted mostly of R&B with a token novelty rap verse from some two-bit expensive-chain-wearing, gold-toothed stereotype with beginner-level lyrics. Even Eminem had begun to falter, sounding more and more tame with each venture. The genre was going backwards while we were intent on going forward in the aim of creating something fresh. So we turned to our first real love, punk rock. On the way to gigs, the tour-van speakers pumped only rock, everything from the Eagles, the Police, Motörhead, Metallica, to Dead Kennedys, At the Drive In and NOFX. But it was the new bands on the scene that really whetted our appetite, luring us back to a life of thrash and distortion. Bands like Story of the Year, Thrice, My Chemical Romance and particularly Billy Talent. We realized that if we couldn't listen to our own music and feel the way we felt while listening to these bands, then we were wasting our time. Besides, the music scene on both sides of the Atlantic was undergoing another seismic shift. Guitars were making a comeback in a big way, so the decision now to plough this course felt entirely natural, one which we could convince the record company was logical and *commercial*. They would come to realize this in time, I'd make sure of it.

Potentially this decision could also solve our biggest dilemma. We'd always known that the moment we released a single as a rap outfit would be the moment the game was up, our Scottishness revealed to a mocking world that simply wouldn't accept hip-hop lyricism in an accent like ours. But in the context of a punk-rock act, our true nationality perhaps wouldn't be such an issue. Rock was far more encompassing a genre: you could be black, white, American, English, Chinese. You could sing in a mid-Atlantic accent, or with a Welsh inflection. Punk rock, for us, represented who we really were and it also represented safer ground. If and when we were exposed for what we really were – Scottish – big deal, move on. In fact being a punk-rock band would allow us to tell the real story musically in a louder, more colourful way. That was my rationale, anyway, and I was sticking to it.

As soon as we started to play together as a band, it felt fluid, instinctive and natural. It was as if we were always destined to end up together. Each of them had seen Silibil N' Brains live, and each thought the prospect of us becoming punk rock was an inspirational idea. One afternoon, we invited them to the studio Sony had in the basement of their Great Marlborough Street offices, and, with just an engineer on board, quickly and seamlessly re-recorded seven tracks, putting them down live, just to see how they would sound. They sounded out of this world,

Gordon's rampant hip-hop grooves now complemented by Greg's ferocious guitar hooks and some powerhouse drumming from Colin. The five of us, plus engineer, sat at the sound desk and played back our efforts. The hairs on our necks stood up. It was the best moment I'd yet experienced in a studio.

Despite the confusion this caused, it all felt overwhelmingly *right*. This was the fresh impetus we had been searching for all along, and I belatedly realized that as a duo we had only been scratching at the surface of our potential. But this, *this* was the real deal.

Shalit took more convincing. Initially he was furious, felt he was being messed around, his generosity taken advantage of. We hadn't wanted to deal with him until the re-recorded tracks sounded as good as they possibly could, so it was only after a week of avoiding his successive calls that we pitched up at his office and insisted he hear us out. Purple-faced, he summoned Del into the room. Both of them glowered at us, and for the first few minutes it felt as though we were trying to convince a couple of judges to keep us out of jail. I slipped the CD into the tray and turned the sound up loud. 'Losers' was first, a song now completely hijacked by growling guitars and a satanic bassline. Even in the office on a bright, late-spring day you could tell just how well this song would go over in a murky live setting, Bill and I launching ourselves across the stage, up on to the speakers to spreadeagle into the frenzied crowd below. It sounded like a juggernaut of pure sonic momentum, rough around the edges, *werewolfian*. By the time it reached its nuclear climax Del was on his feet, whooping and howling, and wildly applauding. I was beginning to like him more and more. Bill did a theatrical bow as I pressed Stop. Shalit began to smile.

'This isn't half bad,' he conceded.

We then played him 'Cunt', our ode to George W. Bush. A song compounded with fresh punk fury, the chorus of 'He's a cunt, George Bush/A cunt cunt cunt cunt' all but stripped paint from the walls. For its three-minute entirety Del was right up there on the imaginary stage alongside us, ready to launch himself from the speaker stack.

'It's definitely called *'Cunt'*, is it?' Shalit asked warily afterwards. He sighed, but the smile wouldn't leave his face. It couldn't; he was impressed. He grabbed for the phone with his fat fist and called our A&R. 'Ruth? Jonathan Shalit. Ruth, I need to see you right now. I've got Silibil N' Brains in with me. There's been a development.'

She said she couldn't find time to see us immediately, so he and Del took us for a boozy lunch at a restaurant around the corner while we waited. Afterwards, very kindly, he paid for the breakages, which Bill smilingly insisted had been an accident. We arrived at Sony jubilant and pissed. When Bill was asked to sign in, he drew a big smiley face.

Ruth clearly hadn't wanted to face us alone, because when we arrived in her office there were several people squeezed in alongside her – back-up, perhaps. These were the new Sony people. Introductions were made, supercilious smiles exchanged. Bill and I sprawled over a pair of the nearest chairs, burping up beer fumes, while Shalit remained on his feet to give our new pitch, which he did with all the style of a game-show host talking about the cash prizes on offer for the victor.

'*Punk?*'

Poor Ruth, she looked so tired.

'Just listen.'

The CD went in, and 'Losers' filled the room. The new additions to our *team*, and what a laughable phrase that was, couldn't help themselves. They were grinning, bouncing in their seats, getting jiggy with it in an unbecoming fashion. Some of the older ones, however, just looked confused. When it finished, and before anyone could say anything, Shalit quickly skipped on to a second song, explaining that this was 'Play with Myself' re-imagined into something else entirely. But he cued up incorrectly and instead found 'Cunt'. The volume level remained the same, but it somehow sounded much louder. Ruth put her head in her hands when the song reached the chorus, and let loose a whimper. Somebody hit the Stop button halfway through. I didn't recognize him, but judging by his age and dress sense he had arrived into the company directly at executive level.

'Correct me if I'm wrong,' he began, 'but this is not what we signed?'

Shalit opened his mouth, but Del jumped quickly in, telling them to think about Lost Prophets and Linkin Park, loud American rock acts who were cleaning up on the live circuit in the US, as were all those Green Day acolytes like Blink 182, Sum 41 and Good Charlotte. Each, he explained, boasted similar musical elements but each paled when compared to Silibil N' Brains.

But they remained unconvinced. Instead, they wanted the small print. They wanted to know how many people were in our band now. We told them.

'And you expect us to pay them as well?'

Shit. This was something we hadn't even considered.

Bill grinned, arms spread wide like a benevolent politician's. 'Hey, this kind of talent doesn't come for free,' he told them.

Before the shouting could begin, Shalit intervened, suggesting that he would pay their expenses for the time being, that this was something we could fine tune later down the line. The important thing, he said, pointing to the CD player, was that *this* was genius, our future success all but guaranteed. What Sony had here was their next world-slaying act. Did they really want to look a gift horse in the mouth, he asked. Because if so, then say the word. Say the word, and he'd take his boys elsewhere, all five of them. The executives held up their hands, a placatory white flag. Ruth exhaled.

The following day, Sony informed Shalit that they wanted us to go out on the road again, but this time on a proper tour of proper venues right across the country. How better to test just how good a five-piece we were than in front of the great British public? Let them decide.

We were to leave the following Monday. On Sunday I chose to spend the day alone, suddenly craving solitude. After all the effort of the reinvention, I was exhausted, sapped of all energy. I felt feverish and found it hard to leave my room. I couldn't stop thinking of Alison. I had tried to call her several times after she broke things off, but only ever got voicemail; my messages, my pleas, cruelly unacknowledged. But, now that the band was about to explode into the big time, I wanted her, only her, right alongside me. If only she'd give me another chance. Missing her was like an open, suppurating wound. And I wanted to pour salt on it.

Shalit had just bankrolled us for another week, so I was flush with ready cash. I went to the off-licence and spent most of it on beer, Jägermeister and Jack Daniel's. I was so laden down with bottles and cans that I had to take a cab for the journey back, which was less than half a mile. I dragged my plastic carrier bags into my room, and started to drink, and to cry. My stomach had been percolating all week, so I drank with a manic determination now to kill all pain, all thoughts. I had never felt so bitterly alone. I put on some music, Billy Talent, and cued up 'The Ex', a song that now meant more to me than it ever had before. I had it on repeat, and allowed it to play itself to death – possibly taking me along with it. I drank and I swallowed several of my painkillers, and then swallowed some more.

I must have passed out, because the next thing I became aware of was being dragged by Bill and Gordon across the hall and down the stairs. They were shouting at me, grabbing at my hair and slapping my cheeks, asking me over and over again what I'd taken.

When I woke up again, it was in by now quite familiar sur-roundings: a hospital ward. My sister must have been called, because there she was, Michelle, at the end of the bed, in con-ference with a nurse. I lowered my eyelids and listened as the nurse told my sister that I clearly had a problem and that it would be wise to tackle it now before it became serious. Once again, I heard Michelle play it all down; but I could hear the underlying fear in her voice, and it upset me. The nurse gave her a bunch of leaflets, and urged her to encourage me to call the number at the bottom of one of them to schedule an appointment.

'It could make all the difference, if you know what I mean,' she said.

Michelle drove me home and, perhaps recklessly, left me in Bill's care. Bill bundled me up into a bear hug that very nearly asphyxiated me. He reminded me that the tour was now just twelve hours away, and said that this would provide the perfect opportunity for me to get over Alison once and for all.

'We'll get you wasted and laid every night,' he promised, laugh-ing. 'We'll have the time of our fucking lives, just you wait and see.'

Around eleven o'clock the following morning, Greg, Colin and Gordon already congregated in our living room with bags packed, the tour van arrived. We opened the front door to be greeted by our tour manager, a man we would come to know as Big Mark, a proper Cockney geezer who had been around the block and could talk you into a coma, but who was funny and filthy. We would come to love him as one of our own.

'Men,' he said in a broad East London accent, 'your carriage awaits. Come on, let's scarper.'

With the five of us, plus equipment, squeezed into it, the van felt claustrophobically small and heroically uncomfortable. Soon, it would smell something terrible. Moulding pizza crusts, dog ends, feet.

Seven

Shalit had pulled strings. In his words, he'd *made nice* with them. The record company were now willing, he explained in an expansive phone call full of good cheer and barrelling optimism, to fund all five of us on the university tour. In other words, we wouldn't be expected to doss down in the van every night but would instead be put up in hotels. Nothing fancy, and never with swimming pools and spas attached, but perfectly decent Travelodges nonetheless. We were happy, grateful, even excited at the prospect. Meanwhile, the promotions team had done a good job: at each venue we saw people wandering around the campus in Silibil N' Brains T-shirts, while there were also Silibil N' Brains stickers and enough Silibil N' Brains flyers to wallpaper the entire university building. Album promos had been distributed to student and pirate radio stations, and a bunch of our tracks were on heavy rotation. All of which meant that at each university our arrival was anticipated. Being anticipated felt tremendous.

Our first destination was Bristol University's Freshers' Ball, which was held in a low, cramped venue that, should health and safety be conveniently overlooked, could comfortably cram 500.

It took us the better part of three hours to get there after several wrong turns and far too many pit stops for the toilet, for food, for beer. We arrived mid-afternoon, and could no more find our way to the building that housed the venue than we could get out of a paper bag. We wandered through half-deserted corridors, we poked our heads into classrooms and lecture halls and ended up, purely by accident, in one of the dorm buildings. Its dwellers were clearly crime conscious. All the doors were locked. (Bill checked.)

Eventually we found the place. Silibil N' Brains flyers led us there in a sort of Hansel-and-Gretel trail. The hall smelt of yesterday's spilt beer, and there was no sound desk to speak of. But there was a proper stage, elevated at least four feet from the floor; and, as of ten o'clock that night, for half an hour or so, it was to be all ours. We took a running jump at it, then bounded all over it. We slam danced and freestyled while Big Mark watched us from the floor, a paternal grin on his face.

'Um, can I help you, gentlemen?'

A man had wandered in through the far door, security by the looks of him.

'We're the band,' I told him. *Boy*, did that feel good.

'Ah, OK, good. You've arrived. I'll go and get, um . . .' And off he went to get whoever it was that needed to be alerted to the fact that Silibil N' Brains were in the building.

Sound-check was a shambles at five in the afternoon, and we spent what was left of the day retracing our steps through the various halls of residence, stickering girls left, right and centre, making sure absolutely everybody knew that we were here, and that everyone was going to be coming tonight. Bill made a point of approaching any good-looking girl he spotted and promising to get them on the guest list. Admission was all of £5, but Sony had allotted us a guest list of five each for every show, twenty-five in total. By seven o'clock that evening, we'd already put upwards of fifty people down, all of them female. We had a word with the folk on the door later to ensure that they would definitely get in free of charge. If they had any problems, we told them, bill the record company.

That night, as a still newly minted five-piece, we were astonishing; the stage could barely contain us. We ran amok in the heaving crowd, too, trailing microphone leads and guitars. Bill sprayed off-licence-purchased champagne into the throng, and we played them 'Losers', 'Stalker' and new songs like 'Medicine for Rejects', 'Let's Get Naked', 'Spaz Out' and 'Your Moms'. We ended with 'Cunt', by which time dozens of fans had clambered up on to the stage alongside us. As the song came to an end one of the girls from the front row pulled me off stage. With my mouth full of Heineken, I kissed her, a golden shower of alcohol dribbling between us and making us sticky and wet. She smiled at me provocatively, and pushed herself against me.

In the five years I had been with Alison, I had never once been unfaithful to her, never even entertained a desire to do so. I was going to make up for that now.

The Heineken girl came out to the tour van with me after the show, and while my four bandmates stood signing breasts and midriffs, and Big Mark waited patiently on the pavement outside, smoking and talking to other students, she fucked my brains out, my arse biting into the van's cold floor while her head banged the ceiling.

We played a different university each night, Liverpool, Manchester, Derby, Cardiff, Aberystwyth, Bath, Preston, Leicester, York, and each night we played our hearts out, and with a chemistry that entirely validated Silibil N' Brains as a punk-rock five-piece. When Big Mark couldn't take any more, bless him, Ian Martin, the only other tour manager to survive us (and a diamond geezer, I might add) took over and made sure nobody got killed. The tour was great for bonding and eventually I felt I had as much of a bond with Colin, Greg and Gordon as I did with Bill, and they were as blazing up there on stage as either of us were. Every night after a show, we would walk out into the crowd immediately, unshowered and readily available. We signed autographs. We were mobbed, cheered, jeered. Colin had a habit of approaching particular girls and carrying them in a firemen's lift back to the dressing room. Few resisted, even those with boyfriends. The rest of us would simply invite anyone back who wanted to come, doors thrown wide open. These were tiny dressing rooms, the size of cubicles, mostly, and daubed with the graffiti of a thousand previous visiting bands. We found no privacy in such places, unless we used our initiative. Sometimes, it was wise to do so.

One night, I tumbled into the backstage area with a girl surgically attached to my face. Her tongue was in my throat, and her hands were all over me. As we fought our way in, I placed my palms on her buttocks and lifted her up on to my waist. Freeing my lips from hers, I shouted for everyone to mind their backs. 'Coming through!' We squeezed into the bathroom, as small as any you'd find on a low-cost plane, and forcibly shut the door behind us. The toilet had been recently used. Pee marked the circumference of the seat, and whoever'd just shat in it – Bill, in all likelihood – had failed to pull the chain. We tumbled into the adjacent shower cubicle, still locked together, impervious to the filth. I pulled aside her knickers, and freed my cock, and we were fucking so hard that even when my elbow knocked the taps and freezing water came on, we didn't stop, we just kept deliriously at it. Her fake orgasm was something to behold.

In Derby we were treated like royalty. Perhaps Derby doesn't get many visiting superstars, because the reception wherever we went that day was enough to make you think that Sony had already released 'Losers' without our knowledge and it was sitting at Number 1 in the charts. However, it was 'Cunt', I was told, that was currently the Number 1 track on student radio, and was keeping Westlife from the top spot. We couldn't move without causing a frenzy, five good-looking guys with girls all around us. The Student Union bar had already been Blitzkrieged with Silibil N' Brains stickers, thousands of them. By the time we took the stage, it was pure carnage, the place dangerously packed and the crowd lurching heavily forwards. Within minutes there was no oxygen left in the room. I saw spots before my eyes. During 'Drunk Too Much', I fell over the drum-riser and cut my forehead. Bill pulled me back up again and, with blood pouring down my face, we started pulling girls out of the crowd and dissing their boyfriends, rearing sharply back whenever a bunched fist was thrown out in anger from one of them. The sound was soup but the atmosphere electric. Sparks flew from the speakers, and everything went dead. We'd killed the venue.

Backstage afterwards, we could barely move for girls. Greg had one on either knee. Bill, Colin and Gordon were sitting on the collapsed sofa, a girl on each of their tented laps. I watched on with amusement until somebody tapped me on the shoulder. I turned.

'Hello.'

She was tall and beautiful, with blonde hair, blue eyes, an athletic body clad in a too-tight T-shirt and tiny miniskirt. Her legs were golden, her manicured toes exposed by sandals. She was sweating, her face still in awe, clearly, from the sheer spectacle of our performance. She had a hot pink mouth, and she was smiling it at me.

'I've got one of your stickers,' she said, 'and I'd like to give it back to you.'

I wasn't quite sure how to respond to this, so I shrugged.

I followed her eyes down and watched, with mounting incredulity, as she began to lift her skirt. The mêlée around us had somehow fallen away into nothing more than background noise and unfocused blur. We were now the only two people in the room. In the place I would have expected to see her knickers, I saw only a Silibil N' Brains sticker, my face and Bill's gurning from a trim patch of pubic hair that confirmed her as a true blonde.

'It's yours,' she said. 'Take it back.'

I did what any man would do in this situation. I took my sticker back. I watched my hand reach out towards it, brushing her pubic bone as it did. I felt the sticker beneath the pad of my index finger. She was warm to the touch. I extended a middle finger, and pressed. She was wet already, and gasped lightly, her eyes smiling at me, her pointed tongue clamped between perfect white teeth.

We were back at the Travelodge in no time. In the lift I fumbled through my pockets for my key, tossing tissues, sweet wrappers and coins to the floor. We got to the room to find a 'Do Not Disturb' sign hanging from the doorknob. I threw it down the hall and slid in my key. It remained locked, from the inside. From the bedroom came Colin's voice. While Sony had generously agreed to pay for our accommodation, they hadn't been generous enough to give us a room each.

'Fuck off!' he shouted.

I put my face to the frame and whispered frantically. 'Col, dude, I've got a girl out here.'

I heard rustling, giggling. 'So have I!'

I turned to my blonde beauty. 'Sorry about this.' She didn't hesitate. She pushed me against the wall and began to dry hump me. I didn't resist. Ten minutes later, the door finally opened. Two middle-aged women, forty years old, perhaps as old as forty-five, came out. They had clearly dressed in a hurry, bright blouses still half undone, zips gaping open on their tight leather skirts, red stilettos in hand. They looked up at me, and smiled.

'Night, dear.'

They tottered off unsteadily, laughing loudly. I looked towards the room. Framed in the glow of the bedroom lamp's low light stood Colin, stark naked, hands on hips, and still wearing the condom.

Time, it quickly became clear, was of the essence in situations like these. Beds were a luxury, privacy, as I've said, an impossibility. We became experts at living in the moment. There was no hotel waiting for us in York. After our show there, we were to drive overnight to Newcastle, and the final night of the tour. It was another amazing show. We were getting better and better, and reports were filtering back to the record company, who were now sounding, Shalit told us, more positive about us than they had at any point since we'd signed.

In York, the usual quota of girls followed us back into the dressing room, but I was late in arriving, having hung out by the bar to do an interview for the student paper. It was invariably me who did any local press, with Bill's insistence that he was happy to let me do the talking compounded by the fact that he was always busy with more pressing, more conjugal matters. I answered questions dutifully, swearing all over the place just as our media trainer had warned me *not* to do, then darted backstage. The final song of any show was effectively now an aphrodisiac for me: I knew that sex would follow it soon, often within a matter of minutes. By the time I reached the cramped space, the others were already locked in messy embraces. I looked around to see who I could claim. She came at me so quickly, and with such determination, that I didn't have time to even clock her face. She kissed well, though, and I was hard in seconds. I became aware of movement around me. People were filing out. Outside, the van was ready and waiting.

'No time, Gav, not tonight,' shouted Big Mark. 'Come on, let's go.'

At first I ignored him, because they were never going to leave without me. But then I realized that that was precisely what they would do, their idea of a big laugh. I zipped up again, and ran.

Newcastle came and went in a blur, the end-of-tour celebrations merging with the celebrations we had had the night before and the night before that. In fact, every night had been a celebration, heady and drunken, full of sex, so much sex. I'd kept a list: my two-week tally could cast into shadow any self-respecting Premiership footballer. No STDs, mercifully, just a mild and constant crotch hum to remind me just how active I'd been, and what fun I'd had.

When we finally arrived home to Eagle's Nest at six o'clock on a crisp Thursday morning, bidding Big Mark a farewell that almost brought tears to my eyes, I was ready to sleep for a week. I staggered upstairs to the bathroom, where I stuck my head under the tap and drank deep, then popped two, no, three sleeping pills, went to bed and did something I'd so very rarely managed to do: fell into an instant, and dreamless, sleep.

It took me some time to work out what the sound was.

Nagging, and high-pitched, like a needle repeatedly inserted into my head and out again. It was the ringing of a car alarm. No, a phone. I couldn't understand why Bill wasn't answering it, and even half conscious I felt myself becoming furious with him. The ringing stopped eventually, and I gave it my silent thanks. Then it started again. Only gradually did I begin to realize that it was in fact *my* phone, and that it was coming from the pocket of my jeans. I rolled over from my front to my back, groaning with exhaustion.

'Hello?'

'Brains? Del. Hi.' Del's voice was unnecessarily loud, his enthusiasm clearly something he'd caught from Shalit. Perhaps it was a requirement of the job. I pulled the phone away from my head and kept it at a safe distance from my ear. He was still talking. 'Good news and bad, mate. We've landed you another tour. That's the good news. But this time it's a bigger one, the kind of tour you'd kill your own mother to be on. The kind of tour that could transform Silibil N' Brains overnight into something massive. No, I am not shitting you.' He was laughing, giggling almost, his voice a hiccup, a tall glass of fizzing Coke. 'The bad news?' he said to a question I hadn't asked. 'The bad news is it starts tonight.'

My heart sank. '*Tonight?*'

'Tonight.'

'Del, *Del*, you've got to be kidding? No way, no way. I'm in no fit state. I'm knackered, Del, fucked. Don't you know we've only just come back off the university tour, like, *an hour ago?*'

His smile was so bright that I could almost hear his teeth. 'I do, I do, but there's nothing I can do about it. Sorry. That's just the way things work. Listen. You have to be at the venue by two this afternoon.'

I groaned. Why didn't he bother Bill with this news instead of me, Bill who was no doubt still sleeping soundlessly in his room.

Del chatted on. 'Anyway, you haven't asked me who you're supporting yet.'

I hadn't realized he was talking about us *supporting* anyone. I became suspicious.

'Who?'

His voice was scaling consecutive octaves now, increasingly girlish, a helium squeal.

'*D12*! That's right! D12! Your old friends!'

I sat up straight in bed now, and dropped the phone. Then I held my head in my hands, and began to rock ever so gently back and forth.

When you spin a lie as grand as ours, you do not hold back. What's the point? You dive in, you add layers to the lie, add depth to it in order not simply to bring it to vivid, believable life but also to maintain its momentum to such an extent that you too believe it to be true. It is difficult not to get carried away in such situations, not least when the lie effectively bags you close to £200,000 with so much more promised, and that I suppose is what had happened to us. We got carried away, and one lie begat another one, and another one still. We had added so much colour to our story to so many people these past few months that it was difficult to keep up: what we had told, and to whom, when and how and why, but particularly that: *why*?

This whole *friends with Eminem and D12* thing – started in the boardroom at Sony, the day we signed, Friday the fucking 13th of February 2004 – was a perfect example. While entertaining the ladies and trying to steer all the guys' questions away from holes in our story we got caught up in the moment: *Eminem, D12, yeah we go way back.* This lie had grown legs, enormous fucking mutant legs that were running amok. It didn't help that every time we were out drunk and someone mentioned it I just kept fuelling the flames with more ridiculous stories. The next thing you know, we're Eminem's best friends, third cousins twice removed. In truth, we had no more met D12 or Proof than we had Eminem himself or, for that matter, Elvis Presley, Gandhi, or any of the popes. This didn't matter. Lies don't always have to catch up with the perpetrator, especially not if he is clever and cautious with them. But how was I to know that circumstances would ever conspire to have us actually *meet* D12 for real, much less to tour with them so early on in our career? Del's news derailed me. On the one hand, it was amazing news, the fullest summation of our wildest dreams, but also it was awful, terrible, a sure disaster. I felt my sphincter ripple in anticipatory fear, and I checked my watch. Later tonight, in a matter of hours, we were to open for our idols before 4000 members of what were very likely our target audience. There were rumours Eminem was going to make a guest appearance.

Could things get any better for us? Could they get any worse?

I rushed into Bill's room and shook him forcibly awake. I told him the news and his face opened like a flower. Pacing, I told him not to worry, that it would be fine, we'd pull something out of the bag – come on, let's face it, we always did. I grabbed him by the shoulders and shouted at him to calm down, to calm the fuck down, for fuck's sake. But Bill was already perfectly calm. In fact, he was radiant, his eyes impossibly wide. He jumped out of bed on a pair of nimble feet and skipped around the room, rubbing his hands together as if he had just hit the jackpot. Which, in a manner of speaking, he had.

'Don't worry,' he winked. 'Follow my lead, and we'll soar.'

I went back to my room and called the guys to break the news. Then I went to the bathroom to sit on the toilet. For what was about to happen, I didn't need to strain.

We got to Brixton Academy bang on two o'clock, as instructed, still exhausted but preternaturally pumped up, and raring to go. The place was cavernous and empty, the temperature inside far cooler than it was outside. As we loaded our gear in, we could hear D12 sound-checking. I looked for a place to hide and considered climbing into one of the empty drum cases. We waited by the side of the stage as Proof and Kon Artis finished their mic checks. I had been biting my fingernails all the way to the venue and by the time we got the call to load in, I was down to the bone.

Over my shoulder Del whispered: 'It's him!'

As I turned back to face the stage I saw Proof walking our way. I became unusually heavy, torpid, as if my blood had abandoned the top half of my body and settled in my feet, which were now solid concrete blocks. This was it, my gut continued to whimper. Everything was now in slow motion. To the left of me I spotted Del's face – he had the expression of a five-year-old on Christmas morning about to wet his pants; I was about to shit mine. To the right, I saw the guys gawking nervously at me and Bill. The look on my cousin Byron's face, if anything, left me feeling a hundred times worse, it being the look of pure fear. Then out of the blue, in a moment I will never forget, Bill whooped confidently and launched ahead into the path of the D12 superstars. Fuelled by adrenaline only, I followed him.

'Dude!' Bill approached him, arms spread wide. 'Well, shit, it's been too long, too long! How you bin, dawg?'

Proof, so big and solid a man up close that he appeared indestructible, carved from stone, his face creased in mild confusion, was now stopped in his tracks. We were about fifteen feet away, just out of listening range, from our team of roadies and bandmates who looked on, binocular-eyed.

My turn now. 'Mah man!' I went to high-five him and, instinctively, he held up a palm, which could have been as much for protection as welcome. 'Bro, it's been – what? – *years*. When was the last time we saw you?' He opened his mouth. 'No, wait. Lemme think.' Silently, I performed some quick calculations. I'd seen *8 Mile*, of course, the biopic of Eminem's life, more times than I could count. In my mind, I fast-forwarded through the film, stopping off at the battle raps that made up the best moments of the movie, and instantly I recalled the name of the main venue, the Shelter. 'It was two, maybe three years ago, in the—'

Bill interrupted me. 'Barrowlands . . . In Scotland,' he added. I reared round at him in momentary shock. *Scotland*?

Proof opened his mouth again. 'OK,' he said. 'Sure.'

Talking fast now, Bill told them that, yes, that's it, we'd met up with them in Scotland a couple of years back. We were there visiting distant relatives and they were there playing Glasgow's Barrowlands, and they couldn't possibly forget Barrowlands, could they? Nobody forgets a Scottish crowd, the best in the world. Proof was nodding eagerly now. 'Best damn show of the whole tour, that,' he agreed.

Bill explained that we were a crew ourselves now, recently signed to Sony for megabucks and on the brink of stardom, and that we were supporting them tonight. This was clearly news to Proof, but he was by now caught up in the enthusiasm Bill always generated everywhere he went; now D12 were warm and friendly, and wished us luck before heading off towards their dressing room.

'Let's party later,' Bill called out as they left.

'Sure, sure . . .'

And that's when it all became clear to me. Bill and I were magicians, pure and simple, capable of magic, of opening every door, turning any situation to our advantage, and imprinting our larger-than-life characters on to anyone we met, no matter how illustrious. Frankly, who would bet against us?

We had never sound-checked at somewhere so big before, and an empty Brixton Academy seemed absolutely vast: Wembley Stadium with a roof on. Bill and I stood by our microphone stands, grinning at one another. The guys, plugged in and ready, stood behind us, twitching. Across the main floor opposite us was the sound desk, at which stood our very own sound engineer, someone we had never previously met who had evidently been dispatched by Sony just an hour before. He raised his thumb, and we launched into 'Stalker'. The sound was huge. It bounced off the far walls and came back on us like a physical thing, reverberating in the pit of my stomach and the very deepest parts of my ear canal. I could feel Gordon's bass in my gums, and all the electricity on the stage itself seemed to run up my feet and make my spine tingle. I almost pissed myself with delight.

Though various D12 folk were ambling about, we had an audience of just one for our sound-check: Del. He stood several feet in front of the sound desk, hands behind his back, leaning forward in anticipation. For those twenty minutes we played exclusively to him, a performance interrupted only by the sound engineer as he messed with sound levels and asked us to stop and start over again. It was a strangely naked experience, but also visceral. Del gave the impression that he loved every minute of it, our biggest fan. I could have hugged him.

It is difficult now to recall all the details of the hour before we went on stage that night. I remember only flashes of our chaotic dressing room, the rider mostly untouched (unusual for us), a lot of silence and the kind of loaded stares that would normally close an episode of *EastEnders*. Bill cracked jokes, I remember, because that is how Bill always dealt with stress, and I had diarrhoea, as well as the worst follow-through smell I think I've ever been responsible for. The hour seemed to last a minute, full of the most exquisite anticipation and the most utter dread. One thing I was sure of, though: we hadn't arrived here by mistake. Right here right now was our destiny.

They say that the mark of a true sportsman is the capacity to up his game on the world stage, when it really counts. Well, that is precisely what Silibil N' Brains did that night. We upped our game in front of an international audience. No nerves as the call came for stage time, that was until I peeked around the curtain and took in the size of the crowd. All of a sudden it felt like I was walking a tightrope without a safety net and had just looked down. A pre-show huddle. Then a sixty-second excruciating wait at the side of the stage listening to the growing murmur of the audience, 5000 strong and already baying for the headliners. A door opened, and suddenly there was light, a stage filled with fat leads and cables, a drum-riser, guitar and bass, a pair of microphones up front. On the floor, our Sellotaped set list. Six songs written out in permanent black marker on a piece of paper, capital letters, my handwriting. I grabbed the mic and shouted into it: 'Yo yo yo yo. *Brixtoooon!*' A cheer rose, thunder, an earthquake, until the rumble was swiftly cancelled out by the band, *my* band, launching loudly into 'Stalker'. Bill and I went at it instantaneously, running laps of the stage, left and right, and leading the audience into a chorus that was always designed for call-and-response. The crowd went wild for it, for *us*. I wish I could have seen them, every last face, but I was blind to them all, the stage lights so strong I could see nothing but a blanket of blinding white, as if this wasn't Brixton Academy at all but the entry way to heaven itself. It certainly felt like paradise.

We commanded the stage for thirty-five minutes without a dip. I'd never sweated so much, never covered so much ground. Every song overlapped the next, the pair of us freestyling with quicker and more ferocious wit than we'd ever previously managed. I didn't want it to end, I wanted D12 to come down with some debilitating illness that would necessitate us to carry on alone, for hours, all night if the audience so demanded. 'Losers' was our last song. It was gargantuan. At its conclusion, we dropped our microphones to the floor, and the five of us strolled off stage with one arm each held aloft like Black Panthers, quelling any desire to run around like headless chickens while squealing with excitement. We were cool, we were calm, we knew exactly what impression we needed to make on Brixton, and we made it in style.

We had barely opened a second beer each in our dressing room afterwards when word came from the booking agent that he wanted us to support the band again in a few days' time, in Birmingham, this time to an even bigger crowd.

In my memory now, Birmingham happened almost instantaneously after Brixton, as if we walked off one stage and right on to another, with more dazzling lights and the eyes of thousands of new fans upon us, the five of us surfing a wave of their adulation just as we had done in London. We played for another half-hour, every second of which pulsed through me like electricity, then we staggered off stage, ecstatic. In our dressing room we opened a beer each, then another, then decided to go and watch D12 from the side of the stage, where, perhaps, they would invite us out for more, give the crowd what they so clearly wanted. But everywhere now were security goons, stalking the corridors as if under military orders. This convinced us that the rumours were true: Eminem was in the building. You couldn't move about the backstage area now without bumping into one of his heavies, and they didn't take the collision lightly. We were ordered back into our dressing rooms, and, like meek schoolchildren, we obeyed. Correction: four of us did. Bill had other ideas. For the majority of D12's performance, he hung his head out of our dressing-room door, monitoring the goons' movements. When one of them finally ambled out towards the stairs and showed little sign of returning imminently, he seized the moment. He tiptoed into the headliners' room. Through a crack in our door no greater than four inches, the rest of us observed his progress. A minute passed. A raised voice came, and the goon made his lumbering way back. Bill appeared, something large and bulky barely concealed beneath his T-shirt. He ran towards us, we opened our door more, and he fell inside. From underneath his T-shirt he produced two bottles of the band's champagne, still cold. We popped the corks and polished them off in minutes.

An ominous knock at the door had us scurrying to hide all evidence of our stolen goods behind the sofa, and prompted a flurry of drunken giggles. Colin was pushed to the front, and reached to open it. One of the goons loomed large, his bulk filling every space of the door frame.

'Proof says you wanna come party?'

We very much wanted to come party. We went immediately.

I'd always heard that you should never meet your heroes, that you can only come away disappointed. This may well be true, but the way I saw it then was like this: why deny your heroes the opportunity to meet *you*?

D12's room was bigger than ours, but in no way better decorated. It had the air of an old staffroom gone to seed after years of nicotine abuse. Alcoholically, however, it was very well appointed, and everywhere we looked we could see beer and champagne on ice. No wonder they hadn't missed a couple of bottles. The room was packed, with band members, with crew, record-company types from both the UK and US, and the kind of fat-bottomed girls who populated hip-hop videos, many of them local judging by their Brummie accents. Drinks were thrust into our hands, and suddenly Proof was in front of us, freshly showered and changed into a sky-blue Sean John tracksuit, complimenting us forcefully on our show.

'You guys make one helluva noise,' he told us, smiling. 'I'm impressed.'

'Me too,' Bill grinned self-reverentially.

As we chatted away, Kon Artis, Bizarre, Swift and Kuniva joined us: members of our favourite hip-hop act, gathering around us swapping tour stories. Their laughs were bear-like, low, rumbling and dark, like tar.

The first I saw of him was his peroxide hair just peeping over the right shoulder of Kon Artis. He was sitting down and surrounded by people I didn't recognize, goons to the left of him, goons to the right. Where everyone else was shouting and yelling and laughing and braying, there was a stillness to him that made his presence somehow even more startling. He was smiling slightly at something somebody was saying, but the smile never reached his eyes. He had a glass of champagne in his hand, but I never saw him drink from it.

I was vaguely aware that Proof was talking now, but somehow I couldn't take my eyes off *him*. Presently, Proof followed my gaze, and smiled.

'Want an introduction?' he asked.

I looked at Bill. Bill shrugged, affecting a cool that none of us bought. We then shuffled over with Proof, tension mounting visibly. Ignoring the girl who was still talking directly to him, Proof leant over. 'Hey, Em. Remember these guys? They came to our show in Scotland – *Glas*-gow – couple years back, we met them afterwards? These were our support act tonight. They rocked.'

Eminem looked up at us, but didn't stand. He said something but his voice was barely above a whisper. I didn't hear him, and couldn't quite bring myself to say *Pardon?* He stretched out his fist in greeting, and I prayed that Bill wouldn't try to hug him instead. There were a million things I wanted to say to him, but I couldn't find the words. I didn't want to come across as just another fan; I wanted to be a peer. But I could never be that – not yet, at least. He turned his gaze from us and back to the girl, whom he seemed to stare right through as if she wasn't there. One of his security man-mountains inserted himself between us and his charge, signalling that our audience with him was over. Proof melted into the crowd to talk to somebody else. Surrounded by hip-hop royalty, the five of us stood there huddled together, watching everything around us as if on some kind of exotic nature watch. This was us, and we were here. *Unbelievable*. Me and Bill hugged. It was spontaneous, without warning, neither of us saw it coming. We must have looked odd, two grown men embracing so tightly in an environment where, strictly speaking, men didn't really embrace one another so openly. But it was a moment for us, a monumental one. We wanted to savour it. It was unreal. It was beautiful.

Eight

By now, I wanted to remain Brains McLoud for the rest of my life. No longer was he just a caricature through whom I could become famous, but rather he was the person I felt myself truly to *be*. He had everything I didn't: the gift of the gab, the skyscraping confidence. He had Proof's cell-phone number. He wrote better songs, and certainly performed them with more conviction. He was better-looking, more popular with girls. He was good on the drink, not maudlin. He loved a ruck, and could handle himself. His wit was quick, his creativity boundless. He was invulnerable, and now he was on the brink of superstardom. Nothing could touch him.

But when the brink of superstardom was then put back again, subject to further infuriating delays by a record company so obsessed with its schedules it no longer knew its arse from its elbow, Brains McLoud ebbed away into the margins, leaving me with – well, with myself, Gavin Bain, a young man with bitten-down fingernails, a stomach ulcer and several nervous twitches. Frankly, I wished him dead.

In comparison, Bill had managed to lose himself to Silibil

entirely, in a manner so comprehensive I could only stand back in awe. I was amazed he could do it. The man was so joyfully carefree, so immune to all the risks we were running. He was bulletproof. At night, after he'd drunk until he dropped, he slept like an immovable log. I envied him his snores, but felt increasingly bewildered by him, and at ever greater odds with him. I still loved the guy, but I was starting to hate him, too.

But being on the road managed to obliterate my neuroses, at least for now. I drank to party and I drank to lose myself. Mostly, I succeeded.

A few nights after the D12 Birmingham show, we arrived in Winchester to headline a show of our own, a date of which Del managed to give us a full thirty-six hours' notice. Sony were adamant now that we spend as many nights as possible on the road before they would even consider releasing what was fast becoming our semi-mythical debut single. This was another entirely necessary test, Del said, of whether we really gelled as a five-piece, and of whether the public had a genuine appetite for us. Yes, the Brixton and Birmingham shows were positive, but Sony needed more evidence. They would let us know their findings in due course.

It was difficult to complain too much because we were having such a brilliant time. I'd never been to Winchester, but in my memory I now think of it in much the way I expect Paul McCartney does Shea Stadium in 1965. Two nights previously, we had been playing in front of 5000 Eminem fans. Tonight the crowd was just 300 strong, but every one of those 300 people were there to see us. We were now packing out venues. Our MySpace page had been inundated with visitors and postings, receiving more hits over the course of forty-eight hours than we'd had in the previous six months. The messages were not only in praise of our music, our support slot, but also told us how good-looking we were, how sexy, and how much so many of their authors wanted to fuck Silibil and Brains and all the rest of us. Some of them were coming to the Winchester show specially to do so. We were looking forward to it.

If we hadn't suffered from tinnitus before Winchester, then we certainly did afterwards, the sound of frenzied screaming ringing persistently in our ears for weeks afterwards. The crowd was two thirds female, three quarters of whom were stunning. Bras and even tampons were thrown up on stage throughout our performance, and that hadn't happened before. When we came to play 'Cunt', the guys in the crowd shouted along with every word while the girls pointed towards their crotches and tried to make eye contact. At one point, I fell to my knees to serenade someone and was promptly pulled into the crowd, bundled and manhandled, searching fingers scouring my most private places. Bliss.

It felt good to be back in such close confines after the enormity of Brixton. Backstage afterwards, we barely had space to breathe, the cramped, fetid room wall-to-wall with women. I found myself facing one in particular, blonde and tall and looming down on me with a purpose I had come to anticipate, and also to expect. The music that was being pumped from the in-house speakers was so loud it rendered conversation impossible, and so without the foreplay of friendly conversation, she simply popped open the button flies on my jeans in a manner that suggested this wasn't her first time. Before I knew it, her hand was on my cock and my cock was standing to attention. Bill chose that moment to turn from his own embrace and appraise me. He grinned.

'I'd know that cock anywhere,' he said, looking at the girl. Adding, 'Careful, girl, he never washes it.'

We never spent enough time on the road for it to feel like work, a dull daily grind that would drain the very lives out of us. If, by night, we were acting like rock stars, then by day we were full-time pranksters, goofing off because there was nothing else to do, because we felt as if it were somehow expected of us, and because, well, why not? Before checkout at each hotel, we would make crank calls to everyone we worked with, pretending to be Australians, Russians, Mexicans and even Scots, although by now our Scottish accents were beginning to sound pretty ropey.

We existed on a mostly liquid diet of beer and spirits to chase the hunger away, though we rarely managed to go a full day without at least one mandatory visit to a Little Chef, where an all-day breakfast proved perfect for our perennial hangovers: sticky and congealing, disgusting and very possibly carcinogenic, but it did so wholeheartedly hit the spot. We played drinking games in the back of the van, and pissed into the empty bottles afterwards to cut down on all the toilet stops. I had never been more proactively unhealthy, and had never felt more vibrantly alive.

When we finally arrived home, our on-the-road bad behaviour often came back to bite us. We had a rule of never giving girls our real phone numbers, much less our home addresses, but when you are trying to get into somebody's pants you'd do pretty much anything required. Plus, when drunk, it was all too easy to fall in love and convince yourself that this was The One. Consequently, there was always someone either calling for us or, occasionally, knocking for us in person. I remember one time smuggling a Czech girl I had been seeing out of my bedroom one morning while Bill detained my new German girlfriend in the kitchen after she had unexpectedly shown up on the doorstep. I became serious with only one girl during this time, a beautiful girl called Belinda, who told me that she was twenty-four years old and worked in the City. The sex was incredible, but so was the conversation. I hadn't been able to talk to a girl like this since Alison. I fell head over heels, and was ready to give up all tour sex for her, perhaps even bring her out on the road with me if she could get the time off. But then her father came to the house early one day, his fist a cannonball at our front door, waking us up in a sudden rush of terror. Bill answered it, and I listened as he told the father that I'd left the country a couple of days previously, a family emergency back in Hemet. No, I heard Bill say as I crouched at the top of the stairs, Gavin had had no idea that Belinda wasn't twenty-four at all but only sixteen, but he, Bill, would be sure to pass the message on that she was, in fact, barely legal. Belinda's father punched him full in the face. It was one way to get over a hangover, Bill noted afterwards.

But then all our personal problems began to pale, as professional ones took over. Sony, we learnt, had delayed the release of our debut single, now definitely 'Losers', yet again, this time for reasons I was never fully to discern. There were rumours afoot that, since merging with BMG the previous year, Sony wasn't what it once was, its outlook different, with an emphasis now to promote far less insurrectionary bands than us. But Shalit was adamant. Keep plugging away at what you are doing, he told me repeatedly, and everything would work itself out. He himself would focus on the finer details; he would be the one to make everything that needed to happen happen. *Trust me*, he said time and again. But even he was becoming impatient now. There was a new strain to his voice that he could no longer conceal, as if he had been pushed as far as he was going to on this project before he started pushing back.

We had almost completed the re-recording of our debut album with its new, punkier edge. Any time I began to despair about the futility of our stop-start progress, I needed only to go into the studio to play back what we had so far committed to tape to know that we were still sitting on an amazing product here, something that would explode all over the world. Even in my lowest moments, I never had any doubts about that.

And Bill? Bill had created a monster. Though he was mostly present for our daily recording sessions, music had very much taken a back seat for him. Now, he wanted only to party. To look at Bill was to believe that the Môtley Crüe biography was his bible, a pre-rehab Anthony Kiedis his god. While I would meticulously tweak each of our songs, either in the studio with the producer, or on my laptop back at Eagle's Nest, Bill was somewhere else entirely, a pub, a club, our front room, with a new group of friends, faces I only ever vaguely recognized and had little desire to get to know. These people were a distraction, and I didn't need distraction. I'd come home in the dead of night after a long day's recording to find him prostrate on the sofa, sitting alongside dodgy-looking guys in hoodies and girls too beautiful for a scene like this, all of them monged out, fighting, arguing, laughing, and playing music constantly. Whenever I had to step over them in order to get into the kitchen, I experienced a deep and profound hatred for them all, and an increasing alienation from the man who was clearly their leader. Bill would watch me passively from the sofa, his body sunk so low into it it looked as if the cushions were giving birth to him. He always wore a crumpled smile of unearned self-satisfaction, but the light in his eye was out. I had no idea who he was any more, or quite what he wanted. It was as if we had fast-forwarded in our career to a point at which, after all the millions of sales and all the adulation of a fawning world, we had grown old and disillusioned, desperate to recapture the spirit of that initial naivety but with no firm idea of how to do so.

Off the road, and occasionally on it, I had become really close with Rob Bayley, who was one of Greg's best friends. I had lived a few miles from him in Montclair as a child but it wasn't until Greg joined the band that we became the closest of friends. Our relationship grew in a similar fashion to that in which mine and Bill's had in Dundee. And, just as Bill and I had Porcupine, Rob and I had Jack Daniel's and the Crobar. On any given night of the week, you could find us in the Crobar drowning hundreds of pounds at a time, comfortable enough in each other's company just to talk the whole night away. It was good just to talk. I had no idea that my friendship with Rob would cause problems with Greg, and therefore add to tension in the band.

It was Rob who pretty much saved me from myself. Because Eagle's Nest had become some kind of caricatured den of iniquity, populated by lowlife scum on the make, whenever I did encounter Bill alone, we'd argue. If either of us were in the mood, we'd fist fight. It settled nothing. And so Rob, along with my cousins Warren and Byron, took it upon themselves to help us bond all over again, keen that we didn't piss such an incredible opportunity up the wall at this late a stage, when, they insisted, we were still so close to making real the stuff of dreams. One Saturday lunchtime, they herded all the stragglers up and out of the house, cuffing them on the back of the head, kicking them up the arse, slamming the front door behind them. They ordered Bill into the shower, and me to switch off my laptop; they suggested a night out on the town, a night that was intended to wipe the slate clean, to clear the air. I should have known it would end in blood.

We went into town on a wave of sudden enthusiasm, Bill and I somehow reborn in one another's company, friends again, if only temporarily. En route we plundered our bank accounts of what was left of the Sony advance, and began a marathon bar hop that stretched from early afternoon until well into the night. We took them to all the best places, where all the future foot-ballers' wives drank, and everywhere we went women flocked to us, often without any kind of visible preamble.

'Like flies to shit,' Bill winked.

By mid-evening, we were deep in Soho, surrounded by new friends and flanked by flashing neon signs. It was now time to penetrate the velvet rope, something me and Bill could do with the finesse of bomb-disposal experts. The music-industry guest list is a much-fabled thing. If you are of a certain age or deport-ment, then you want nothing more than to have a plus one on this artist's guest list, or that record company's after show. There is no ignominy on earth worse than the legendary *Your name's not down, you're not coming in*. Despite Del's Herculean efforts to get us on every guest list for any media event that mattered, we preferred to target those to which we weren't invited. Gatecrashing was *so* much more fun, and to us it was easy. If we could scam a record company out of a six-figure advance, then we could sure as hell blag our way into a party at which we knew no one and where our presence was very likely not desired. The process of actually *getting in* thrilled us. It meant getting past a meathead on the door, usually a man with more brawn than brain, simply by exercising our charm. In this game, a winning smile, coupled with a supernatural conviction, can take you far. So we'd descend on these meatheads, dropping the names of high-ranking record-company folk, TV-production types or fellow pop stars. We'd pretend to be other people whose names were sure to be down, or else we'd simply employ the charm, laughing and joking with them until a smile spread across their faces like butter on toast and they'd stand helplessly aside. *We were in*.

First up on this particular night, we blagged our way into an MTV party. The cocktails were free, and came served with multicoloured umbrellas. Within minutes we were spotted by several VJs who recognized us from that initial *TRL* appearance, and we were swiftly spirited to a cordoned-off area. Here were congregated the most beautiful girls they'd ever seen, and some of the most underdressed. These were the kind of girls you vaguely recognized from television but couldn't quite put a name to. Names, we explained to my cousins, rarely mattered. Very quickly we endeared ourselves to a whole bunch of them, making sure everyone had a fresh cocktail in their hand, and then we kept them giggling with our patter, our routine. They were putty.

'Do I recognize you?' one asked Bill, a hand on his shoulder.

'You will,' he replied.

The cocktails kept on coming, lurid sweet drinks coloured blue and green and pink, not the kind of drink any self-respecting Scot would ever be seen dead with, but since when had we been self-respecting Scots? We got joyfully drunk on them.

Had Warren and Byron had their way, the girls we'd picked up here would have come straight back home with us to Eagle's Nest, but the night was still young and so we cast them aside, threw them back into the pond for others to fish. We had other places to go. Our group was now ten and making our way through the crowded streets was becoming impossible. We decided to split up and took Rob, Warren and Byron to see the studio we were rehearsing in. This was state-of-the-art stuff, where genius happened. I knew they'd be impressed. Gaining entry here was no problem. By now we were firm friends with the Ghanaian security guard, who always claimed loudly to be one of our biggest fans while, I'm sure, never having heard a single note of any of our music. He greeted us like returning heroes tonight, and waved us down into the basement with his boisterous bonhomie. Rob was appropriately awed by the studio, *our* studio, and spent a good half hour pressing buttons and playing with faders. We then took the lifts up to the A&R department, still fully lit but eerily empty, and we ransacked the cupboards of many of their promotional CDs. We rearranged desks and left rude drawings of penises on notepads and if our Ghanaian friend was in any way suspicious of just what it was we were carrying in our Sony-branded plastic carrier bags, then he said nothing. He simply remained behind his desk, his eyes trained on the all-night poker channel on TV while he waved us out.

From there, it was back into Soho and some more of our favourite bars. Intrepid Fox, Garlic & Shots, Borderline and inevitably Crobar, where we were reunited with Colin, Greg, Gordon and the rest of our motley crew. We lined up shots across the entire length of London's loudest establishment and went at them. It was an expensive way to cut the numbers down but it worked. We left whoever couldn't walk in the corner of the Crobar, half conscious, to wake up being molested by some kinky black-hot temptress if they were lucky, and hailed cabs to take us to Tufnell Park where this night was to come to a bloody end.

We ended up in the Dome, a heavy-metal nightclub where everyone was tattooed from head to toe and dressed in black. At first we took no notice of the fact that we stood out like a handful of sore thumbs and continued our binge drinking. Until Bill, of course, decided that a night out without a fight was an unsuccessful and altogether boring prospect. Our group of about six were hovering near the bar when all of a sudden a ruckus broke out on the opposite side of the club. It was Bill and Colin, and they seemed to be fighting, well, everyone. Apparently Bill had flicked a shot glass at a guy who turned out to be one of the club's bouncers, celebrating his birthday on his night off. Big mistake. Suddenly, the whole club was at it, a mass brawl. The security guards began a stampede. We rushed over to find Bill being stamped and Colin taking punches from everywhere but just managing to hold his own. We got Bill back to his feet and found ourselves cornered and taking a lot of punishment. I was punched by three or four fists before I even felt mine connect. Bill spat what looked like a pint of blood from his mouth, let out one hell of a roar and went straight for the biggest bouncer he could find.

It quickly spilt out into the streets. I saw one guy punched to the kerb, convulsing with what looked like an epileptic fit, saliva foaming at his mouth. From a distance came the encroaching blare of a police siren. People began to run. That's when I was pushed from behind, and my feet were lifted up out from under me. My head cracked on the pavement, hard, and everything went black. Moments later, Rob was leaning over me, slapping me awake, screaming at me to open my eyes. The sirens were louder now, almost upon us. Rob managed to wrap his shirt around my head and make sure an ambulance was on its way. I could tell how bad it was by looking at him, he was covered in blood, my blood, so much of it, litres of it in fact, running down the concrete like piss. Everyone was still running, legs everywhere. I felt drunk and light-headed. I could taste the blood in my mouth, and could hear Bill's warrior cry, a sound I could pick out anywhere. Everything went black again, this time for longer, much longer.

At least it's a different hospital.

That's the first thing that came to mind when I woke the following morning. A nurse was leaning over me, plumping up my pillow, which had gone flat overnight. Her face loomed into my vision as she sat me up and gave me a cup of lukewarm water to drink through a straw. It was this nurse who told me, with a pinched expression, that I had received thirty-six stitches to my head. I was lucky, she said. It could have been worse. A sudden sense of déjà vu: every time I ended up in hospital I was proclaimed *lucky*. Surely I had been anything but? I raised my hand gingerly to my head and felt the padding of a bandage. It was soft and spongy. I couldn't wait to see what I looked like in the mirror. Frankenstein's monster? I reached across my bedside table, where one of my cracked mobile phones sat. I asked the nurse to take a photograph of me, making sure to get all the bandage in. The wounded-soldier look suited me. Bill, I knew, would *love* it.

I was almost sorry to see it go, a week later, when I returned to the hospital to have it unwrapped. As another nurse slowly unwound it, the first thing I felt was the air on the side of my head, still freshly shorn and boasting its Action Man scar. I brought my fingers up to touch the stiff, thick stitches arcing on the right side of my head, just above my ear. I asked for a mirror and surveyed my new, uneven hairstyle, long on top, shaved on just one side. The scar looked brutal, crusty with dried blood, the stitches themselves long, brittle and insect-like. It looked good, but the hairstyle didn't work at all. I resolved to even it out once home, to give myself a mohican. This would perfectly suit someone who called himself Brains, I thought.

Bill was deeply impressed by the scar, so much so that he wanted one himself.

'You're going to make quite an impression tomorrow night,' he said.

Tomorrow night was the 2005 Brit Awards, and the fact that we hadn't been invited wasn't about to stop us. We spent a small fortune on new clothes in preparation, and turned up on the night radiating confidence, celebrity swagger and my fantastic new scar. As we approached the VIP entrance, we had ourselves a little bet. Bill was convinced we'd be in within three minutes. I, erring on the side of caution, plumped for ten. In truth, however, this was going to be our biggest challenge yet. Earls Court was swarming with security, wannabes and very genuine VIPs. There was a distinct chance we'd end up watching the ceremony from the pub next door.

'I'll do the talking,' said Bill.

Halfway up the steps to the entrance, he developed an undeniable *mince* to his walk. We joined the long, snaking queue, and smiled at those in front of us and those behind. Bill placed one hand on his hip. Somebody watched him, amused. 'I'm a little teapot,' he grinned. Pointing at me, he added: 'And he's short and stout. Want to see my handle?' I had no idea what he was doing. Silibil N' Brains had never previously employed a camp side, but whatever he was trying to pull off here he was doing so with aplomb. Soon we were chatting to everyone as if they were dear and cherished friends, Bill insisting on ramping up the unexplained femininity while I did my best to follow suit, despite looking like someone so recently stamped upon. The queue shuffled forward, and presently we were standing before a tall woman who was wearing full evening dress and holding a clipboard. Across her cheek was taped a flesh-coloured microphone, the earpiece for which was sunk deep into her ear. Both were wired to a small box that sat in a discreet belt on her hip. Bill cleared his throat.

'Darling, you look divine.'

To fully appreciate many incidents in life you need to have been there; a written account of what really occurred just doesn't look entirely plausible. But believe me when I say that Bill was superlative that night, ridiculously theatrical but somehow believable with it. Charming, even. He told the woman with the clipboard that we were Jamelia's hairdressers. Jamelia was one of the nominees, and, he said, she had arrived just moments before and scooted on inside (he made rapid walking movements with his index and middle fingers for this) without us while we were overseeing the parking of the car. 'Check the list and you'll see,' he said. She did, and nodded. He explained that we were needed backstage now, *pronto*, our scissors, our tongs, our styling gels being already in her backstage dressing room awaiting us. 'You wouldn't expect us to bring such dangerous equipment through your metal detector, would you? In this day and age?' He smiled and flirted, and the girl with the clipboard was helpless in amused admiration. He mentioned Jamelia again, the mood she would so quickly fly into should we not materialize before her *imminently*, and mentioned also the phalanx of record-company people who would sack us on the spot if we weren't permitted entry to do what we simply had to do. The woman with the clipboard pressed a button on her hip box. A moment later, she was talking into her microphone. I watched her glance intermittently, but always smilingly, at Bill. Soon we were given laminates and wristbands and ushered through – all in under three minutes. Bill, the victor of our bet, strode forward, I minced behind, and now here we were, in the main auditorium, which was dark and noisy and thrumming with celebrity activity. People were taking their seats, and we milled casually in the middle aisle, watching like hawks. We found a pair of seats halfway down that were currently free. We claimed them, resolving to move the moment somebody challenged us. Nobody did.

That night, we cheered the losers and booed the winners with as much volume as we could muster, and we cracked so many loud jokes about the proceedings that those around us couldn't help but laugh, even the ones who secretly wished we'd just shut up. Bill, no longer the camp hairdresser, introduced himself to everyone in his immediate vicinity.

'Remember the name,' he boasted. 'It'll be us up there next year.'

Afterwards, as people filed into the lobby area, we caught sight of one of our A&R team, the bovine guy we'd first met on the day we signed. He powered over to us.

'Guys! I, um . . . I didn't know you were coming.'

I beamed back at him. 'Wouldn't miss this for the world, Dirk.'

'Dave.'

'That's what I said. Wouldn't miss this for the world, Dirk. Now, are you going to get us some drinks?'

I pointed over to the bar, which was at least six deep.

'Of course, of course. What would you like?'

'The occasion rather calls for champagne, wouldn't you say?' I said in a mock English accent.

Bill leant in. 'A bottle.'

'What happened to your head?' he asked me.

'War wound, Dirk. War wound.'

He scurried off.

The bottle didn't last long, and Dirk, who had now been joined by several other Sony types, our very own Ruth among them, explained that everyone was going on to separate after-show parties. Were we going to the Sony one, they wondered. Try stopping us, we responded.

'But have you got tickets?' said Ruth, hesitantly.

Bill bundled her up into a loving embrace. 'Ruth, baby. Why do we need tickets? We have *you*, our very own entry to parties, to heaven and beyond.'

Ruth blushed, and exchanged an awkward glance with Dirk that only I caught. We all made our way outside to awaiting cars, while I recounted my recent night in hospital to them. Out front there was chaos, hundreds of overeager, overdressed record-company employees desperate to make their getaway and start the party proper. We mingled deep within the heaving throng, Bill all eyes, me all ears. I overheard someone talk about a Madonna party. *Madonna*. Why would anyone want to attend a Sony party when there was a Madonna party to go to instead? I grabbed Bill, waved goodbye to a clearly confused Ruth, and began to ingratiate the two of us with some of the Warner team, each of them Madonna-bound. We charmed them effortlessly (I peeled back the plaster to reveal my scar, then let them touch it), and it was only as their people carrier pulled away from the crowd that they seemed to realize that not only were we in their car with them but also we now fully expected to be permitted entry into the party alongside them. The force of our smiles and the exaggerated nature of our American friendliness meant that they couldn't possibly disappoint us. And the fact that Bill had from somewhere managed to get his hands on another bottle of champagne, unopened but ready to pop at any moment, meant that they were now even more predisposed to our wishes. *Easy*.

From the outside you wouldn't have known it was a party for the world's biggest pop star. But that, presumably, was the point. There was plenty of rigmarole involved in getting us past the bouncers, but we were with executives here, and so we soon found ourselves in, down the stairs, past the hat-check girl and into the velvet-lined club. Drinks were served on silver trays by gorgeous waitresses. All the cocktails had olives in them. The music was oppressively loud, a dull, heavy throb that made your diaphragm bounce and your gums itch. We shouted pleasantries to everyone who caught our eye, and my mohican had a lot of people looking our way. When a waitress squeezed past bearing a bottle of Krug for somebody more important than us, Bill swiped it and sent her away with a dismissive wave of the hand. We were drunk in *seconds*.

You can always tell when someone properly famous has walked into the room. The atmosphere changes instinctively, as if the temperature has dropped a degree or two. Dust motes appear to slow down, and conversation falls away as everybody cranes their necks for a better look at whatever it is that everybody else is gawping at. I felt this in the dressing room at Brixton Academy when I suddenly became aware of Eminem's presence, and I felt it now as Madonna walked into the room. She was wearing a little black dress out of which her bare arms and legs seemed unaccountably porcelain. Even from across a crowded room you were aware of her musculature, her *power*. She was radiant, beautiful. I turned to Bill and watched as he unconsciously squeezed his crotch. He downed his glass of champagne in one gulp and strode towards her. She was angelic up close, more handsome than beautiful, more masculine than feminine, and she looked as if she knew how to use whips and handcuffs, and to have you begging for more. A halo danced a few inches above her bottle-blonde hair, or at least that's how it appeared. It was like watching a ghost materialize before you. The hairs on the back of my neck stood to attention.

Madonna's bodyguards were in a different class to that of other pop stars. They were like CIA, FBI, men in black: tall, chiselled and strong, dressed impeccably, silent but ominous. I glanced automatically to their waists to see if I could make out the outlines of partly concealed guns. They looked like they could dispatch us with the flick of a wrist and the bare minimum of effort.

Which was why I was so terrified as Bill made his drunken beeline towards her. He was going to get shot, no question. Although his back was to me as I hurried to keep up, I could feel the force of his introductory smile make its way to her. By the time only a few feet were separating them, his arms were already open wide in anticipation. Abruptly, he went for his pocket. My mind reeled: the men in black would think he was going for his gun, and so they would go for theirs. Everything inside me tightened, and I called out for my friend but my words were drowned out by the music. Bill now had his mobile phone out of his pocket, and he was taking a picture of her. I was by his side in seconds, but he didn't register me at all. We were in front of Madonna now, and he was talking to her: 'Well, well, if it isn't Madonna, or can I call you Madge like all the Brits do? Ha ha, no but seriously. What an absolute pleasure it is.' He extended a hand in greeting. 'I'm Bill, Billy Boyd, but you probably know me better by my professional name, Silibil, of Silibil N' Brains. The pleasure's all mine.'

Madonna's curious smile was all the encouragement he needed. He now turned to stand right alongside her. One hand he casually draped across her shoulder, while his other held out his mobile phone to take a photograph of them together.

'Say cheese.'

To my considerable surprise, and no little relief, Madonna smiled, the most famous woman in the world grinning helplessly next to my oldest friend. Our most surreal moment yet, surely. Bill introduced me. She winced as she took in my scar, but said a polite hello. For a minute, possibly two, we made the smallest of small talk. Yes, she said, she thought that she had perhaps heard of us, good things too. She recommended a pub in Mayfair for good British beer, her local, and we told her we'd definitely stop by as long as she promised to stand us a round. This she unhesitatingly did. It meant nothing to her, and everything to us. The men in black ushered us back then, and she moved on. We fell back, happy and dazed. The people we'd arrived with, whose names I never did learn, looked on at us with new admiration.

Nothing could touch us.

Nine

But then it all began to unravel.

First up, 'Losers' was no longer going to be our debut single. Sony had changed their minds *again*. It was now 'Play with Myself' (no, but really, *definitely* this time . . .), the label having convinced themselves, despite earlier concerns, that the controversial lyrics could now only work in our favour. Parental-advisory stickers were all the rage, we were told. Hadn't we heard? Mysteriously, however, we'd now missed another release-date slot: the endless perils of scheduling. This meant that we had performed on MTV's *Brand Spanking New*, appeared on *TRL* and MTV *Hits* interviews, toured with D12, headlined three university tours, made festival appearances, had national radio play, done a bucket-load of press and delivered Sony not one but two albums, and they hadn't managed to capitalize on any of it. This didn't go down well with any of us. Shalit was out of his mind, constantly furious and spluttering into telephones, exploding in capital-lettered emails. The man was always shouting now, furious about how long everything was taking and just how protracted it had all become. His stomach ulcer must have been twice the size of mine. Our advance, meanwhile, was fast running out, the bulk of it having gone on day-to-day expenses, new studio equipment, on booze and girls. The tighter things got, the more generous our manager became, continuing to bankroll us – and our three other members. He helped out with rent (we needed to live), with gym memberships (we needed to look good), and bar bills (all humans need watering). But he was tiring of it. He'd covered virtually all our expenses for months now; he was due at least some kind of return, and the only way that would happen was if we started selling records. Since the tour, we had ceased making any money whatsoever, which meant that Greg, Colin and Gordon were seeing no financial return at all. They'd been living off us, which was fine when we were able to cover for them, but we were no longer solvent enough for that. Colin was talking about getting a day job. Greg and Gordon were threatening to take their session skills elsewhere. I told them repeatedly I would sort it out, to be patient. But patience was running out.

Meanwhile, it felt as though our cover was almost continually on the brink of being blown – if not by ourselves via a careless quip, a word spoken out of turn, *out of accent*, then via a bizarrely comedic moment when, in a city of six million, we'd bump into someone from back home. What are the chances? Well, mathematically speaking, one in six million. But it happened. To me.

We went to a birthday drinks party for one of Shalit's workforce one night, and the West End venue was crammed with record-industry types. Bill and I were in our element, with people queuing up to buy us drinks and watch us drink them down in one. I came up from one long swallow of a hideously colourful cocktail, my vision swimming, and I saw, or thought I saw, of all people Catherine Perkins. Surely not? Catherine Perkins had been a girlfriend of mine back in Dundee. I closed my eyes, and purple pinpricks swam beneath my lids like tiny fireworks. I opened them again, but she was still standing there, Catherine Perkins, ten, fifteen feet away, perhaps a dozen people in between us. She knew me as Gavin Bain, of course. If she found out I was now Brains, and American, then this could be bad, very bad. I could count on the discretion of close friends, but Catherine Perkins, someone I hadn't seen in years?

I thrust my empty cocktail glass into the nearest hand, then hit the deck and crawled across the dirty wet floor through a nest of legs to the men's room, where I sat in a locked cubicle convinced that at that very moment, outside, Catherine Perkins had spotted Bill and that our game was up. I was shivering. Was it cold in here, or just me?

I spent half an hour in that cubicle, half an hour of smelling toilet bleach and unflushable unpleasantness. I felt sick. I texted Bill repeatedly, but received no reply. I couldn't take it any more. I crept out of the stall and opened the door to find that the party was still in full swing, no obvious controversy apparent. Everyone was drinking and laughing. I couldn't see Catherine Perkins. Neither could I see my purported sparring partner. Head down, I bundled my way out and into the dark street where I quickly melted into anonymity, and gulped down as much fresh air as I could.

Phew. Close one.

I became convinced that the record company's continued indecision meant that they were losing interest. There were too many new people at the company now, and most of our main supporters had left. Yes, the tour had gone brilliantly, better than anyone could have expected following our rebirth, but its success hadn't quite whipped them into the frenzy of re-motivated energy I had expected, or craved. We hadn't played live for several weeks now, and we were told that Sony's studio was fully booked for the foreseeable future. In other words, we were to stay away. If I wanted to add anything new to the songs now, I would have to do so alone, producer-less, on my laptop. This I did, but no one showed any interest in listening to the results. Ruth stalled us inexpertly, stuttering into a phone she clearly couldn't wait to put back down into its cradle. I whinged at Shalit endlessly to kick her arse a little harder, but Shalit was already doing all he could. I told him I was going out of my mind, that I couldn't drag myself out of bed in the morning, because what was the point? I was becoming depressed and depressive. Alison haunted my thoughts. I missed my mum, too.

Two days later, Del called. I was stewing in front of daytime TV, biting my nails, and he was full of his customary good cheer and puppy-dog excitement, as if he'd just won a tenner on a scratch-card or something. He explained that Sony had found us a last-minute gig at some out-of-town nightclub. It was nothing great, and it would never get reviewed, he admitted, but at least it would get us out there and playing again, and that was the important thing.

We were told to arrive not before nine o'clock in the evening, which meant that we wouldn't be getting a sound-check. That was the first bad omen of the night. There would be others. We were told a tour manager would not be dispatched for just this one show, and so we were to make our own way there. Shalit would pay for the hire of the van, which Colin could collect. We arrived some time before ten. The club, located in a drab commuter-belt town an hour from London, was tiny. Outside, posters advertised forthcoming events for acts I'd never heard of, all of them Indian. The doormen who initially refused us entry were also Indian. Eventually, one of the management team arrived, a dapper thirtysomething dressed in a silk suit, with a turban on his head. He looked at us as if we were a bunch of neo-Nazis, then shook his head, shouted at someone sat innocently behind a little box-office window, and reluctantly led us to the smallest dressing room we'd yet been in. There was no rider. The five of us sat bemused among our instruments, wondering quite what to do. We had three hours, we had been told, until we were on. Management said that we had a thirty-minute set but added, looking us up and down, that we'd 'be lucky to make it past fifteen'. The club opened, and we listened as it filled up. The music sounded to me like the soundtrack of a Bollywood movie. I went to find the manager.

'What kind of club is this?' I asked.

'Bhangra, of course. What did you expect?'

'You do know we're a punk-rock act, don't you?'

His eyes travelled the length of my body before settling on my face, his gaze derisory. 'I do now. Good luck.'

One o'clock in the morning took an age to arrive, by which time we were bored and bad-tempered, and thoroughly un-drunk as we'd been told alcohol was banned backstage. Eventually somebody came to fetch us. He too greeted us as if we were a bad joke, a prank booking made by some fool at our expense. From somewhere we tried to conjure up a little enthusiasm. We failed. The crowd, exclusively Indian, stared back at us in silence as we filed on to stage and plugged in.

'Let's have some motherfucking noise!' Bill roared into the microphone. Nothing, not a sound.

'Losers' went down like a lead balloon. 'Play with Myself' fared even worse. By the time we reached 'Cunt', the crowd was openly booing and throwing bottles. Somebody pulled the plug quickly, and the sound died. The manager had been right. We didn't make it past fifteen minutes.

Back in the dressing room, I called Shalit. I woke him up, of course, it being the middle of the night by now. I heard him fumble for his glasses on the night stand and switch on the lamp before he came properly to the phone.

'You'd better have a good reason for this,' he growled.

I let loose, swearing and screaming about the worst show of our lives, about fucking Sony, and just what the fuck were they playing at? Did they have any fucking clue, etc., etc. I must have ranted for a good quarter of an hour, bouncing off the walls while my bandmates goaded me on and watched me turn blue. Shalit listened patiently and then, to my relief, sounded just as apoplectic. He was going to get answers, he promised. First thing in the morning, he would force an emergency meeting with the record company. If those idiots didn't realize what they had in us, the breadth of our talent, the scope of our potential, then he would just have to take Silibil N' Brains elsewhere. They'd fucked with him, with us all, too much now and for too long. Enough already. Tomorrow would be D-Day.

I hung up feeling immeasurably better.

The following lunchtime, an emergency meeting did indeed take place. Shalit was a bull in a china shop, shouting and pointing an accusatory finger at Ruth and a variety of her seniors, of whom I recognized only one, Paul Ellis, the executive who had proffered the pen on the day we signed. This surprised me; I thought he had long gone from the company. Our manager conveyed just how disappointed, how bitterly disappointed, we all were by the lack of progress. We had fulfilled our requirements, we had recorded the album not once but twice, and it was ready, ready to go. And what were Sony doing? Prevaricating, procrastinating, stalling, having a fucking wobble; whatever, it wasn't good enough. Shalit brought a clenched fist down on the table in front of him and sent four Sony-management mobile telephones jumping several inches into the air. Ruth looked at us, distraught and sorrowful. Bill stared back at her blankly. Shalit suggested to everyone that he was now ready to get us out of the contract, whatever it took. Counter offers, he told them, had already been made for us. (If this was true, it was news to me. If it was a bluff, it was brilliant.)

'Guys, guys,' said Paul, employing the fake smile of all record-company types; the smile I now knew so well. 'Don't get us wrong here. We still have every faith in you, every absolute faith. You are a phenomenal act. You know that, and we know that. Trouble is, you've confused quite a few people here. One day you are straight-ahead hip-hop, the next punk. You're a duo, you're a five-piece. We remix your songs – *brilliantly*, I might add, and expensively – and you throw a fit.' He paused for breath before continuing. 'Now, as you know, there have been some changes here these past few months, and so we've had to run you by a whole new team, but let me assure you once again that we are all on the same page right now. We think you have the potential to do brilliantly, and we really do want to push forward, and to get back that first spark we all felt when you first signed with us.' Shalit tried to interject here, but Paul didn't let him. 'You guys want to release singles full of objectionable themes and swear-words, while we want you to have daytime radio play and hit singles. We need to find a middle ground, cool?'

To my barely contained fury, I watched Shalit shake his head yes.

'But we were full of objectionable themes and swearwords when you signed us,' I pointed out.

'Yes, true, that's all very well, but at the end of the day, this is a business, and good business sense tells us that we will not have a hit with "Play with Myself".'

'But you were the ones who wanted "Play with Myself" over "Losers" . . .'

He smiled here, and I had no idea why. 'Ah. Not any more. We had a meeting, took an executive decision. We are thinking now of the original remix of "Losers".' He held a hand up to silence us. 'Seriously, guys. It's a hit single waiting to happen. It'll be huge on the dance-floor, *huge.*'

Bill leant back in his chair and put his feet on the table. All eyes swivelled towards him. He told them about the latest song we had been working on, which he proclaimed our best and certainly most commercial to date.

'It's called "Spaz Out",' he said.

'"*Spaz Out*"?'

'Yes, "spaz" – short for spastic.'

Shalit glowered. 'Guys,' he told us, his eyes beady, 'could you just wait for me downstairs? I'll handle things from here.'

We spent the next quarter hour waiting on the pavement outside before it hit us: what the hell were we doing? 'Fuck this,' said Bill, and stalked off to the nearest pub.

We were still there at nine o'clock that evening, now joined by the rest of the band. The mood was gloomy, our own meeting having dragged on interminably over the past several hours, and made no easier by the constant supply of beer, which polarized our melancholy. Colin, Greg and Gordon weren't happy. They felt increasingly disillusioned. Convinced that we were taking advantage of them. At one point Colin told us to fuck off back to

California. Greg calmed him down. But then Bill upset him, and Greg stormed out. I checked my phone. Eleven missed calls from Shalit. I was in no mood to talk to him or anyone else until we had reached some kind of conclusion, a happy ending. Greg came back, sheepish and apologetic. We group hugged, and got another round in, convinced we were still the best band in the world. Everybody else just had to realize it, that's all.

By ten o'clock we had regained some lost momentum, and were back at Sony's HQ, talking our way past the building's night-watchman and getting back in the studio, our home from home. It was empty except for the five of us. Creativity was humming right through us, mixing with the beer fumes and creating a heady atmosphere. It was suddenly clear just what we had to do next. We had had enough of 'Losers', 'Play with Myself', with 'Cunt' and even the brand-new 'Spaz Out'. All of them had been tainted now by the indecision of Sony. We needed to do something new, something fresh, something that would mobilize the troops. And so we did what perhaps any act would do in our position, when their backs were against the wall and they were in fear of losing everything. We recorded a punk-rock version of 'Footloose', Kenny Loggins' 1984 pop classic. We nailed it in one take, and trust me when I say that it absolutely fucking rocked. Put simply, 'Footloose' had never really existed before we came along to breathe drunken life into it. Colin nipped out to the off-licence for more booze. This was something worth toasting, our first sure-fire future Number 1 single, and with no swearwords, zero obscenity. Just wait till Shalit heard it. Sony would rejoice. We played the song back time and again, and turned the sound up loud. The soundproofed walls vibrated with it. Greg called me his saviour. Then Bill, steaming drunk, said something. I barely even heard what it was, really, but somehow I knew it to be negative, a slight on my personality, and just like that the entire mood in the studio had changed from positive to negative, from day to night. I looked over at him, ignorant as to what had suddenly got his goat, and loathed the smug, self-righteous expression on his face. I went for him. We were rolling around the studio floor now, fists flying, Colin and Gordon trying to pull us apart.

'Come on, guys, this is no way to end a memorable evening,' Greg implored.

But I'd hurt Bill. He staggered out of the studio and up the stairs without a further word. I didn't see him again for three days.

When you first meet him, it is difficult not to fall for Billy Boyd in some or other fashion. The man is a charmer but arrogant with it, the best fun of anyone in any room you could hope to stagger into. He was everybody's best friend, and in the time we'd spent in London he had gotten to know so many people that the address books on his mobile phones were full. People were always calling him and leaving messages, girls and guys, pop stars, actors and models, each of them remembering a legendary night out, Bill the life and soul of the party. They wanted another one soon; when was he free? Half of London, it seemed, had a story about Silibil, the more apocryphal the better, though all of them had at least some basis in truth, simply because that was the way it was with Bill. The more outlandish, the more exaggerated the tall tale, the more likely it was to be true. In Bill's company, things *happened*, the world came alive. Trouble was, he was also the most combustible force I had ever come across and could go off at any time. He frequently did. The last twelve months in London may well have brought him countless friends, but he'd also notched up

214

as many enemies here as he had during his shagging days in Arbroath. He had lost focus on the band.

Of course, he could have accused me of comparable crimes, but I didn't care what he thought. Couldn't afford to. I had enough voices in my head busy shouting me down at any opportunity and making me more neurotic still. I had no intention of letting him add to that. There was no way I could continue Silibil N' Brains without him, of course, and yet keeping the band going with him in it was slowly killing me. I had always thought that the borrowed time we were living on was borne exclusively of the fact of our lie and our fear of it being exposed. But now I knew differently. It was borne of the fact that I could no longer cope with Bill being Bill. Something was about to give.

For the record, Shalit *loved* 'Footloose'. He had certain reservations, however, because strictly speaking new bands didn't come out with a cover version for their first single unless they were, and wished to remain, disposable, interchangeable, anonymous. But he was convinced that it had the potential to be a smash hit right across the Western world, if not with Sony then with any number of major-label record companies, all of whom, he insisted, would be clamouring for some of our action the moment he advertised our availability.

Meanwhile, the atmosphere at Eagle's Nest was becoming more poisonous by the day. We had failed to settle our fight, and instead were simply pretending that it had never happened in the first place. The paranoia Bill and I felt towards each other had rubbed off on Greg, who had grown suspicious that I was conspiring to end his friendship with Rob. When Bill finally showed his face back at the house, he settled himself on the living room sofa for days and nights on end, constantly receiving strange new friends and acquaintances, who would turn up at the door at all hours. Colin, Greg and Gordon no longer knew quite who to side with. If they joined Bill on the sofa, I'd sulk and silently rage. If they hung out with me instead, Bill would mock them for not knowing a good time when they saw one. Soon, none of us could have a conversation together without it descending into petty bickering, the house cancerously full of brooding and incipient hatred.

Some of which I turned on to the others. Colin and I agreed he should leave the band. He was tired of the arguing, and anyway he needed to return to his real band, PMX, as they had a European tour booked. Greg and Gordon rallied round at first, and even Bill realized that this was serious, but after another night of boozy recriminations, Greg's problems with me came flooding out and the following fight, which took place in our kitchen at the Eagle's Nest, pulled Rob innocently and unfairly into the middle of his two best friends. Rob decided wisely to walk away without choosing sides and Greg chose to leave the band. The rifts were deep and it would be two years before I would even see Rob again. Suddenly, we were down to three. Gordon was looking increasingly conspicuous by his continued presence now, but Gordon wasn't a quitter. Gordon hung around, and I'm grateful to him that he did. While he remained a part of our increasingly dysfunctional band, his presence at the Eagle's Nest was crucial in itself, because he effectively became a kind of referee, intervening in arguments between me and Bill and separating us when those arguments turned physical. Gordon was a peacemaker, constantly removing knives, sharp objects and anything that could be transformed into a makeshift weapon in the heat of an insane fight. If it hadn't been for

Gordon's many interventions, Bill or I might have ended up behind bars.

I had always suffered from anxiety, but this was something else. My whole body felt as if it was under attack from hives. I couldn't stop scratching. My heart beat out an irregular rhythm in my chest, always slightly too loud, painful against the ribs. I didn't sleep for days on end. I was downing too many pills, drinking too many spirits. My stomach ulcer was a forest fire, and I was in constant mourning: for Alison, for the band. I put off telling Shalit about our latest development because I couldn't face it, couldn't face him, this ultimately sweet man who had invested in us, unwisely as it had turned out. I could imagine him coming at me with an axe, his mouth open in a silent scream.

Whenever the house emptied of the latest batch of hangers on, I would attempt to have serious meetings with Bill over cups of black coffee. I wanted him to see the band for what it really was today: anorexic slim, on the verge of irrevocable disaster. Did he want that? But mostly he seemed to sleep through my requests until one morning, to my great surprise, he sat down in the kitchen, a steaming mug in his hands and said, 'I'm all ears.' He was looking bad, tired and drawn. He'd lost weight and was pale. Before I could even say anything to him, he started talking. He told me that he was sick of it all, the whole thing, and that he wanted to come clean. I told him no, no way, that we couldn't, we'd be sued by Sony, sued, ruined, bankrupt, a laughing stock. He was adamant. We were so good at turning every opportunity to our advantage, he argued, that we would be able to do so with this as well. Over the last year, nothing had stood in our way. Everything we had wanted – a recording contract, money, girls, drinks, entry to many parties, to so many parties – we'd got, so why would this be any different? We'd go in and make our confession, no more bullshit. Also, we'd be a more sellable product this way, the guys who had duped the entire British recording industry coming clean and cleaning up. Which record company did I know, he asked, that would turn away such a commercial proposition? Everyone would want to hear our story. They'd make a book of our lives, a film. People would marvel at our cheek, our cunning. We'd sell records, we'd sell out tours. Those TV-production companies would come back to us, begging. Madonna would recount the night Silibil N' Brains convinced her they really were Americans. Eminem, furious at having been taken for a ride, would issue a fatwa, Proof too. *Come on*, he urged, *let's do it*. I had to concede that, though I'd thought all this through myself, many times, Bill was able to make it sound eminently more appealing. How could we fail? *It's you and me,* Bill said. *We* never *fail*.

OK, I said. *OK*. I looked at my hands. They were trembling.

But then we received some unexpected news. There had been another staff overhaul at the record company. Those few allies who had survived the most recent cull were now gone, history. The new regime, Shalit told me in the gravest phone call I'd had with him yet, were going through the existing roster one by one and getting rid of anything that didn't immediately appeal. In other words, we were on the brink of being dropped, game over.

'You'd better come in,' Shalit said, sounding unusually nervous. 'Crisis talks.'

There was something unnatural about his smile as he stepped out of his office to greet us. It was too wide, too forcibly bright, damage limitation disguised by a dazzle of enamel, gold caps and complicated bridge work. Suddenly I knew not to trust him any more, that everything he would say would come necessarily sugar-coated. These really were crisis talks, then.

'Tea? Digestive biscuit?'

He sat back in his executive leather chair at its customary tilt, and stretched his legs out before him. His trousers rode up his shins to reveal bright-yellow cashmere socks and, of all things, sock suspenders. His shoes were very likely alligator skin. He explained that the new main man at the record company was a guy called David Marcus. He knew David Marcus well. They'd done a TV show a few years back and had gotten along famously. The new MD, by Shalit's account, was *cool*.

'I've spoken to him already and don't worry: you're still a buzz act.'

Leaning forward now, he brought his hands together. His gaze bounced between us as if watching the back-and-forth rally of a tennis match.

'But look at you, look at the pair of you. *Oyyy*. I can under-stand you want to burn the candle at both ends but surely to Christ it's about time you got hold of yourselves – right, Del?' Del had sneaked into the office behind our backs, almost on tiptoe. He looked timid, but made an effort to high-five us enthusiasti-cally. Shalit continued. 'Billy, you look dreadful, wasted. You've lost weight. Are you eating? You're not on drugs, are you?' He turned to me. 'And Gavin? Gav, when was the last time you slept? Your eyes are on stalks. Seriously, my boys, if I saw you out on the street, I'd give you 50p for a cup of tea. You're supposed to be pop stars – *rap* stars.' He grabbed the remote control on his desk, and turned on the television, surfing through the music channels and clicking on to Usher, Kanye West, 50 Cent, each man buff and shiny, freshly exfoliated, the picture of radiant good health. 'Now *that's* what you want to look like.' He noted Bill's scowl, and immediately amended the sentiment. 'OK, OK, if not *exactly* like them then at least a close approximation of. Instead,' he said, growing flustered now, 'instead you look like ... Del, what do they look like?'

Del smiled, and wisely chose not to answer. Shalit continued.

'Now, I've arranged a meeting for you with David Marcus tomorrow at two. I won't be there myself – other commitments, I'm afraid – but Del'll accompany you. I don't want you to be late, and I don't want you to fuck about with him. None of your nonsense this time, boys, because this time it's serious.' He reached for the phone, his mind already leaping towards his next job of the day. As he dialled, he pointed the receiver at us. 'Oh, and if you must bring the rest of the band along, keep those lads of yours in line, understood?'

I exchanged a loaded look with Bill, as if to say, *Will you tell him or will I?* Shalit, picking up on it immediately, carefully replaced the phone. 'Tell me what?' he barked. 'What now?' I explained that there had been a development, that Colin and Greg had left the band. They hadn't walked, I told him, incapable at that moment of speaking the truth. No, we had kicked them out, and good riddance, too; Silibil N' Brains were reborn once more as a duo.

Jonathan Shalit's face went purple, the richest, fattest-of-in-season-blackberries purple. He swore at us then, a string of long, hollered expletives. When he finished, there were flecks of saliva all over his desk. He wiped them carelessly with the back of his shirt sleeve and let out a long sigh, like a tyre with a slow puncture. He picked up the phone, and resumed dialling. Then he dismissed us.

Sony/BMG was now located in a swanky part of West London, 4×4 territory, all miniature dogs and expensive handbags,

Botoxed women trailing children called Tristram and Tamara. Its entrance was sunk back from the main road and looked out towards the river, but once inside it was a familiar story: silver, gold and platinum discs on the walls, self-consciously dressed young guys in wasted Converse sneakers shuffling across carpets, and pretty young girls gliding through every department as if gliding was what they were primarily employed to do. Rubber plants sprouted from every corner, and there was always a work experience person who materialized out of nowhere to offer coffee, tea, sparkling water with a twist of lime.

We signed in, and headed for the lift. A man joined us, and leant forward to press the button we'd just that minute pressed ourselves – presumably in case we hadn't actually bothered to, as if calling for the lift were the very last thing that would ever have occurred to us to do. Why do people do that? He looked over, smiled curtly, then looked back down at his BlackBerry. At that moment, I had a sickening sense of déjà vu. His face was familiar, eerily so, a face from our recent past. I dared a glance over, and this second glance was all I needed. This was Robbie Bruce, from Sony A&R, the very first record-company guy ever to have contacted us, back when we were fresh off the bus from Dundee. I had a further flashback: us in his office, newly American and unsure of our accents, our back-story, *everything*, and convinced that he – a Scot – was on to us, and that our cover was blown. Already. And now here he was again. Christ. This was bad.

I glared at Bill, who slowly took in my terrified expression.

'What's up, dude? Seen a ghost?'

The lift arrived. I decided, there and then, that we would take the stairs instead, but Bill strode into it, leaving me helpless but to follow.

'Which floor?' he asked Robbie Bruce.

'Third, please.'

I watched Bill looking at Robbie Bruce more intently now, and watched, almost with satisfaction, as recognition began to dawn. His eyes bulged. Then I saw Robbie Bruce having a little recognition of his own. A succession of comedic double-takes took place. I audibly swallowed. *Any minute now . . .* I thought.

I could sense the words in his throat, our names on the tip of his tongue. He looked up once, then down. He frowned, then looked up again.

'Sorry, but do I know you two?' he said. 'You both look familiar.'

I opened my mouth, fully expecting Silibil to come tumbling out. But I was panicking, wildly, not thinking rationally. My heart was a tin can across my ribcage. I started speaking to him in *Australian*.

'No, mate? We just got in from Adelaide yesterday? We're here visiting friends?'

The dubious look he afforded me was the very same one he had given the both of us last year in his office. But he started nodding.

'Oh. OK. Sorry. But,' he added, now shaking his head, 'you both look *really* familiar.'

The third floor couldn't come quickly enough.

'G'day, mate?' I said as he stalked out.

The lift doors closed. I collapsed. Bill burst into laughter.

'*G'day mate?* Nice recovery, dude! But Australian? Where the hell did that come from?'

I shrugged my shoulders. But, oh, the relief, the sweet merciful relief.

We were greeted in the hall by a minion, and instructed to wait in a small corner office, as small as a gerbil's cage.

'You know,' I said to Bill, resuming our recurring theme, 'this still could be the mother of all get-out clauses.' We had talked endlessly about finally coming clean and starting over as Scots, but we were still stalling for all sorts of reasons, many of them to do with fear and the likelihood of reprisal. There was no way we could bring ourselves to tell Shalit in his current mood, but if this David Marcus guy was as decent as he claimed, then perhaps *he* could tell Shalit on our behalf. This could be the day we finally revealed the full story of Silibil N' Brains, a day of belated reinvention. David Marcus would see the funny side. He'd promote us to the top of the newly merged company's to-do list, and make us overnight stars – at last.

But right now Bill was frowning. He began to shake his head. 'Actually, I've been thinking about that. You know what? I *like* being American. I sometimes think I'd like to be American for the rest of my life. I mean, think about it. Who the fuck wants to go through life being a Scot?'

Slowly, I lowered my head towards my hands, which were open and ready to catch it. I should have anticipated this, because this was how all our conversations went now. We always contradicted one another, as if addicted to confrontation, perhaps for the simple sake of it. One of us wanted to come clean, the other didn't; perennial indecision. And so we were stuck with our lie, the anvil around our necks.

I picked up a copy of *Music Week*, the industry bible, that was sitting on the coffee table in front of us, and started flicking through it. Browsing through the charts, I learnt some particularly painful news. Our *TRL* peers, Kasabian, Bloc Party, Natasha fucking Bedingfield, whose names seemed to haunt us now, were all proper established pop stars these days. One of them had already sold half a million albums. One had had two *NME* covers. The other was about to be launched in America, for fuck's sake. How I despised them all, each of them robbers of what was rightfully ours.

Twenty minutes later, I was browsing still. Where the hell was this David Marcus guy? Was it cool to keep your talent waiting? Bill paced the room, increasingly agitated. I called Del, but all I got was his voicemail. Eventually, he showed up, full of apologies and a sheen to him that suggested he'd been running. Bill started shouting.

'Dude, for fuck sake, what's fucking going on here? We've been here – what? – almost an hour now. You're late, and this new big-cheese cunt hasn't even the decency to turn up to a meeting *he* arranged? What's up with that?'

Del went to find out what the problem was. He came back a quarter of an hour later, now cradling three cups of coffee in his hands. 'Apparently he's in a meeting that overran. He sends his apologies. Another five minutes and he'll be here.'

'I've not even met him yet,' Bill said, 'and already I want to kill him.'

Eventually, a secretary came to fetch us, her smile in lieu of an apology. The room we had been waiting in was not David Marcus's office at all, merely a holding cell for undesirables. We crossed the floor, the rubber soles of our trainers sucking up all the static electricity in the place until we sparked, and were led to the man at last. He was on the phone. David Marcus's office was huge, with floor-to-ceiling windows that gave over to Putney Bridge and the million-pound apartments beyond. There were signed Alicia Keys picture discs on the wall, and a giant framed poster of John Lennon sitting before his white piano, an adoring Yoko Ono by his side. Marcus beckoned for us to sit down with an extended index finger, while he continued with his phone conversation. He was fortysomething and nonspecifically good-looking, all brow and jutting chin, dressed in pressed jeans and an expensive white linen shirt. The top two buttons were undone to reveal Tom Jones's chest hair. He wore a wedding band and, on his pinky, a fat signet ring probably left to him by a late father I liked to think he never fully bonded with. He was smiling, both at us and into the phone. A contented smugness radiated from his every pore like something nuclear.

By the time he located the good manners to bring his phone conversation to what seemed like its conclusion, I hated him too. This was not someone you confessed your sins to. There wasn't a trace of sympathy in his eyes, which were instead hard as jewels. He was simply a record-company executive, an automaton, a number-cruncher. If he had even a whiff that we were fucking with him in any way, he'd surely guillotine us from his books without compunction. And so I knew, there and then, that our fate was sealed: we would always be American. At least until Silibil N' Brains ceased to exist.

The phone hadn't yet quite left his hand. He was still winding the call up, lots of *yeah*s and *absolutely*s and *catch you later*s, but no firm *goodbye* as yet. Bill started crooning Christina Aguilera's 'Beautiful', and I joined in. Del cleared his throat nervously and said, 'Um, boys . . .?' Dutifully, we fell silent.

'Don't you just hate it when that happens?' was the first thing David Marcus said to us.

'What's that, dude?' Bill said. 'Being kept waiting an hour, an hour and a half?'

His smile thinned out and evaporated on his lips. 'Anyway.' His eyes searched for a piece of paper on his neatly organized desk. He lifted it and scoured it quickly, as if searching for our names. 'Silibil N' Brains, right? I've heard a lot about you guys, a lot.' He pulled open a drawer and brought out a sleeveless CD. He waved it at us. 'I've watched this,' he said.

'Porn?' Bill asked.

'No, no. Your EPK,' he said, referring to the electronic press kit we had filmed several months ago now, which contained all sorts of Silibil N' Brains footage: some of our concerts, but also of us generally goofing around – in hotel rooms, the back of tour vans, with girls backstage – and also a selection of filmed sketches for the TV show that never got commissioned. David Marcus looked at the disc, as if written on it were those lines he had to speak next. The pregnant pause stretched out like elastic.

'I'm . . . confused. What exactly were you trying to do here?'

'Dude,' I said, 'it's an EPK, you know?'

In the entire history of Silibil N' Brains, David Marcus was the only man to make me feel tongue-tied.

'Right . . . right.' He dropped the disc on to the desk, and focused somewhere just over my left shoulder. 'You signed to Sony – when? – almost a year ago now, but no release yet. I wonder why, exactly . . .'

Del opened his mouth to talk, then closed it again.

'You've changed a lot in that period, I understand? First hip-hop, then punk. Quite a stretch, no?' He picked up the disc again. 'But this . . . I still don't really know what you were trying to do with something like this. I mean, what does it tell us about you? That you're – what, exactly?'

Del spoke up now. He explained that it showcased our *multi-media* skills, that it showed we could be as funny and entertaining in a TV studio as we could in our music, and how many acts could you say that about today? Del talked with a stridency and passion about us, and I appreciated it, I really did. I still couldn't stop wishing Shalit were here in his place, though.

David Marcus nodded, but he appeared far from convinced. A little v had formed between his trimmed eyebrows. 'Thing is,' he said, 'I just don't think it's *believable*, you know?'

'What's not *believable*, exactly?' Bill sneered.

'I just don't think you make for particularly good actors. And this,' he was holding the disc now as if it were incriminating evidence, 'this just confuses the issue as to who – or what – exactly, the both of you are.'

My blood was beginning to boil. I had a brief vision, almost like an outer-body experience. I pictured myself lunging over the table and wrapping the phone chord around David's neck, strangling him until his eyes bulged out of his skull and his nose exploded like a volcano, blood all over his records and framed pictures on the walls of his squeaky-clean office. Back in the real world, I could feel a tingling in my arms and legs, and also at my temples. I leant forward, beseeching. 'Look,' I began. 'This is a *music* meeting, right? If you don't like the TV stuff, the goofing-around stuff, fine, let's get rid of it, no problem. But let's just focus on the music here, shall we?'

As he offered up another insincere smile, he picked up another disc. It was our un-mastered album, the same album that had been knocking around Sony's offices for several months, but with a recently added bonus track, 'Footloose'. We had been told previously, by Shalit, that David Marcus had heard our music and had loved it, was as convinced as everyone else that we had the potential to become massive. But now I was wondering whether any of that was true.

'I see you have a song here called "Cunt". What's that all about, then?'

'It's a love song to George W. Bush, our president.'

'But "*Cunt*"? A bit harsh, wouldn't you say?'

'Wasn't Iraq?'

His eyes went back to the track list.

'And this,' he pointed. 'Presumably this isn't *the* "Footloose", is it?'

Bill said, 'No, of course not. You think we'd really do a fucking Kenny Loggins song? You serious? No, our "Footloose" is an anti-war protest song. It's about people who have lost body parts – feet, for example – in landmine explosions. You know, where your good Lady Diana led, we now follow. Think of it as our Rage Against the Machine moment.'

David Marcus looked confused, unsure whether or not to take us entirely seriously. We were Americans, after all, and you can never be sure with Americans and irony. The light was dimming in his eyes by the moment.

'OK, well, anyway.' He brought his hands together, as if in prayer. 'Obviously there have been a lot of changes around here these last few weeks, and there will doubtless be more to come – it's the way of the world, after all. But I want you both to know, and you, Del, that we remain committed to Silibil N' Brains, and that you remain very much a priority act on Sony/BMG – or, as I like to call it, BMG/Sony. Ha ha, I'm joking, of course. No, we have every faith in you becoming big sellers in the international market. It's a good record, this,' and he held up the disc I was by now convinced he had never played, and likely never would, 'though I'm not yet able to offer you a release date just yet, if only because we have a number of previous priority BMG acts already scheduled and ready to go. But that shouldn't be a major problem, because you are very much in my long-term picture. What we need to do right now, I feel, is to get you into the studio with a proper producer and knock things into shape, right?'

Again? 'But . . .' I began.

'Chief among my concerns,' he continued, 'is that we polarize exactly what Silibil N' Brains *is*, you know? Who will your core audience be, who we should be aiming at; that kind of thing. You've already cost this company a lot of money, so now we need to focus, focus, focus, streamline you into a marketable commodity, and then I'm sure we'll be ready.' He clapped his hands once. 'So, good. Thanks for coming.'

Bill stood quickly, as if to attention. He leant over the desk, and for a moment I was convinced he was about to deck the guy. But no. He offered his hand to shake instead. Insincerity lashed out of him. 'It's been a real pleasure, sir. I look forward to working with you.' And he saluted him.

In the lift on the way back down, Bill hatched a plan.

'I say we find the nearest hardware store, buy an axe, then go back and chop the motherfucker to pieces. Who's in?'

Del laughed, but this was uneasy laughter. Out on the street he hugged us warmly, then hailed a taxi and swiftly, perhaps a little too swiftly, disappeared into it. He didn't offer us a lift. We watched him go, now pitilessly alone and unprotected. I glanced over at Bill and was shocked by what I saw. He looked thoroughly defeated, his bubble burst. I thought for a moment he would cry. He did his best to recover.

'Fat lot of good you did us up there,' he said accusingly. 'I thought you were the brains of the outfit?'

I wanted to thump him, but I couldn't muster the energy. Though we didn't fully appreciate it just then, a tectonic shift had occurred between us. Because of forces now out of our control, we were in the process of being shunted further and further apart. Soon, we would lose sight of one another completely.

Bill took to his bed. He stopped going out altogether, and no longer answered his phone. He must have spent weeks in his room, until his bed reached a level of squalor Saatchi would have paid millions for. He refused to talk to me, would yell at me even when I opened his door just to see if he was OK, if he needed anything, some food, drink, a little company. If he ate at all during this time, I never saw him do so, but then I was deep into my own neuroses by this point. While he stewed in his room, I stewed in mine. Mere feet separated us, but we may as well have been in different universes. My own personal stresses were manifesting themselves in interesting ways that kept me more than occupied. The night terrors were vivid, of course, but various old pains came back at me now, sporting injuries I'd developed back in my teens re-manifesting themselves now out of stress. My legs hurt, my ankle, my lower back. I had a constant headache. My stomach burnt, my eyes felt raw. The doctor upped my medication until I was popping pills for my ulcer, my old foot-ball injury and all sorts of panic attacks. I had pills to help me relax, to slow down my galloping heart rate, and pills to pick me up again when I felt low and alone. I was always feeling low and alone. I was on sleeping pills, which I would swallow with cough syrup. I'd developed a taste for cough syrup. Combined, they made me calm, but they never quite brought me the uncon-sciousness I so craved. Instead, I spent night after night hunched over my laptop, messing with every track on the album until one beat became indistinguishable from the next, until I forgot which songs were which, until I took to hating everything I was hearing and everything I'd ever written. Shalit called intermittently, just to report on his progress with Sony (which was sounding like precious little progress at all, David Marcus still hunting for the appropriate producer), but his phone calls soon stopped. 'Don't let it all get you down,' was the last thing he said to me. 'This sort of thing happens all the time with record companies. We'll get back on track soon enough, trust me.' But did I trust anyone any more?

Early one Saturday morning, I dared to knock lightly on Bill's door. I'd not seen or heard anything from him for several days; and, though I knew he was never the sort to do anything stupid, Bill ultimately being too in love with life to ever consider extinguishing it, I nevertheless wanted to see for myself that he was still alive. I pushed open the door to be greeted by fetid black gloom, the stench as thick as porridge. I braced myself, anticipating a sudden holler for me to get the fuck out, but there came only silence. I switched on the light to carnage, the room ransacked as if recently burgled, clothes tossed here and there, a damp towel on the duvet, half-empty pizza cartons and a dizzying array of crushed beer cans. I could smell smoke, armpits, farts and feet. Picking my way carefully through the mess, I approached his bed and pulled back the covers. There were stains, and a long vertical rip in the bed sheet, but no Bill. I checked the bathroom, the kitchen. The living room. I called his mobile, and left a message. I went back upstairs, helped myself to the few remains in one of the more recent pizza boxes, and returned to my room. I sat on my bed, then stood up again. I walked over to the window, which looked down upon the garden, overgrown and overrun with weeds, vodka bottles and cigarette stubs. The pizza tasted awful. I swallowed it without chewing. I went back to the laptop, and worked some more because what else was I going to do? Presently, I fell asleep. A great many hours passed.

From downstairs, I heard the door slam shut. *Bill*. I shook my head awake, then made my way down to find him in the kitchen. He was wearing what looked like new clothes: new jeans, a clean T-shirt and bright-white trainers. He looked fit and healthy. He'd shaved, and had had a haircut. And he was smiling.

'Dude! Good to see you. You're looking dreadful, though!'

He gathered me up in a hug as I tried to work out what was out of place here. Something about him was different. I couldn't quite put my finger on *what*.

'I'm making tea. You want one?' he asked.

And suddenly it dawned. He was talking to me in a Scottish accent. I wasn't used to it. It sounded wrong.

He filled two cups with boiling water, and added the tea bags. I followed him into the living room. He told me to sit down. He had some good news. I filled with dread.

'Where have you been?'

'Back home. You should have come. I had a fantastic time. It's so much nicer up there than London.' His grin was almost religious in its zeal. 'Mary's pregnant.'

This took several moments to sink in.

'*What?*'

He laughed. 'Yep! And we're getting married.'

A million questions leapt into my mouth, but I couldn't find my voice. What, why, but . . . Mary was Bill's first true love, his on/off, endlessly long-suffering girlfriend who had chosen, wisely, not to follow him down to London chasing cockeyed dreams a year previously but instead to stay in Dundee, where she was studying to be a teacher. Mary was a beautiful girl in every way, and almost too tolerant of Bill. I'd thought they were history. Evidently not. Bill explained now that actually they had been seeing more of each other recently. This was news to me, but by this stage we were virtually leading separate lives. Anything he'd have told me would have been news.

'You're coming to the wedding, right?'

'But what – I mean . . . *when*?'

'Soon! The sooner the better!'

I reminded him that we had at least one more show booked before the end of the year, and that, now that it was only the two of us, we would have to prepare scrupulously for it. Our entire future depended on it. But Bill didn't seem to be listening. He was up and pacing the room, talking as if to himself.

'It'll be fine, fine. I'm getting married! I'm pretty stoked, man. Me, a married man! Fucking mental, eh?'

I wondered whether I'd imagined the previous few weeks, a depressed Bill adrift in bed, wailing all hours of the day and night and teetering, for all I knew, on the brink of suicide. I looked up at him, a complete stranger to me all over again.

'Bill, Bill. What are you doing? Seriously, what the fuck are you doing?'

He looked at me, genuinely perplexed.

'What do you mean, dude? Come on, don't spoil my buzz. Let's go out and celebrate.'

'I mean, Bill, *what about us*, Silibil N' Brains? You can't just go and get fucking married, for Christ's sake. I mean, where did this even come from? You've not mentioned Mary to me in months, in a *year*.'

'Gav, dude. It's happening. I'm going to be a *father*.'

'A father? You're a fucking animal. Take a fucking look at yourself, man. You're all over the place. You can't take care of yourself, how the fuck are you going to raise a kid?'

He turned on me now, aggressively. 'Me, I'm a mess? How many pills have *you* popped today, you fucking hypocrite.'

I pointed out that they were prescription pills.

'Stop kidding yourself, Gav. Everyone knows. You're coming apart.'

I hadn't yet touched my cup of tea. Now I threw it at him and, in a second, was on top of him. I beat him about the face with my fists before he even had time to protect himself. But then he flung his own teacup which clipped the side of my head, and while I was checking for blood he was up and kicking me in the face, shouting about my stitches, my fractured skull, that he was going to kick my stitches and open up my head all over again. But then he changed his mind and ran, to the hall, the front door. I pursued. The fight spilt out on to the street, on the pavement, on the small patches of dog-shit-strewn grass that surrounded the neighbourhood trees, still wet with last night's rain and heavy with mud. We rolled on the ground and into parked cars, and we fought until the both of us were sapped of everything we had left. My nose was bleeding. His eyes were pink, and already swelling to purple and grey. I looked at him and smiled, ready to laugh it off because we needed to laugh it off; it was imperative. But all I got in return was an expression of the very gravest disappointment. I'll never forget it. Then he took me down, I struggled for a few minutes before breaking out of his grip. But before I could get up I felt a thud on the back of the head. I hit the mud face first and then down he came, his whole body, his full weight now holding my face in the mud. I couldn't breathe. This was it. He was screaming, then I heard sobbing. And then he was gone. I rolled over and gasped, swallowing mud.

I lay there on my back looking up at the sky, and slowly the energy started returning to my arms and legs. Anger, more forceful than I had ever felt before, mixed with heartbreak and betrayal washed over me. I had feared he was going to kill me – Bill, my best friend, the only enemy that ever mattered.

I picked myself up out of the mud and ran. I ran as fast as I could back to the house, bashing my way through the unlocked front door, lunged up the stairs, four stairs at a time until I reached Bill's room. I kicked Bill's door open and jumped at him, mud flying everywhere, all over the white walls, TV and bed. In that moment, I wasn't myself or Brains McLoud any more: I was a killer. I was on Bill's back and I had his neck locked with my forearm wrapped around it. He bashed me around his room, smashing me into his wardrobe, his mirror, cutting both of us, but I wasn't letting go. He fell, slapping at my face and arm, I felt him weakening with every slap, he was nearly done. I could see his face reflected on a piece of the broken mirror, his eyes bloodshot. I fully intended in that moment to kill him. And if Gordon had come home from work five minutes later I may well have done so. Gordon shouted but Bill and I couldn't hear. But he easily separated us. While Bill gasped for air, I couldn't stop thinking that we might even have killed each other. It was over.

The next morning I panicked, and felt terrible. I wanted to apologize, to be the bigger man and be the first to make amends. I showered, and picked away all the dried blood on my painful face. I passed Bill's bedroom and could hear him snoring. Downstairs I left a note and stuck it to the fridge: *Gone to the shops to buy breakfast. I'm sorry, can we talk over lunch?* It was a beautifully crisp summer's morning. I walked slowly, taking my time, feeling full of guilt and remorse and contemplating failure for the first time. After thinking about everything we had been through, all we had sacrificed, how far we had come, it suddenly hit me how ridiculous we were to falter at the final hurdle. I told myself I could fix it, that I wasn't going to let us throw it all away. I had a new determination to get us back on track. We'd needed the fight to realize just what was at stake here. Bill and I had come this far, and had faced greater obstacles than marriage and fatherhood. Mary could move into Eagle's Nest; we'd be one happy family. I'd phone Shalit later and joke with him that Mary could be the new member of the band, the bun in the oven a possible future backing singer. We'd sort it all out. We'd be fine.

At the supermarket, I bought eggs, sausages and bacon, and big fat beef tomatoes for grilling. I bought orange juice and sparkling water, a six-pack of lager and a bottle of Jack to share. I walked back home humming 'Footloose', Kenny Loggins' version, an absolute pop classic for good reason.

Back at home, my note was untouched and there was no sign of Bill having surfaced, so I started cooking. I got the grill going, and the frying pan. I filled the kettle with water, then set the table. I'd never set a table at Eagle's Nest before. It felt like a special occasion, somehow, like my folks coming round for Christmas Day. I switched the radio on to some mindless nonsense. Natasha Bedingfield, of all people. Soon, the smell of bacon was filling the air, and my stomach told me I was ravenous. The kettle started whistling. I stuck my head out of the kitchen and shouted his name.

'*Bill!* Bill? Get your arse down here! I've got breakfast on the go.'

After five minutes, I switched everything off and skipped up the stairs, wincing at the pain in my legs, my chest and arms. I knocked on his door, loudly, and went in. His bed was empty again, the cupboard door open and hanging by a hinge. All his clothes were gone. I looked for his suitcase, but that was gone too. Downstairs, his coat was missing from the peg. His laptop wasn't where it had been just before I left for the store, behind a cushion on the sofa.

I went outside, looked left, then right. I ran, fast now, up our street and around the corner. It was still early, and the Sunday-morning streets were empty of people. There was no one about, no cars, no bikes, no little old ladies walking dogs. In one front garden I passed, I saw a small child, maybe six years old, stroking a cat. The cat bolted and, for a while, followed me as I ran, dancing about my ankles. Still running, I reached for my mobile phone and called him. Voicemail. I ran back the way I came, suddenly panicked, desperate to find my friend. Perhaps something had happened, something bad. He wasn't at the bus stop, nor on the tube platform, nor at the minicab office. I didn't know where else to look and so, reluctantly, I returned home.

Bill was gone, I presumed back up to Scotland, to marriage and to family life, though this wouldn't be confirmed to me for some time to come. Breakfast was still in the frying pan, his and mine. I dished it out on to one plate, and sat in the deafening silence of the front room, eating it all up while the walls stared back at me impassively. Eagle's Nest, always so full of people and incident, had never felt so empty. I hardly recognized it.

I finished eating and checked my watch. Almost eleven o'clock on a late-June day in 2005. I sat where I was and tried to imagine how this would all play itself out. Bill, I decided, had stormed off in a foul mood. He would be back in a few days, a week, maybe; two at most. We'd never had such a serious fight before, and I couldn't imagine him being the one to break the deadlock first. I'd have to do it, be the one to call and apologize before he would even consider rejoining me back in the studio where we could resume the music. This didn't concern me. I would apologize a thousand times over if only it got us back on track.

What I didn't know there and then, on that desolate Sunday morning, with nothing but blackened bits of curling bacon fat left on the plate to keep me company, was just how wrong I was. I would never see Billy Boyd again.

Ten

It was self-belief that had got me here in the first place, and it was self-belief that would see me through this current trough of despair. Or so I told myself, repeatedly. Silibil N' Brains, I knew in my marrow, would still go on to become one of the biggest rap acts in the world. It was only a matter of time.

When a full month went by with still no word from Bill, but rumours from friends back home that he'd been seen in Dundee, with Mary – and that he looked, of all things, *happy* – I decided that, OK, fine, Brains would do just as well without him. Bill was only ever baggage to me, after all; now I would be free. They were mostly my songs, anyway, the product of *my* toil and *my* creativity. I could perform them just as capably as he could, and if I didn't find a replacement for him, then I'd do the songs myself, my vision at last undiluted. Of course. Why hadn't I realized this before? With no one now to rely on, the sky would surely be the limit.

What remained of my self-belief took a further nasty knock on the morning I decided finally to come clean to Shalit and Del about Bill's departure. I'd received many calls from them both over the past four weeks, with no real news to impart, but just to check that everything was OK, because our extended silence was, as Shalit put it, *uncustomary*. I'd been putting off talking to them, allowing their calls to go to voicemail, occasionally texting back a morsel every now and then, the least I could do: ALL GD. SPK SOON. But they deserved the truth now, or a portion of it. Perhaps they'd even welcome it. They had grudgingly accepted Silibil N' Brains changing from a two-piece to a five-piece and then back to a two-piece, and so they would be fine when informed that I was now a solo project. Yes. They'd be fine.

I decided not to call ahead to announce my arrival. That would require an actual conversation on the phone, and I wasn't ready for one of those just yet. Instead, I set out early one Monday morning after a sleepless Sunday night, walking half the way into town, convinced that the fresh air would do me good. But an hour's worth of fresh air had done terrible things to my lungs, and so I hailed a cab I could barely afford. I arrived at an office that was still closed, and sat on the pavement to wait. I rested my head on my knees, and the heat of the early-morning sun on my back warmed me and made me drowsy.

Some time later (ten minutes? an hour?) a taxi pulled up, disgorging an immediately voluble Shalit, resplendent in black-and-white silk, sky-blue socks and bespoke Jermyn Street boots. He was shouting at somebody on the phone while thrusting a twenty towards the taxi driver's outstretched fingers. Then he turned and strode right past me, a blur of keys and rolling motion. I had to shout out his name to get his attention. He swivelled on his heel in alarm.

'Gavin, good Christ! You gave me a shock!' He snapped his phone shut without telling the person at the other end *goodbye*. 'I thought you were a homeless whatsit.' He took a proper look at me, and a wave of concern crossed his features. 'You look awful. Come on, come in.'

We went in and he switched on all the lights. His secretary hadn't yet arrived, and so he went to the kettle himself, impatiently filling it with water and throwing spoonfuls of coffee, then sugar, into two available mugs. I stood back and watched him, boisterously industrious even when making an early-morning drink. He filled the cups, then ushered me into his office, where he appraised me silently as if trying to put off what he knew was going to be bad news. There was no reason for preamble, for small talk, and I certainly didn't want to drag things out for any longer than need be. I came out with it, my voice flat and toneless. There was no more Silibil, only Brains.

I had seen Shalit angry on many occasions since he had first signed us. In fact, I often believed anger to be his default setting. It suited him so very well. But this morning was something new. After swallowing my news wordlessly, no trace of emotion on his face, he erupted. It reached his nostrils first, which flared like a bull's. He then bunched his fists and grabbed what hair remained on his temples as if suddenly fearful his head would spin clean off. I let him get on with it because, frankly, he'd earned it. The money he had invested in us was now lost forever. Wasted. I bore the brunt of his rage as he shouted and swore and bounced around in his seat. I felt tiny opposite him, minuscule, a gnat. Once he finished, I tried to explain that I planned to continue alone, and that I would fulfil the upcoming show, but he seemed no longer interested. I reminded him about 'Footloose', about 'Spaz Out' and several other (non-existent) ideas I had up and running on the laptop at home. He looked at me like a small child who understands nothing. Then, very quietly, he spoke, wringing his hands together as he did.

'But what do I have to sell? Don't you understand, Gavin? The band is Silibil N' Brains, not Brains Mcloud.'

Del walked in, a take-away coffee cup in his hand. He saw me and grinned.

'Brains, my man! What's up?' Quickly, because nothing gets past Del, he noticed an absence alongside me. He looked from me to Shalit and back again. 'Where's Sili?'

Shalit had gone beyond the call of duty for us – I realized this, I really did. He had put up with a lot of shit we'd thrown at him, when most managers would have simply walked away. He was a man of endless patience and a lot of faith. And so he was to prove again, even now. We'd had a gig booked for several months now, something that Del was convinced would do Silibil N' Brains a lot of good in terms of profile-raising. It was an out-of-town extreme-sports festival, NASS, the line-up crammed with a bunch of promising up-and-comers alongside the *original* hip-hop act, the Sugarhill Gang, who, no, weren't dead after all. I begged Shalit to allow the booking to go ahead despite Bill's departure, telling him I needed it for my sanity but also to prove to him, to everyone, that Brains could do this on his own. To his credit, and my eternal gratitude, he did just that, spinning the fact that I was now a solo artist to make it sound to the promoter like a positive rather than a negative. The promoter granted permission.

I was gainfully employed, still, and that was the important thing. It gave me strength. I popped pills, the little red ones, and these helped me see my predicament as it really was: a bonus, a boon, nothing but good news. This could be the beginning of everything for me, a solo artist and a genuinely major new force in music, a post-rap, postmodern-punk outfit with a wit, craft and

sonic splendour otherwise lacking in today's charts. Del had managed to get me a bunch of session musicians to join Gordon on
bass, all of whom knew exactly what they were doing. We steered
the others through two weeks of frantic rehearsals, and had no
reason to complain once. This really was a do-or-die situation for
me. It couldn't have been anything less.

The festival was an indisputable success. The headliners, now
well into their dotage, performed well enough, and such was
their charm that you couldn't help but love them. And for me?
The show I performed that late afternoon with Gordon and a
bunch of other guys I hadn't known until just a couple of weeks
earlier was perhaps the most important forty minutes of my life,
because I proved, at least to myself, that I could do it on my
own. I don't know what came over me, but I was possessed, the
uppers and downers mixing with the alcohol and a level of
excitement that made me feel like a teenager all over again. I
baited the audience, who brayed and cheered right back at me.
I did both my and Bill's lines, barely remembering to breathe but
never dropping a single word. It all felt effortless, natural, a sus-
tained white-knuckle thrill. The roar of approval from the
audience came at me in a huge, relentless wave. I lapped it up,
I loved it. I didn't miss Bill for a single second, and I crashed off
stage and into the arms of my new comrades afterwards on the
biggest high I'd ever had. Everybody came up to congratulate
me. Gordon, bless him, was all emotional. 'This,' I told him, '*this*
is the future.'

The rest of the night passed by in a blur. I popped more pills
to slow down my heartbeat, but the whisky made my blood sing.
I eventually went to bed somewhere around dawn, and I
wrapped myself up in the sheets until I lay there in that hotel

room completely cocooned, reliving the night before on the cinema screen of my closed eyelids. I hadn't disappointed my audience. My audience – and they were *mine* alone now, nobody else's – loved me. It was a new beginning.

And so it was rather a rude shock to find out, later that same morning, that my brand-new bandmates had already departed for their next gigs, being session musicians who had seen their stint with me as a one-off, nothing more. I'd convinced myself that they'd want permanent positions, such was our chemistry.

Eagle's Nest was mockingly quiet when I got back. I collapsed on to the sofa, and switched on the television. And there I stayed.

Weeks passed, the hours and days blurring into one. I'd spend a whole morning lying on the carpet in the living room, gazing into its pattern and pulling apart its tiny fibres. Occasionally I would half-heartedly wank, discarding the balled-up Kleenex tissues behind the sofa. Afternoons would inch by while I bit my finger- and toenails down to the quick. I could sit on the stairs for hours at a time and stare into space. I could spend whole chunks of the night opening and closing the fridge door, trying to catch the fridge light out. I never did. (The milk went off, though.) I saw no one, and spoke to no one. The only time I ventured out was for food, and to get repeat prescriptions from the doctor's. But one of these required consultation with the GP before the bitch felt prepared to sign her illegible scrawl. I accepted this necessity with great reluctance.

'Tell me how you feel.'

'I feel like shit.'

'Could you perhaps be more specific?'

'Where would you like me to start? I feel upset, depressed, so very tired. I don't want to see people. I don't want to see you. I don't want to talk. It hurts my throat. I just want you to give me my fucking pills.'

'Have you considered psychiatric help?'

'Why would you ask a question like that?'

'Because it seems to me that psychiatric help would be of great use.'

'I don't want to be referred for any psychiatric help, OK? I just want you to sign a piece of paper, and I'll be on my way.'

'I'm sensing some hostility, which often, in my experience m—'

'Just give me the fucking pills. *Please*. I'll be all right. I just need the pills.'

She reached for a box of tissues on the table, and handed them to me. I wiped my wet cheeks.

'Look,' I told her, doing what I always did when things got awkward: lying. 'My friend just died, my very oldest friend. He was stabbed in the throat. I watched him die, right there in front of me, and it sucked out all the life force from me. Will that do?'

As they often did, the lie worked wonders. The doctor just gawped back at me in horror, then apologized hurriedly and autographed my precious prescription. I was on my way.

A week later, feeling better, I braved turning on my heavily Sellotaped mobile phone. I had been incommunicado for more than a month now. I expected a deluge of missed calls, frantic text messages from loved ones, family, friends. But there was nothing. No one had tried to get hold of me at all. My disappearance had passed by in utter ignorance. I called Shalit, spoke to Del when I couldn't get hold of him, and told him, with as much conviction as I could, that I was back, back, back, and told him that I wanted to get some kind of new incarnation back out on the road. I told him I wanted Sony/BMG to understand that Silibil N' Brains were history and that my new act was now the present and the future. I was aware that I was talking very quickly indeed, and I was also aware that Del was sounding strange – wary somehow, as if keeping himself at a cautious distance. He said he would see what he could do. A couple of days later, he called back and told me he had landed me a couple of bookings; but this time they were for tiny clubs, the back rooms of suburban pubs. 'How did Sony react to news of my return?' I asked him. They didn't react, there was nothing. I may as well have been fucking dead.

When you sign a recording contract, it's a huge deal. Champagne is involved; a party invariably follows, the kind at which you half expect a brass band to be present, blowing trumpets loudly in your honour. It requires signatures and lawyers, and a management team to check over the fine print, and some of the biggest promises imaginable, all of which act like an anticipatory drum-roll. Life becomes dreamlike. The moment you sign, everything you've ever worked towards falls into place: you get press and promotion, a marketing department to streamline your image; you get access to a state-of-the-art studio, with engineers and producers at your beck and call. People buy you drinks, ply you with drugs. A great deal of money is spent on you, and everything appears to be free. Girls open their legs for you. You become talked about, celebrated, hyped to the hilt. When we signed to Sony, we instantaneously became the centre of the universe. *Everybody* knew of our existence. We were the new kings.

But when you are released from your contract, there is no ceremony, no sense of occasion, no drum-roll. The phone simply stops ringing, its silence mocking, taunting, deafening. When you phone, you no longer get put through. Suddenly everybody is in a meeting, currently unavailable. You are free to leave a message, but the call will never be returned.

I decided to redouble my efforts and ingratiate myself back in with Shalit and Sony/BMG whatever the cost. I was desperate now, and looking for a lifeline. Hell, I'd even be their puppet; they could pull the strings. I'd let them do anything so long as I was given another chance to prove my worth. I called Shalit, and I called Del. I called the A&R department, suddenly yearning for Ruth's kindly voice. I called David Marcus. Not one of them was available. I left voicemails, and sent text messages, emails. Even Del, who I had thought of as a close friend, failed to respond. I became convinced they were avoiding me. I called Del again, this time placing 141 before his number in order to conceal my own. He picked up on the first ring, but the enthusiasm drained from his voice the moment he heard mine. He began to stutter, telling me he was about to go into a meeting and . . . Could he possibly call me back afterwards? Like a fool, I believed him. He never called back. Nobody did.

I could only presume, then, that Silibil N' Brains were no longer a Sony/BMG concern, and that I was no longer represented by Shalit Global. But nobody ever made it official. I desperately craved some kind of written testimony to the fact, if only to silence any creeping sliver of hope that may have reached me in the middle of the night (and it came to me in the middle of *each and every* night), but no such confirmation was forthcoming. To all of these people, I no longer existed. Now, I was an annoyance they would get rid of simply by ignoring me until I went away.

I sat on my sofa at Eagle's Nest, and wondered how long it would be before the bailiffs came. I was no longer earning money, and I had spent so freely and for so long now that I had practically nothing left in my account. All the friends I'd made in London were suddenly off radar, having gone off to become friends with other sure-fire next big things instead. Bill was lost to me. I was alone.

I got up one morning with the belated realization that affirmative action was needed. I had to do something, for survival, for sanity.

I needed a job.

The man on the plastic orange seat beside me was snoring. I had no idea how he could fall asleep so soundly on such an unforgiving chair, but he was doing it expertly. A truck couldn't have shifted him. Across the room, in a corner, a woman was loudly berating her baby, who itself was loudly crying in a pram held together by masking tape. A man came in, dressed in a parka, hood up despite the summer heat. Of all the empty chairs he could have chosen, he decided to sit in the one next to mine. I was now sandwiched between him and the snorer. Claustrophobia pressed at me from both sides. After a while, the hoodie leant towards me.

'Draw?' he whispered.

I looked up at the CCTV camera, and shook my head no.

'Gak?' I shook my head again. He leant in, until I could smell him. 'Look, I'll buy whatever you're selling, yeah?'

Confused, I got up and moved to another seat. I had been here for two hours already but nothing here was about to happen in a hurry.

I'd never signed on before but now I had no other option. The dole office was a half-hour walk from Eagle's Nest, all uphill. It was difficult to miss: an ancient municipal building to which no one had ever got round to applying a second coat of paint, outside of which congregated old men and young mothers smoking cigarettes. Inside it was hot and clammy. The air conditioning didn't work. People smelt of smoke, alcohol and desperation. Most of the job-hunters seemed to be my age, but none of us fraternized. It was the loneliest club I'd ever been to. When I finally got to the counter I was faced by a middle-aged, heavyset woman with a dour expression, to whom I found myself being openly Scottish, which surprised me. I filled out a succession of forms, and answered questions that came as if delivered by machine. She asked me in which area I would ideally like to find gainful employment. I told her that I was a musician and had recently had a record deal. If I was trying to impress her here, I failed. Her face revealed nothing. She flicked through an archaic Rolodex, and picked out a small card.

'Then I might have just the thing,' she said.

Ridiculously, I perked up at this. I have no idea why. What could this woman possibly have offered me that would be of genuine interest? Another Silibil? She handed over the card, upon which was typed out a job description. The font size was tiny, and it swam before my eyes. The only thing I could focus on was the name of the company: Sony/BMG.

'It's a job in a record company,' she said, smiling. 'In the post room. Should I schedule an interview?'

I looked into her face, lined and broken and old before its time, and I guessed she had been in this job for years, possibly decades, with the selfsame Rolodex no doubt, and so I'm sure she was used to abuse. Mine was of no surprise to her. She simply took the card back, replaced it, and gave me a form to fill out. When I stopped shouting, she told me that I would receive £110 every fortnight, but that in the meantime I would have to show proof that I was actively seeking gainful employment.

'You're a young man with your whole life ahead of you,' she said. 'Shouldn't be too long before we have you settled some-where.'

I opened my mouth to say something back to her but then a thought sprung into my head paralysing my tongue. Just a few months back I'd been on tour with D12, laughing with Madonna and taking advantage of the VIP lifestyle; now I was in fucking Palmers Green Job Centre. I didn't regain the use of my tongue for the rest of the day.

Byron and I use to joke about being male escorts. The job seemed deceptively simple: to be taken out by women, and to be charming to them. For this, you would be wined and dined and richly rewarded. 'The easiest money we could ever make,' we joked. Now I was the joke and I needed the money badly, and so the prospect of making it easily inevitably appealed. One night, in the mood for browsing, I went online and quickly came across a whole host of escort agencies crying out for fresh meat. Me. I found myself filling in a form, then clicking Send. A week later, I was an escort for an long-established agency located in one of Soho's more upmarket squares. My profile was sent out to a thou-sand women, and I was told to sit back and wait. I didn't have to wait long.

'So, do you do this often, then?'

Dolly asked me this as the French waiter poured a centimetre of wine and waited for my approval before pouring out two glasses and leaving the bottle on the table.

'No, actually this is my first time.'

She drank in my smile, then reached for her wine. 'I bet you say that to all the girls.' When she replaced the glass, it was rimmed with her lipstick.

Technically, Dolly was right to doubt me. This wasn't strictly my first time. I had turned up for two other dates, but both had been no-shows – a fact that had sent me back in a fit of paranoia to my online profile, wondering what kind of wrong signals I was sending out here. The agency later explained to me about last-minute nerves, and told me how common no-shows were. Dolly was the first to actually turn up for me. There she was, outside the Green Park restaurant, with the requested *Daily Mail* folded under her right arm. I approached her, we compared newspapers and laughed. Dolly was a pleasant surprise: in her late thirties, slim, well-dressed, though perhaps a little too made-up and too eager to have a good time. But she looked sane and sound, and not at all frightening. I'd been expecting a bunny-boiler. What I got was someone ruined by her first marriage and now looking into the tunnel of encroaching middle age, suddenly afraid by her loneliness. Loosened by the wine, she became increasingly candid about her life and its disappointments, and it was only when we were on to the second bottle, and one of those death-by-chocolate desserts (one plate, two spoons), Dolly by now drunk, that she began to flirt with me and make slurred overtures about *afterwards*. The escort agency were deliberately enigmatic on this; I guess legally they had to be. The escort was to be paid £50 per hour, but was not in any way obliged to become intimate with the client. The suggestion, the way I understood it, was that if the client and the escort were of a similar mind, and didn't necessarily want things to end once dinner was over, then, well, the escort was on his own, acting of his own volition and free to do as he pleased. This was the point, I imagined, at which the escort had to choose whether to remain a chaste date or turn to prostitution – because, were the evening to continue, then surely so would the rate of £50 an hour.

Straight Outta Scotland

I had no desire to sleep with Dolly, and awkwardly I made this clear to her. She had been good company, but I don't think I'd ever experienced a more dispiriting evening in my life. Here was a woman who had been ruined by a man and wanted another one to reinvigorate her. I couldn't even reinvigorate myself. And, although the £150 I had made sugared the pill somewhat, I got home that night feeling bad for her and wretched for me. If all I had to look forward to now was a succession of Dollys, then I really had nothing to look forward to at all.

I managed just two other dates, both of which coincided with and were consequently prompted by the arrival of red letters and a further threat of bailiffs. Jenny was a Dolly clone, a sweet, sad lady in her late thirties who just wanted to be held, while Vanessa was a former bodybuilder, no longer competing (at thirty-five, she was deemed over the hill) but still terrifyingly ripped, the veins on her massive forearms as thick as rope. Vanessa told me that men were always too scared to approach her. I could see why, and I didn't know what to say to make her feel better. At the end of the date we didn't kiss, we shook hands. The rigid formality of it made me squirm. The following day I removed my profile from the agency's website. I've a feeling my absence went unnoticed.

Michelle was starting to worry about me. This was nothing new, of course. My sister had been worried about me for much of my adult life, and, because at this point she was my only contact with the outside world (we spoke intermittently on the phone), she became increasingly convinced that things would end badly unless I could bring myself out of my depression. She was furious that everyone had abandoned me, and so took it upon herself to be there whenever I needed; all I had to do was ask. I never got the chance. She inundated me with self-help books, which soon lined my shelves, all of them ignored and unread. She gave me telephone numbers – for counselling, for alcohol abuse and addiction. I called none of them. She turned up unannounced with soup and hot chocolate, full of good cheer and forced empathy. But Michelle's concern only made things worse for me. I hated her kindness, and spurned all her efforts, determined instead to keep on the path of self-destruction, perhaps to its inevitable conclusion.

A Friday night came, late August. It had been another hot day, and the sun was only now, at nine o'clock, starting to set. London's West End was filled with party people who congregated outside every pub, spilling off the kerb and into the roads, drinking and flirting and getting drunk. I had spent much of the day walking through the streets of Soho alone, looking with envy at everyone around me, people with places to go and friends to meet, their nights just beginning and ripe with possibility. To torture myself, I revisited some of my old haunts, drinking dens that dated back to the earliest days of Silibil N' Brains, each of them representative of happier times. With money I could barely afford to spend, I had a drink in each of them, waiting for the recognition that never came from bar staff. Everywhere I went the mood was celebratory, everyone keen to drink and fuck the steamy night away. What was I, wretchedly alone, doing here? I boarded a bendy bus at Oxford Street, and stood in the revolving central carriage for what would be the long journey home. I was drunk, and the constant rotation of the floor beneath my feet amused me. I laughed, stupidly and loudly, then looked up to see somebody looking back at me, derision in his eyes.

'Got a problem, pal?'

I expected him to look away, but he didn't. Instead, he took the two steps towards me and, as the bus turned its sharp left from Oxford Street into Tottenham Court Road, he punched me. My head snapped back. He then took two steps back and resumed his previous conversation with his friend, as if that was all that was needed to put me in my place.

'Motherfucker,' was all I said as I launched myself at him. His friend was on me now, punching me hard in my face. I fell to the floor, still revolving as the bus snaked its way up the busy street. The two guys became four, and they surrounded me. One of them pulled a knife. I saw it glint in the late sunshine that filtered through the window. *Let it come*, I thought. *Let it come and slice me in two.* But ultimately I'm a coward, and so, when the bus stopped to open its doors, I bolted. I hit the pavement running, and carried on running long after the bus and its knife-wielding passengers had overtaken me and disappeared. I ran up Tottenham Court Road, across the Euston Road, along Mornington Crescent and into Camden Town. My lungs screamed. My mouth dried, my leg muscles burnt. I fell to the ground on the bridge, and sat against the wall among the beggars and the dealers. It took the better part of a quarter of an hour to get my breath back, to slow my racing heart. When I finally stood up, my head still spinning, my left hand pressed into the fierce stitch at my side, I saw the MTV building further up the canal, where, so long ago now, a very different future had seemed destined for me. I closed my eyes to it, and turned away. I headed home, another bus, this journey without incident. That night I slept the sleep of the dead – long, dreamless and unbroken for a full thirteen hours. I woke up not refreshed but bone-achingly exhausted, spent of all energy, my body grey and wasted, peat and mush.

Saturday passed in a state of torpor. I didn't leave the house, nor could I imagine, right then, ever doing so again. My bed moulded itself around me, and I clicked through a selection of TV channels without focusing on any of them. I must have slept again, because when I opened my eyes it was dark. I fetched a glass of water, but being upright didn't suit me so I quickly flopped back down again. The television was still on, the Reading Festival, thousands of people having the time of their lives in front of the world's biggest bands. Much of the action washed over me like so many waves, nothing registering until Muse came on, to the biggest reception of the night. Suddenly I sat up and took notice. Muse, the band who, just a year or so previously, had predicted our own meteoric rise to superstardom. And now there they were, and here *I* was.

My bed became a slippery slope, a slick slide. Gravity took over and I shot down it like something greased, and I fell further and further down. Then I landed with a bump. I opened my eyes to find that I hadn't moved at all. Muse were still on the television, and I was still in my bed, my reality unchanged. I reached for a bottle of whisky that lay half empty under the mattress. At first I thought I'd toast the band its deserved success, but I was in no mood for benevolence. I drank for me, only me. It went down like water. It was then that I felt the pain, the searing pain, and with it panic, the need for obliteration. It was the pills next. And then the blackness, from which I never wanted to return.

The day Michelle checked me out of hospital was the day I began leafing through the self-help books that she had by now littered right throughout the house. I had decided to browse them because, frankly, I had nothing else to do; I didn't even have the courage to do away with myself successfully. I read pages and pages of spiritual psychobabble, and all manner of waffle and nonsense. I read about the power of thought and therapy, hypnosis and transcendental meditation, yoga, tai chi, and cosmic ordering. I have no idea why, but it was the cosmic ordering that snagged me. I read on. Cosmic ordering, I learnt, was the belief that individuals can use their desires to fully connect with the cosmos, to make dreams a reality. In the past, I'd have crossed a road full of oncoming traffic to avoid such new-age bullshit, but now, quite suddenly, this all seemed like the most glaring piece of common sense I had ever come across. How could it not? You don't need to do very much to allow cosmic ordering into your life. You don't have to give your life over to the church of Tom Cruise, or donate great chunks of your income to some or other spurious organization, and you don't have to shake a tambourine up and down Regent Street in nothing but a toga and sandals. You simply write down a wish list of things you want to come true. You then submit this list, not physically but mentally, *spiritually* – in short, you close your eyes and concentrate – to the cosmos, and you wait for it to come true.

The book gave pages and pages of examples of people for whom life had been transformed as the result of such lists. I'd never heard of any of these people, of course, and some of them, judging by the accompanying photographs, were the kind of Americans who gobbled up any old shite as if it were the gospel truth. I hated Americans. But then I read online about someone I *had* heard of, a gnomic TV personality who had not been seen on British television screens for almost six years. After all kinds of personal upheaval in his life, this particular chinless wonder wished for a new challenge to come his way. Within months, he was back on our screens, successful all over again, and was now an enthusiastic supporter of cosmic ordering. It had changed his life; it could change mine. What better ringing endorsement could I have hoped for?

I called my sister to discuss it, fearing she would laugh at me.

But it turned out that cosmic ordering had worked for Michelle as well. She was convinced, she told me, that she had landed a job promotion out of it. She also had a new man in her life, another of her wishes. She was living in a nice flat in a nice part of town, and she was happy. *Happy*. I slammed the phone down and raced for a piece of paper and a pen. I sat at the kitchen table and felt a rush of excitement that I hadn't felt in months.

I started to write out all the positive things in my life, to be followed by all the negative. At first I struggled. In the positive list, I included: *I'm alive*. I couldn't say I was happy, because I wasn't. Nor could I say I was particularly healthy. Nor in gainful employment. I wasn't in love, and nobody loved me. I began to cry at this point, just a brief jag, but uncomfortably noisy, and so I put the positive list aside in favour of the negative. I rather enjoyed filling out the negative list. Within a quarter of an hour I'd filled four sheets of paper. Both sides. It felt cathartic.

Then I fetched another piece of paper. Upon this would be my wish list. I wrote down that I wanted something, or someone, to drag me out of my pit of despair. I put the pen down, then re-read what I had just written. This was all I really wanted in life right now. More than fame and fortune, and global adoration, all I really wanted was to be pulled out of my depression. And so I left it at that. I didn't want any watching cosmic god to think me too greedy too soon. I added *please* at the end of the sentence, then put the cap on the pen and laid it beside the piece of paper. I closed my eyes and began to will the wish up, up, up into the cosmos, where it would fly and flap and briefly flutter before being assimilated into the ether, its plea duly noted. Then, after an appropriate period of time, the great galactic cogs would start to turn in my favour. Yes?

Yes.

Straight Outta Scotland

Guess what? It worked. I fell in love, properly.

Skye was in many ways my ideal woman, and of everyone I knew during this most chaotic period of my life Skye was the only person who knew me as I really was. We'd been friends years earlier, as children, back in South Africa, and had maintained regular contact ever since. But it had increased recently, to the point where we were emailing one another every day, sometimes for hours on end. Skye was creative and gorgeous. She was also a fighter, a survivor. She'd had a bad childhood, had run away from home at the age of sixteen and spent the next couple of years travelling the world, seeing things most of the rest of us never would, even if we'd spent an entire lifetime looking. In every city she briefly settled in, crazy things happened either to or around her; but invariably *because* of her. She had Bill's energy, and his easy way with people, but also a profundity to her that touched everyone she met. I was led to understand that she fell in love easily, and then out of it painfully, her life an unfolding drama that it was sometimes difficult to keep up with. But her emails were amazing, full of events and happenings and exclamation marks. She wrote beautifully, so vividly that every written message was a picture to dive into right alongside her. I read her voraciously. She was even better on the phone, her voice first calm then shrill, full of sadness then joy, but she was always entertaining. We could talk the night away, and often did.

I told her everything about Silibil N' Brains. She loved it. The scam thrilled her every bit as much as it would had she been living it instead of me. And, now that I had crashed and burnt, she was the one who gave me the belief that I could bounce back. I couldn't do without her.

Recently, she had returned to South Africa, convinced that it was time to settle down. She was an alcoholic but was actively fighting to overcome it, and her career as a photojournalist was soaring.

Perhaps the most exciting aspect of our relationship, or rather about its progression towards being something more serious, was distance. As Brains, I was so often able to fuck any girl I wanted to that doing so had virtually been part of the job. But with Skye everything went deeper. It was Gavin she loved, and she made me see him in a whole new light. She was always ready to talk or email, whatever time of day or night. She never failed to make me smile, to lift me up and away.

Soon it seemed as though our relationship could develop into something far more tangible than mere online chats. Skye was talking about coming to London – possibly for a visit, perhaps for more. Though neither of us ever found the guts to actually put it into words, much less type it out in an email, the reason she wanted to come was obvious: *us*. Neither of us had ever felt quite like this before. If it was even half as good in the flesh as it was online, our relationship would be incredible; we could be the perfect couple. I encouraged her to come as much as I could. She began working all hours to raise sufficient funds, refusing any offers for me to pay for her trip. It was important she did it herself, she said. We started to talk about the autumn, perhaps the perfect time for her to arrive into the capital. She would write me long rambling emails detailing what she expected of me as a guide from the moment her plane touched down, and I wrote back telling her that I'd make the city her own private playground that she would come to know, with me, like the back of her hand. I was promising her the world here, and would have given it, too. I was also promising her my heart.

I didn't worry when she failed to email one day. When she

didn't for two more, and then three days after that, I put it down to the fact that she must be busy with work. A photojournalist often works unsociable hours, just as a punk-rock act does. I called and left voicemails, but nothing. It was then that I started to panic.

I contacted the few friends we had in common, and they promised to do a little detective work for me. It didn't take long before one of them reported back.

Skye was ill. She had a rare form of cancer, diagnosed too late and already spreading virulently inside her body. She had found out a while ago, a few months, but had said nothing to anyone, and now here she was, my age, twenty-three, and she was dying. She was in hospital, I was told, having lost almost half her weight in the space of two weeks alone. She hadn't told me because she didn't want to upset me, and because she was awaiting a firm prognosis. The doctors then pronounced the disease too rampant, too far gone, for chemotherapy to be a viable option. The only hope left now was hope itself, which of course was no hope at all.

I booked a ticket to Durban immediately, but I never got to board the plane. Skye died just a day later: a small mercy, our common friends told me, given the amount of pain she was in. I was told to come over anyway, for the funeral. They would make a party of it, a celebration of a remarkable life. I travelled to the airport early one morning with every intention of boarding the plane, but never made it to the departure gate. I couldn't. Instead, I locked myself into a toilet cubicle somewhere within Terminal 3. Knees up on the lid, I cried silently, the agony an immense roar inside my head. I started to punch the locked door with my fists, and then to headbutt it repeatedly. I was screaming now, and pummelling hard. Airport security was called.

*

I received a call from Skye's cousin later, passing on a message that Skye had left for me. I couldn't possibly repeat the whole message here, as I believe she intended it for me and only me. But she did say that she hoped that I never give up on my music. And so I never have. But Gavin Bain, I realized, was linked inextricably to death. All around him, people died, many of them friends and peers, all of them gone before their time. Never Gavin himself. That would never be his – *my* – fate, because that wouldn't make any sense. Gavin Bain was here to suffer. He suffered beautifully.

And I hated him. With every shred of me I hated Gavin Bain, wanted to be rid of him once and for all.

I went to ground after that. Didn't resurface again for weeks, months. Sometimes it felt as if I'd never resurface again.

But eventually cosmic ordering came to my rescue again, albeit temporarily. I acceded to it because I didn't want to die, and because I needed something to live for.

An old friend of Silibil N' Brains called up out of the blue. We had an awkward conversation during which I avoided most of his questions while trying to sound as chipper as he had always known me to be. He told me that a band was playing in an East London bar later that night – would I like to come along? I didn't, but said yes all the same. I was going out for the night, a novelty in itself these days. I had a bath especially.

The band was awful and the beer weak. There were too many people present; I felt claustrophobic. But it was at this bar that I met Candy. Candy was, like Brains (and, yes, I still couldn't quite lose him yet), American, from San Antonio, Texas, with all the prerequisites of a high-school cheerleader type: blonde hair, perfect teeth and a fabulous figure of which she was terribly proud.

Straight Outta Scotland

Over the dull roar of the band, her mouth leant into my ear. Her lipstick rimmed the raised ridges of my lobe. I could feel her moist tongue on them, and the heat of her breath.

'Do you want to see my tits?' she asked. 'Men always want to see my tits.'

There was quite a crush of people that we had to snake through in order to get to the women's toilets, but we made it intact, and once there we squeezed into a cubicle. She lifted her top up, and with it her bra. They were *fantastic* tits.

Eleven

And so cosmic ordering had sent me Candy. Not an angel from above by any means, but if anyone was to drag me from my despair, if only for the here and now, then it was Candy Sherman, a small-town former beauty queen who had come to London, much as I had done, to find herself. Winning the beauty pageant a few years previously had brought her local fame. She'd been trotted out at rodeos and state fairs and football games, and also at Thanksgiving parades. She would wave from podiums, her body poured into swimsuits, ball gowns and, once, a mermaid outfit. She had groupies, and they came in every size and shape, from the drunken frat boys in the crowds to the official councillors who had booked her appearance in the first place, heavily jowled men prepared to give her the world, or at least promising it, in exchange for Candy Sherman in the back of the pickup. She had read the weather on a local TV station, and had planned to go into business – funded by her corporate-businessman father, who was only too happy, in principle, to invest in his daughter's nail parlour, or was it a hair stylist's, a day spa, a pet sanctuary? She'd changed her ambitions as often as she did her panties. Her days were busy, her schedule crammed, a personal appearance here, a photo shoot there, no time for food but lots of time, in the back of stretch limousines, for a little snort and a little sip. She was drunk a lot of the time, and also high, but you wouldn't know it to look at her. She had difficulty falling to sleep at night, and so she mostly didn't. Her mother had sworn by cucumber slices, and so did she. Her eyes were *never* puffy. She had a 36D bust. It proved to be quite a calling card.

The breakdown, when it came, was pretty much part of the script for a former beauty queen. Pa shipped her off to that famous rehab place in Arizona, where she got clean – and laid, too, by several famous actors who you would recognize by their first names alone, but her lips were sealed. 'What happens in rehab stays in rehab,' she'd smile.

And then she'd decided that she needed to get out, of Texas and of America altogether, to pursue the dream that all beauty contestants claim to pride above all else: to work with children. Improbable as it sounds, Candy Sherman had arrived in London just a couple of months before our toilet-cubicle liaison to work at a primary school. 'I don't really teach,' she later clarified, 'but I'm, like, a classroom assistant. I help out whenever needed, with arts and crafts, things like that. And they are wonderful, those kids.' Tears filled her eyes.

She was completely committed to her new cause, which she described as her life's passion. But she was also still committed to extracurricular hedonism, hence this East London bar – and me – on a school night. After putting her tits away, she pulled out a wrap from her too-tight stonewashed jeans, and with it a pre-rolled $20 bill. 'Makes me think of home,' she grinned, bending low towards the toilet lid.

I ended up back at her place for a night of acrobatic sex that left me beautifully bruised. I woke with a disbelieving smile on my face the morning after to see her pulling on her day clothes, munching on a granola bar and drinking orange juice straight from the carton. She looked so demure then, so eager to please in a manner comprehensively different to the one she'd shown the night before. I envied those kids for the attention she was sure to lavish upon them.

We became, very quickly, an item, even though you could not have met two more mismatched people. We were different in every conceivable way. She hated most rock music, including that of some of my very favourite rock stars. She loathed all sport, particularly boxing, and thought Mohammad Ali, one of my earliest heroes, to be the devil incarnate. She was pro George Bush ('Daddy knows him real well; they golf a whole lot'). She was not amused by 'Cunt', the song I had written in his honour, and would always refuse to sing along with the chorus whenever I insisted on playing it in her company, to rile her, which I did frequently. She hated skateboarders, hated rap, Eminem especially. The only thing we had in common was that we were a couple of misplaced Americans far from home, and lonely. In bed, she loved to hear me talk because, she said, she missed the accent. She was terribly homesick.

I tell a lie. We had something else in common too: a voracious appetite for hard, crude, often debasing sex. It took us out of ourselves, and we craved this above all else. Candy was amazing in bed, the woman of my dreams: gorgeous and filthy. Cocaine, I soon learnt, was for special occasions only – weekends, mainly – but pot was a daily necessity. She loved strong skunk, and I'd watch, fascinated, as it gave her an altogether different character, and unexpected depth. 'Rape me,' she'd say. 'Call me a bitch, a slut, a whore.' She was a loud lover with an element of theatricality to her cries that I remain convinced had nothing to do with me. But I wasn't complaining. This was like fucking a porn star.

I was completely overwhelmed by Candy, attracted, appalled, and utterly addicted. She came into my life at my lowest moment, a gift from the cosmos, and for the time being she meant everything to me. I no longer thought about my mounting problems, my stalled career. All she did was smoke weed and fuck, almost to the exclusion of everything else. She took time off work, first holiday time, then calling in sick, in favour of a day spent at home, undressed, in bed. Those days she did go off into school, I obsessed over her, wanking furiously over pornographic photographs I'd taken of her on my phone.

But, like in the archetypal country-and-western song (and she *loved* country-and-western songs), Candy Sherman was a complicated girl. She could never be a one-man woman, but was instead pre-programmed to flirt all the time, and with everyone. She needed to be desired, and she was. That brazen opening line she had first used on me (*Would you like to see my tits?*) should have given me an indication of this. We'd be in a bar when suddenly she would catwalk to the toilet and back, all hips and tits and power, encouraging every male eye in the place. She would drink like a fish, and flirt even more. The moment I told her off for doing so, she would scream in my face and throw her drink over me, a cheap femme fatale in a cheap American movie. Then she would flounce off, expecting me to follow in her wake, begging and grovelling, which to my shame I very often did. When we weren't having sex we were arguing about everything: music, animals, climate change, Sarah Jessica Parker. I grew to hate her, to hate *us*, so much that I had to fuck her all the harder, as punishment. We began to split up daily, our arguments spilling over into the physical. She would hit me and I would hit her right back. She never expected that, but it turned her on to carry my bruises. I soon rued the day I ever cosmic ordered the mad bitch into my life in the first place.

Cosmic ordering her right back out again would prove a painful, and protracted, business.

And then I got a job: salesperson, T. K. Maxx, where, as they say, famous labels retail for cheaper. I'd turned down no fewer than thirty-seven jobs in the previous two months, and the dole office was threatening to stop all unemployment payments. I had no choice. Candy was expensive; I needed the money. The job at T. K. Maxx came with its own outfit: Sta-Prest nylon trousers that created static between my knees, and a crisp work shirt complemented by a badge it was company policy to wear. I'M HERE TO HELP. I was on the shop floor each morning, folding and re-folding jeans and shirts and jumpers. There were an awful lot of them, nine aisles' worth in my domain alone. In the afternoon – to keep the mind alert, claimed the manager – I was dispatched to the store room out back, where I was charged with transporting incoming clothes out of their boxes and into piles ready to be taken out on to the shelves, very often by me, the morning after. And so on and so forth, endlessly and forever and ever. It was easy, tedious, mind-numbing work, eight hours a day, with forty-five minutes for lunch, which I was encouraged to take in the upstairs canteen. My co-workers were surprisingly varied, aged between eighteen and sixty-eight, school leavers and the pensionable, and a great many in between who had either been made redundant or sacked from other work, proper careers, and had nothing left but this, the poor bastards. At any one time, at least half of us were going through some kind of quarter- or mid-life crisis.

Straight Outta Scotland

Sick leave was profligate. Staff were forever quitting, often without forewarning. You could see why. I did my best to apply myself here, to make as much of the job as I could, but it wasn't easy. I needed some self-respect and, between them, T. K. Maxx and Candy had robbed me of any I ever had.

In my first month, I broke the store's employee code of conduct no fewer than forty-two times. One afternoon in his stuffy office, my manager, younger than me by eighteen months, counted me through every last one of them.

'If you carry on like this, you shan't be permitted front-till work for the foreseeable future,' he warned. Till work at T. K. Maxx was seen as something to aspire to.

I never made it into my second month. I simply left one day, like so many had before me, and never returned. Back at the drawing board, I realized that I required a new scam of some kind, something to fire me up the way I once had been. I was still capable in all kinds of areas, and I now had to put that capability to work – *somewhere*. I called up Gordon, who had worked as a sales director in a fashion store back in Scotland. I asked him to send me his CV, as I wanted to know how to arrange mine. His was impressive, far more than mine could ever be, and so I simply took what felt like an inevitable shortcut: I scanned it, replaced his name with mine, and sent it off to every clothing distributor in Britain. A week later, I was being interviewed for a senior sales position.

The night before my interview I had a night terror that woke me screaming and scared Candy half to death, and my stomach ulcer flamed in supportive tandem. I welcomed both back like old friends, their presence meaning I was alive again. I bought some new clothes, I bought some breath mints, and I turned into Oxford Street convinced that if I could dupe the entire recording industry, I could do likewise to the fashion industry.

The hard work had already been taken care of. They were impressed by the CV right away, and they loved the fact that I was American. Given that the company itself was American, the appointment of an anglicized Yank might just take its UK branch on to the next level. This was their reasoning, at any rate. I shook hands with the manager, who ushered me into his office, encouraged me to sit down, and began to fire questions. He knew the facts, he said, holding my CV in his hand; now he wanted to know the *real* me. I decided to tell him at least one truth: that I'd been a musician, recently on the road with D12. His jaw hit the floor.

'D12? my kids *love* D12.'

I got the job. A week later, I turned up for my first day. It wasn't a major position, but it was a potentially crucial one. My duties were to get the company's skate-friendly footwear range affiliated with as many underground skate happenings as I could. I was given a desk and a phone, and a bunch of numbers to call. I spent my days talking to professional skateboarders and their promoters, angling to get my company's logo into as many areas as possible. I'd had no previous training in this, but it was plain sailing, ridiculously easy. Professional skateboarders were *desperate* for any kind of promotion. They snapped up my offers before I even had a chance to dangle them properly. My boss was impressed, my co-workers admired me. By the second week, we were heading out each night to bars and clubs and concerts, where I always managed to get them in free of charge, my old guest-list tricks as effective as ever. I was developing a new social circle, and beginning to feel good about myself again.

At home, Candy and I were still fighting like cat and dog. By now I could barely stand the sight of her, and she me. The sex had become tired and grubby. It left me feeling unclean, and whenever we fucked we did so out of spite. But spiteful sex was oddly addictive, and I always wanted more. To end things with Candy was to bring about an end to the best sex I'd ever had. Easier said than done.

If I blamed cosmic ordering for finding me Candy and then T. K. Maxx, then I guess I should have been grateful at least that it got me my new job, because my new job helped prompt within me a resurrection of what was, and always will be, my abiding obsession: music. I was going out every night now, to bars and venues across London, and I was starting to meet the same faces at each. These faces became friends, and all came to know about my past, about Silibil N' Brains. I'd head back to their places after hours and play them my unreleased album, taking profound satisfaction – and also relief, definitely that – when they rated it highly. Several of them wanted us to start up a band, which prompted a childlike excitement within me but also an incipient terror. I didn't want another experience like my first. I'd never be able to survive a second fallout, but I also knew I couldn't walk away from such an opportunity. I needed it.

Inevitably then, as I'd promised Skye I would, I started a band. Gordon joined me and together we found Andy Patrick, an incredible drummer from Boston. Andy was playing the lead in a West End show and was without a doubt the best drummer I'd ever seen. He and I then found Grant Magnus, whose life story inspired us as much as his talent, which was of another world. Not content with us just being a normal punk-rock band, I wanted to create something that would stand alone. Something audacious, something epic, as beautiful as it was monstrous. The answer came a few months down the line in the form of Tony Sabberton, a twenty-two-year-old trained violinist who was inspired more by punk than classical music. He played his instrument plugged into an amp, and loud. He was incredible. The five of us would get drunk together every night, and allow our dreams to bubble to the surface. We found a rehearsal space and the sound we produced was pure helium to my deflated dreams. I started writing lyrics again and with Grant I found a true songwriting partner. We could stay up writing literally all through the night and into the morning after, forgetting all about the day job in the process. My boss, who had initially been encouraging, was now losing his patience. I claimed I was sick, but he came to know exactly the reasons for my continued absence: everyone was talking about Gavin and his apparently awesome new band. I received warnings that I barely registered. I was writing several songs a day, and we were rehearsing them by night. This was no longer rap but rather an epic, motion-picture punk rock. It was the greatest music I'd ever produced. This was me grown-up, come of age.

There was only one sticking point, and it was mine alone: my genealogy. To my new bandmates, people with whom I felt a more profound bond than I ever had with Bill, I was American, a guise I was still fully incapable of dismantling – not just for them but also for myself. I wanted nothing more than to start afresh. I'd just been sacked from the job, and Candy had finally, mercifully left me in a storm of violence and of tears. In principle, now was the perfect time for reinvention. But whenever I resolved to confess to my bandmates I couldn't find the words, fearful that it was my American self who possessed all the talent, something the Scottish part of me couldn't ever hope to compete with. I was stuck.

We came up with a band name that we were all happy with, a perfect fit. We were Hopeless Heroic, so dubbed after a friend of mine described me as both in the same sentence.

'Gav, dude. Face it,' Andy said. 'You're hopeless . . . but at the same time you're heroic as well, you know?'

I *knew*. Hopeless Heroic was the name of my new band. It would now be my life's work to plant it on the whole world's lips.

But, as always seemed to happen with me, Hopeless Heroic's progress was to coincide with personal tragedy. A friend of mine back in South Africa, Ivan, to whom I had been introduced by Rob and Greg, was dying of cancer. *Another one*. Ivan and I shared a special connection: he was the only person I'd ever met who had the same night terrors as me, and could not only describe the same sensations but also would see the exact same demon attacking him in his sleep. One night, hanging at Eagle's Nest with Greg and Rob, Ivan and I decided to each draw the creature of our night terrors; eerily, when we compared drawings, we found both sketches to be identical. I truly felt that with Ivan I was getting closer to figuring out more about these night terrors and why they had haunted me my whole life.

I'd lost contact with Ivan since the Silibil N' Brains split and it was only when I bumped into Rob one night in the Crobar that I found out he was sick. The news was crushing. Rob and I began to put the pieces of our friendship back together and decided that we would try to raise money for Ivan's treatment by throwing him a benefit gig. We would call it 'Rock for Ivan' and we would donate every penny raised to get Ivan healthy again. We believed we could save our friend.

This was to be Hopeless Heroic's first show and the most important of my music career, because this was for something real; it was for a friend who needed my help.

We'd spent several weeks rehearsing for the show, which was to take place in the Water Rats Theatre, an intimate yet legendary music venue in King's Cross. We managed to get a few up-and-coming bands to perform and I knew, this being my first gig in a couple of years, that Rob and I could draw a big enough crowd to raise some decent money. I worked tirelessly to promote the event and managed to inspire Ivan's friends all over the world to hold similar events. I alerted all of those Silibil N' Brains diehards whose contact details I still had. To my great relief, the majority of them mailed straight back saying they wouldn't miss it for the world. The day came, and with it the news of Ivan: he was in a bad way and it was beginning to look like we would be raising funds in vain. I was reeling, and for most of the day remained numb and unreachable.

We arrived back at the venue an hour before we were due on stage. The place was rammed, and that made me happy. All of Ivan's friends in London had come along, as well as the Silibil N' Brains loyal and, of course, our biggest supporters within the music industry.

The atmosphere backstage was the strangest I'd ever experienced – excitement mixed with uncertainty, adrenaline with sadness – and there was an odd taste in my mouth. Perhaps it was the lack of Jack Daniel's, because I was sober. This would be the first time I would take to the stage without being at least slightly inebriated. I began to panic, all sorts of questions racing around my mind. Who was I going to be tonight? Brains McLoud or Gavin Bain? How could I be Brains at an event like this, for Ivan, a friend who knew who I really was? Which voice was I going to use, to sing, to speak? Then came a moment of clarity. My hands were no longer shaking.

The excitement of getting back out there in front of an audience again felt like a pure and physical thing that filled my veins just as surely as blood. I was born for this. Just before we took the stage my mobile phone vibrated. A text message. Ivan, I read, was not expected to see the night through. I would not get to see him again. Tears came to my eyes, and I blinked them away. We had a group hug. We whooped. In my head, I came to a resolution.

We walked out on to the tiny stage to an intense roar from a packed venue. The atmosphere was electric, everyone expectant. Before the lights came on to blind me, I scanned the crowd and saw several familiar faces: Ruth, old fans, old A&Rs, friends and enemies. Behind me, the band launched into our opening song, 'Become the Monster', and it carried me up on a wave of pure momentum. This, I knew, was *it*. I would not fuck things up, not this time. I would do what had to be done. I approached the microphone and gripped it tightly between two clammy palms. Over the sound of a building drumbeat, I spoke.

'We're Hopeless Heroic,' I said, not in my affected accent, but in my broad, *natural* one, and with pride. 'I'm Gavin Bain and . . .' My mouth was dry. I took a breath. 'And I'm not American, I'm Scottish.'

I dared a glance at Grant on guitar, who was watching me curiously, as if waiting for the punchline to a joke he didn't get. I turned to face the crowd again as 'Become the Monster' took off, and I sang out loud in my own voice – at last.

Ivan somehow pulled through that night, and hung on for a few more weeks.

It goes without saying that we went down a storm that night, that my band rocked, and that we won over those who had never heard of us before just as surely as we did my old fans, the loyal ones who had always thought of me as something else entirely.

As the final chords of the last song were still ringing out, I jumped off the stage and into the crowd, making a beeline for the bar. In my head I came to a rapid conclusion: if a beer was waiting for me, like it had been in those early, heady days of Silibil N' Brains, then all would be well; all would work itself out in a way that had nothing to do with cosmic ordering but everything to do with hard work and obsessive commitment. I'd survive this, perhaps even start to thrive. I passed grinning faces and surprised faces, and a lot of furrowed brows. There came pats on the back. People ruffled my sweat-soaked hair. Somebody hugged me. I reached the bar, and there it was – a beer, waiting for me. I picked it up and downed it in one, the cheers rising all around me. And then came the questions, first from the faithful, and then from my band members, who had by now joined me up at the bar. 'Scottish?' was what everyone was saying. Out of the corner of my eye I saw Del. Of all people, Del. He was shaking his head at me, but, I think, smiling with it. I went over to embrace him, so very grateful to see him, and whispered into his ear: 'I'll explain everything, I promise.' 'You'd better,' he said, not entirely hugging me back.

I answered a lot of necessary questions that night. I'm still doing so today, and to all kinds of people. Some have forgiven me, others haven't. I've lost friends, I've made enemies. So it goes. But I have rid myself of my regrets.

Because all along I simply did what I thought I had to do. Tell me, wouldn't you?